T0170616

TITANIC: A SURVIVOR'S STORY & THE SINKING OF THE S.S. TITANIC

TITANIC
A Survivor's Story
COL. ARCHIBALD GRACIE

The Sinking of the
S.S. TITANIC
JOHN B. THAYER

ACADEMY CHICAGO PUBLISHERS

Titanic: A Survivor's Story
by Colonel Archibald Gracie
First published in 1913 as *The Truth About the Titanic*

The Sinking of the S.S. Titanic
by John B. Thayer
First published privately in 1940
Copyright © 2010 by Capt. Richard Fremont-Smith, USCG
(Ret.)

This edition published in 1998 by
Academy Chicago Publishers
An imprint of Chicago Review Press Incorporated
814 North Franklin Street
Chicago, Illinois 60610
ISBN 978-0-89733-452-5

Library of Congress Cataloging-in-Publication Data is on
file with the publisher.

Cover design: Joan Sommers Design
Cover image: Atlantic liner Titanic sinking, bow first, 1912,
by W. Pearson, 1912. Repro ID: PY5224
©National Maritime Museum, Greenwich, London

Printed and bound in the United States of America

CONTENTS

Titanic: A Survivor's Story

The Sinking of the S.S. Titanic

Even before the film TITANIC was released, there was a good deal of interest in the tragedy, a human drama of enormous proportions.

Despite Colonel Archibald Gracie's illness—contracted from exposure on that dreadful night—he was able not only to write an account of his own experiences, but also found other survivors to interview and attended court hearings held in the United States, using court records to augment his own recollections.

He worked on his manuscript throughout 1912 and died in December of that year in New York; the book was published in 1913.

Walter Lord, author of A NIGHT TO REMEMBER, relied on Gracie, whom he called "an indefatigable detective." His book, Lord said, was "invaluable for chasing down who went in what boat."

John B. Thayer was also a survivor; he was only seventeen at the time of the sinking and wrote his own memoir which was published privately for family members in 1940. He committed suicide in 1945. It appears here for the very first time, courtesy of Capt. Richard Fremont-Smith, USCG (Ret.), a cousin of the author.

TITANIC

CHAPTER I

THE LAST DAY ABOARD SHIP

"There is that Leviathan."—Ps. 104:26.

AS the sole survivor of all the men passengers of the *Titanic* stationed during the loading of six or more lifeboats with women and children on the port side of the ship, forward on the glass-sheltered Deck A, and later on the Boat Deck above, it is my duty to bear testimony to the heroism on the part of all concerned. First, to my men companions who calmly stood by until the lifeboats had departed loaded with women and the available complement of crew, and who, fifteen to twenty minutes later, sank with the ship, conscious of giving up their lives to save the weak and the helpless.

Second, to Second Officer Lightoller and his

ship's crew, who did their duty as if similar occurrences were matters of daily routine; and thirdly, to the women, who showed no signs of fear or panic whatsoever under conditions more appalling than were ever recorded before in the history of disasters at sea.

I think those of my readers who are accustomed to tales of thrilling adventure will be glad to learn first-hand of the heroism displayed on the *Titanic* by those to whom it is my privilege and sad duty to pay this tribute. I will confine the details of my narrative for the most part to what I personally saw, and did, and heard during that never-to-be-forgotten maiden trip of the *Titanic,* which ended with shipwreck and her foundering about 2.22 a. m., Monday, April 15, 1912, after striking an iceberg "in or near latitude 41 degrees, 46 minutes N., longitude 50 degrees, 14 minutes W., North Atlantic Ocean," whereby the loss of 1490 lives ensued.

On Sunday morning, April 14th, this marvellous ship, the perfection of all vessels hitherto conceived by the brain of man, had, for three and one-half days, proceeded on her way from Southampton to New York over a sea of glass, so level it appeared, without encountering a ripple brought on the surface of the water by a storm.

The Captain had each day improved upon the

previous day's speed, and prophesied that, with continued fair weather, we should make an early arrival record for this maiden trip. But his reckoning never took into consideration that Protean monster of the Northern seas which, even before this, had been so fatal to the navigator's calculations and so formidable a weapon of destruction.

Our explorers have pierced to the furthest north and south of the icebergs' retreat, but the knowledge of their habitat, insuring our great ocean liners in their successful efforts to elude them, has not reached the detail of time and place where they become detached and obstruct their path.

In the twenty-four hours' run ending the 14th, according to the posted reckoning, the ship had covered 546 miles, and we were told that the next twenty-four hours would see even a better record made.

Towards evening the report, which I heard, was spread that wireless messages from passing stean.ers had been received advising the officers of our ship of the presence of icebergs and ice-floes. The increasing cold and the necessity of being more warmly clad when appearing on deck were outward and visible signs in corroboration of these warnings. But despite them all no diminution of speed was indicated and the engines kept up their steady running.

Not for fifty years, the old sailors tell us, had so great a mass of ice and icebergs at this time of the year been seen so far south.

The pleasure and comfort which all of us enjoyed upon this floating palace, with its extraordinary provisions for such purposes, seemed an ominous feature to many of us, including myself, who felt it almost too good to last without some terrible retribution inflicted by the hand of an angry omnipotence. Our sentiment in this respect was voiced by one of the most able and distinguished of our fellow passengers, Mr. Charles M. Hays, President of the Canadian Grand Trunk Railroad. Engaged as he then was in studying and providing the hotel equipment along the line of new extensions to his own great railroad system, the consideration of the subject and of the magnificence of the *Titanic's* accommodations was thus brought home to him. This was the prophetic utterance with which, alas, he sealed his fate a few hours thereafter: "The White Star, the Cunard and the Hamburg-American lines," said he, "are now devoting their attention to a struggle for supremacy in obtaining the most luxurious appointments for their ships, but the time will soon come when the greatest and most appalling of all disasters at sea will be the result."

In the various trips which I have made across the Atlantic, it has been my custom aboard ship, whenever the weather permitted, to take as much exercise every day as might be needful to put myself in prime physical condition, but on board the *Titanic,* during the first days of the voyage, from Wednesday to Saturday, I had departed from this, my usual self-imposed regimen, for during this interval I had devoted my time to social enjoyment and to the reading of books taken from the ship's well-supplied library. I enjoyed myself as if I were in a summer palace on the seashore, surrounded with every comfort—there was nothing to indicate or suggest that we were on the stormy Atlantic Ocean. The motion of the ship and the noise of its machinery were scarcely discernible on deck or in the saloons, either day or night. But when Sunday morning came, I considered it high time to begin my customary exercises, and determined for the rest of the voyage to patronize the squash racquet court, the gymnasium, the swimming pool, etc. I was up early before breakfast and met the professional racquet player in a half hour's warming up, preparatory for a swim in the six-foot deep tank of salt water, heated to a refreshing temperature. In no swimming bath had I ever enjoyed such pleasure before. How curtailed that enjoyment would have been had the presentiment come to me telling how near it was to being my last plunge, and that before dawn of another day I would be swimming for my life in mid-ocean, under water and on the surface, in a temperature of 28 degrees Fahrenheit!

Impressed on my memory as if it were but yesterday, my mind pictures the personal appearance and recalls the conversation which I had with each of these employees of the ship. The racquet professional, F. Wright, was a clean-cut, typical young Englishman, similar to hundreds I have seen and with whom I have played, in bygone years, my favorite game of cricket, which has done more than any other sport for my physical development. I have not seen his name mentioned in any account of the disaster, and therefore take this opportunity of speaking of him, for I am perhaps the only survivor able to relate anything about his last days on earth.

Hundreds of letters have been written to us survivors, many containing photographs for identification of some lost loved one, whom perchance we may have seen or talked to before he met his fate. To these numerous inquiries I have been able to reply satisfactorily only in rare instances. The next and last time I saw Wright was on the stairway of Deck C within three-quarters of an hour after the collision. I was going to my cabin when I met him on the stairs going up. "Hadn't we better cancel that appointment for to-morrow morning?" I said rather jocosely to him. "Yes," he replied, but did not stop to tell what he then must have known of the conditions in the racquet court on G Deck, which, according to other witnesses, had at that time become flooded. His voice was calm, without enthusiasm, and perhaps his face was a little whiter than usual.

To the swimming pool attendant I also made promise to be on hand earlier the next morning, but I never saw him again.

One of the characters of the ship, best known to us all, was the gymnasium instructor, T. W. McCawley. He, also, expected me to make my first appearance for real good exercise on the morrow, but alas, he, too, was swallowed up by the sea. How well we survivors all remember this sturdy little man in white flannels and with his broad English accent! With what tireless enthusiasm he showed us the many mechanical devices under his charge and urged us to take advantage of the opportunity of using them, going through the motions of bicycle racing, rowing, boxing, camel and horseback riding, etc.

Such was my morning's preparation for the unforeseen physical exertions I was compelled to put forth for dear life at midnight, a few hours later. Could any better training for the terrible ordeal have been planned?

The exercise and the swim gave me an appetite for a hearty breakfast. Then followed the church service in the dining saloon, and I remember how much I was impressed with the "Prayer for those at Sea," also the words of the hymn, which we sang, No. 418 of the Hymnal. About a fortnight later, when I next heard it sung, I was in the little church at Smithtown, Long Island, attending the memorial service in honor of my old friend and fellow member of the Union Club, James Clinch Smith. To his sister, who sat next to me in the pew, I called attention to the fact that it was the last hymn we sang on this Sunday morning on board the *Titanic*. She was much affected, and gave the reason for its selection for the memorial service to her brother because it was known as Jim's favorite hymn, being the first piece set to music ever played by him as a child and for which he was rewarded with a promised prize, donated by his father.

What a remarkable coincidence that at the first and last ship's service on board the *Titanic*, the hymn we sang began with these impressive lines:

O God our help in ages past,
Our hope for years to come,
Our shelter from the stormy blast
And our eternal home.

One day was so like another that it is difficult to differentiate in our description all the details of this last day's incidents aboard ship.

The book that I finished and returned to the ship's library was Mary Johnston's "Old Dominion." While peacefully reading the tales of adventure and accounts of extraordinary escapes therein, how little 'I thought that in the next few hours I should be a witness and a party to a scene to which this book could furnish no counterpart, and that my own preservation from a watery grave would afford a remarkable illustration of how ofttimes "truth is stranger than fiction."

During this day I saw much of Mr. and Mrs. Isidor Straus. In fact, from the very beginning to the end of our trip on the *Titanic*, we had been together several times each day. I was with them on the deck the day we left Southampton and witnessed that ominous accident to the American liner, *New York*, lying at her pier, when the displacement of water by the movement of our gigantic ship caused a suction which pulled the smaller ship from her moorings and nearly caused a collision. At the time of this, Mr. Straus was telling me that it seemed only a few years back that he had taken passage on this same ship, the *New York,* on her maiden trip and when she was spoken of as the "last word in shipbuilding." He then called the attention of his wife and myself to the progress that had since been made, by comparison of the two ships then lying side by side. During our daily talks thereafter, he related much of special interest concerning incidents in his remarkable career, beginning with his early manhood in Georgia when, with the Confederate Government Commissioners, as an agent for the purchase of supplies, he ran the blockade of Europe. His friendship with President Cleveland, and how the latter had honored him, were among the topics of daily conversation that interested me most.

On this Sunday, our last day aboard ship, he finished the reading of a book I had loaned him, in which he expressed intense interest. This book was "The Truth About Chickamauga," of which I am the author, and it was to gain a much-needed rest after seven years of work thereon, and in order to get it off my mind, that I had taken this trip across the ocean and back. As a counter-irritant, my experience was a dose which was highly efficacious.

I recall how Mr. and Mrs. Straus were particularly happy about noon time on this same day in anticipation of communicating by wireless telegraphy with their son and his wife on their way to Europe on board the passing ship *Amerika*. Some time before six o'clock, full of contentment, they told me of the message of greeting received in reply. This last good-bye to their loved ones must have been a consoling thought when the end came a few hours thereafter.

That night after dinner, with my table companions, Messrs. James Clinch Smith and Edward A. Kent, according to usual custom, we adjourned to the palm room, with many others, for the usual coffee at individual tables where we listened to the always delightful music of the *Titanic's* band. On these occasions, full dress was always en règle; and it was a subject both of observation and admiration, that there were so many beautiful women—then especially in evidence—aboard the ship.

I invariably circulated around during these delightful evenings, chatting with those I knew, and with those whose acquaintance I had made during the voyage. I might specify names and particularize subjects of conversation, but the details, while interesting to those concerned, might not be so to all my readers. The recollections of those with whom I was thus closely associated in this disaster, including those who suffered the death from which I escaped and those who survived with me, will be a treasured memory and bond of union until my dying day. From the palm room, the men of my coterie would always go to the smoking room, and almost every evening join in conversation with some of the well-known men whom we met there, including within my own recollections Major Archie Butt, President Taft's Military Aid, discussing politics; Clarence Moore, of Washington, D. C., relating his venturesome trip some years ago through the West Virginia woods and mountains, helping a newspaper reporter in obtaining an interview with the outlaw, Captain Anse Hatfield; Frank D. Millet, the well-known artist, planning a journey west; Arthur Ryerson and others.

During these evenings I also conversed with Mr. John B. Thayer, Second Vice-President of the Pennsylvania Railroad, and with Mr. George D. Widener, a son of the Philadelphia street-car magnate, Mr. P. A. B. Widener.

My stay in the smoking-room on this particular evening for the first time was short, and I retired early with my cabin steward Cullen's promise to awaken me betimes next morning to get ready for the engagements I had made before breakfast for the game of racquets, work in the gymnasium and the swim that was to follow.

I cannot regard it as a mere coincidence that on this particular Sunday night I was thus prompted to retire early for nearly three hours of invigorating sleep, whereas an accident occurring at midnight of any of the four preceding days would have found me mentally and physically tired. That I was thus strengthened for the terrible ordeal, better even than had I been forewarned of it, I regard on the contrary as the first provision for my safety (answering the constant prayers of those at home), made by the guardian angel to whose care I was entrusted during the series of miraculous escapes presently to be recorded.

CHAPTER II

STRUCK BY AN ICEBERG

"Watchman, what of the night?"—Isaiah 21:11.

MY stateroom was an outside one on Deck C on the starboard quarter, somewhat abaft amidships. It was No. C, 51. I was enjoying a good night's rest when I was aroused by a sudden shock and noise forward on the starboard side, which I at once concluded was caused by a collision, with some other ship perhaps. I jumped from my bed, turned on the electric light, glanced at my watch nearby on the dresser, which I had changed to agree with ship's time on the day before and which now registered twelve o'clock. Correct ship's time would make it about 11.45. I opened the door of my cabin, looked out into the corridor, but could not see or hear anyone—there was no commotion whatever; but immediately following the collision came a great noise of escaping steam. I listened intently, but could hear no machinery. There was no mistaking that something wrong had happened, because of the ship stopping and the blowing off of steam.

Removing my night clothing I dressed myself hurriedly in underclothing, shoes and stockings, trousers and a Norfolk coat. I give these details in order that some idea of the lapse of time may be formed by an account of what I did during the interval. From my cabin, through the corridor to the stairway was but a short distance, and I ascended to the third deck above, that is, to the Boat Deck. I found here only one young lad, seemingly bent on the same quest as myself.

From the first cabin quarter, forward on the port side, we strained our eyes to discover what had struck us. From vantage points where the view was not obstructed by the lifeboats on this deck I sought the object, but in vain, though I swept the horizon near and far and discovered nothing.

It was a beautiful night, cloudless, and the stars shining brightly. The atmosphere was quite cold, but no ice or iceberg was in sight. If another ship had struck us there was no trace of it, and it did not yet occur to me that it was an iceberg with which we had collided. Not satisfied with a partial investigation, I made a complete tour of the deck, searching every point of the compass with my eyes. Going toward the stern, I vaulted over the iron gate and fence that divide the first and second cabin passengers. I disregarded the "not allowed" notice. I looked about me towards the officers' quarters in expectation of being challenged for non-observance of rules. In view of the collision I had expected to see some of the ship's officers on the Boat Deck, but there was no sign of an officer anywhere, and no one from whom to obtain any information about what had happened. Making my tour of the Boat Deck, the only other beings I saw were a middle-aged couple of the second cabin promenading unconcernedly, arm in arm, forward on the starboard quarter, against the wind, the man in a gray overcoat and outing cap.

Having gained no satisfaction whatever, I descended to the glass-enclosed Deck A, port side, and looked over the rail to see whether the ship was on an even keel, but I still could see nothing wrong. Entering the companionway, I passed Mr. Ismay with a member of the crew hurrying up the stairway. He wore a day suit, and, as usual, was hatless. He seemed too much preoccupied to notice anyone. Therefore I did not speak to him, but regarded his face very closely, perchance to learn from his manner how serious the accident might be. It occurred to me then that he was putting on as brave a face as possible so as to cause no alarm among the passengers.

At the foot of the stairway were a number of men passengers, and I now for the first time discovered that others were aroused as well as myself, among them my friend, Clinch Smith, from whom I first learned that an iceberg had struck us. He opened his hand and showed me some ice, flat like my watch, coolly suggesting that I might take it home for a souvenir. All of us will remember the way he had of cracking a joke without a smile. While we stood there, the story of the collision came to us—how someone in the smoking room, when the ship struck, rushed out to see what it was, and returning, told them that he had a glimpse of an iceberg towering fifty feet above Deck A, which, if true, would indicate a height of over one hundred feet. Here, too, I learned that the mail room was flooded and that the plucky postal clerks, in two feet of water, were at their posts. They were engaged in transferring to the upper deck, from the ship's post-office, the two hundred bags of registered mail containing four hundred thousand letters. The names of these men, who all sank with the ship, deserve to be recorded. They were: John S. Marsh, William L. Gwynn, Oscar S. Woody, Iago Smith and E. D. Williamson. The first three were Americans, the others Englishmen, and the families of the former were provided for by their Government.

And now Clinch Smith and myself noticed a list on the floor of the companionway. We kept our own counsel about it, not wishing to frighten anyone or cause any unnecessary alarm, especially among the ladies, who then appeared upon the scene. We did not consider it our duty to express our individual opinion upon the serious character of the accident which now appealed to us with the greatest force. He and I resolved to stick together in the final emergency, united in the silent bond of friendship, and lend a helping hand to each other whenever required. I recall having in my mind's eye at this moment all that I had read and heard in days gone by about shipwrecks, and pictured Smith and myself clinging to an overloaded raft in an open sea with a scarcity of food and water. We agreed to visit our respective staterooms and join each other later. All possessions in my stateroom were hastily packed into three large travelling bags so that the luggage might be ready in the event of a hasty transfer to another ship.

Fortunately I put on my long Newmarket overcoat that reached below my knees, and as I passed from the corridor into the companionway my worst fears were confirmed. Men and women were slipping on life-preservers, the stewards assisting in adjusting them. Steward Cullen insisted upon my returning to my stateroom for mine. I did so and he fastened one on me while I brought out the other for use by someone else.

Out on Deck A, port side, towards the stern, many men and women had already collected. I sought and found the unprotected ladies to whom I had proffered my services during the voyage when they boarded the ship at Southampton, Mrs. E. D. Appleton, wife of my St. Paul's School friend and schoolmate; Mrs. R. C. Cornell, wife of the well-known New York Justice, and Mrs. J. Murray Brown, wife of the Boston publisher, all old friends of my wife. These three sisters were returning home from a sad mission abroad, where they had laid to rest the remains of a fourth sister, Lady Victor Drummond, of whose death I had read accounts in the London papers, and all the sad details connected therewith were told me by the sisters themselves. That they would have to pass through a still greater ordeal seemed impossible, and how little did I know of the responsibility I took upon myself for their safety! Accompanying them, also unprotected, was their friend, Miss Edith Evans, to whom they introduced me. Mr. and Mrs. Straus, Colonel and

Mrs. Astor and others well known to me were among those here congregated on the port side of Deck A, including, besides Clinch Smith, two of our coterie of after-dinner companions, Hugh Woolner, son of the English sculptor, whose works are to be seen in Westminster Abbey, and H. Björnström Steffanson, the young lieutenant of the Swedish army, who, during the voyage, had told me of his acquaintance with Mrs. Gracie's relatives in Sweden.

It was now that the band began to play, and continued while the boats were being lowered. We considered this a wise provision tending to allay excitement. I did not recognize any of the tunes, but I know they were cheerful and were not hymns. If, as has been reported, "Nearer My God to Thee" was one of the selections, I assuredly should have noticed it and regarded it as a tactless warning of immediate death to us all and one likely to create a panic that our special efforts were directed towards avoiding, and which we accomplished to the fullest extent. I know of only two survivors whose names are cited by the newspapers as authority for the statement that this hymn was one of those played. On the other hand, all whom I have questioned or corresponded with, including the best qualified, testified emphatically to the contrary.

Our hopes were buoyed with the information, imparted through the ship's officers, that there had been an interchange of wireless messages with passing ships, one of which was certainly coming to our rescue. To reassure the ladies of whom I had assumed special charge, I showed them a bright white light of what I took to be a ship about five miles off and which I felt sure was coming to our rescue. Colonel Astor heard me telling this to them and he asked me to show it and I pointed the light out to him. In so doing we both had now to lean over the rail of the ship and look close in towards the bow, avoiding a lifeboat even then made ready with its gunwale lowered to the level of the floor of the Boat Deck above us and obstructing our view; but instead of growing brighter the light grew dim and less and less distinct and passed away altogether. The light, as I have since learned, with tearful regret for the lost who might have been saved, belonged to the steamer *Californian* of the Leyland line, Captain Stanley Lord, bound from London to Boston. She belonged to the International Mercantile Marine Company, the owners of the *Titanic*.

This was the ship from which two of the six "ice messages" were sent. The first one received and acknowledged by the *Titanic* was one at 7.30

p. m., an intercepted message to another ship.
The next was about 11 p. m., when the Captain
of the *Californian* saw a ship approaching from
the eastward, which he was advised to be the
Titanic, and under his orders this message was
sent: "We are stopped and surrounded by ice."
To this the *Titanic's* wireless operator brusquely
replied, "Shut up, I am busy. I am working Cape
Race." The business here referred to was the
sending of wireless messages for passengers on
the *Titanic;* and the stronger current of the *Californian* eastward interfered therewith. Though
the navigation of the ship and the issues of life
and death were at stake, the right of way was
given to communication with Cape Race until
within a few minutes of the *Titanic's* collision with
the iceberg.

Nearly all this time, until 11.30 p. m., the
wireless operator of the *Californian* was listening with 'phones on his head, but at 11.30 p. m.,
while the *Titanic* was still talking to Cape Race,
the former ship's operator "put the 'phones down,
took off his clothes and turned in."

The fate of thousands of lives hung in the balance many times that ill-omened night, but *the
circumstances in connection with the S. S. Californian* (Br. Rep. pp. 43-46), furnish the evidence
corroborating that of the American Investigation,

viz., that it was not chance, but the grossest neg-
ligence alone which sealed the fate of all the
noble lives, men and women, that were lost.

It appears from the evidence referred to, information in regard to which we learned after
our arrival in New York, that the Captain of the
Californian and his crew were watching our
lights from the deck of their ship, which remained
approximately stationary until 5.15 a. m. on the
following morning. During this interval it is
shown that they were never distant more than six
or seven miles. In fact, at 12 o'clock, the *Californian* was only four or five miles off at the
point and in the general direction where she was
seen by myself and at least a dozen others, who
bore testimony before the American Committee,
from the decks of the *Titanic*. The white rockets
which we sent up, referred to presently, were also
plainly seen at the time. Captain Lord was completely in possession of the knowledge that he
was in proximity to a ship in distress. He could
have put himself into immediate communication
with us by wireless had he desired confirmation
of the name of the ship and the disaster which
had befallen it. His indifference is made apparent by his orders to "go on Morseing," instead of
utilizing the more modern method of the inven-
tive genius and gentleman, Mr. Marconi, which

eventually saved us all. "The night was clear and the sea was smooth. The ice by which the *Californian* was surrounded," says the British Report, "was loose ice extending for a distance of not more than two or three miles in the direction of the *Titanic*." When she first saw the rockets, the *Californian* could have pushed through the ice to the open water without any serious risk and so have come to the assistance of the *Titanic*. A discussion of this subject is the most painful of all others for those who lost their loved ones aboard our ship.

When we realized that the ship whose lights we saw was not coming towards us, our hopes of rescue were correspondingly depressed, but the men's counsel to preserve calmness prevailed; and to reassure the ladies they repeated the much advertised fiction of "the unsinkable ship" on the supposed highest qualified authority. It was at this point that Miss Evans related to me the story that years ago in London she had been told by a fortune-teller to "beware of water," and now "she knew she would be drowned." My efforts to persuade her to the contrary were futile. Though she gave voice to her story, she presented no evidence whatever of fear, and when I saw and conversed with her an hour later when conditions appeared especially desperate, and the last lifeboat was supposed to have departed, she was perfectly calm and did not revert again to the superstitious tale.

From my own conclusions, and those of others, it appears that about forty-five minutes had now elapsed since the collision when Captain Smith's orders were transmitted to the crew to lower the lifeboats, loaded with women and children first. The self-abnegation of Mr. and Mrs. Isidor Straus here shone forth heroically when she promptly and emphatically exclaimed: "No! I will not be separated from my husband; as we have lived, so will we die together;" and when he, too, declined the assistance proffered on my earnest solicitation that, because of his age and helplessness, exception should be made and he be allowed to accompany his wife in the boat. "No!" he said, "I do not wish any distinction in my favor which is not granted to others." As near as I can recall them these were the words which they addressed to me. They expressed themselves as fully prepared to die, and calmly sat down in steamer chairs on the glass-enclosed Deck A, prepared to meet their fate. Further entreaties to make them change their decision were of no avail. Later they moved to the Boat Deck above, accompanying Mrs. Straus's maid, who entered a lifeboat.

When the order to load the boats was received I had promptly moved forward with the ladies in my charge toward the boats then being lowered from the Boat Deck above to Deck A on the port side of the ship, where we then were. A tall, slim young Englishman, Sixth Officer J. P. Moody, whose name I learned later, with other members of the ship's crew, barred the progress of us men passengers any nearer to the boats. All that was left me was then to consign these ladies in my charge to the protection of the ship's officer, and I thereby was relieved of their responsibility and felt sure that they would be safely loaded in the boats at this point. I remember a steward rolling a small barrel out of the door of the companionway. "What have you there?" said I. "Bread for the lifeboats," was his quick and cheery reply, as I passed inside the ship for the last time, searching for two of my table companions, Mrs. Churchill Candee of Washington and Mr. Edward A. Kent. It was then that I met Wright, the racquet player, and exchanged the few words on the stairway already related.

Considering it well to have a supply of blankets for use in the open boats exposed to the cold, I concluded, while passing, to make another, and my last, descent to my stateroom for this purpose, only to find it locked, and on asking the reason why was told by some other steward than Cullen that it was done "to prevent looting." Advising him of what was wanted, I went with him to the cabin stewards' quarters nearby, where extra blankets were stored, and where I obtained them. I then went the length of the ship inside on this glass-enclosed Deck A from aft, forwards, looking in every room and corner for my missing table companions, but no passengers whatever were to be seen except in the smoking room, and there all alone by themselves, seated around a table, were four men, three of whom were personally well known to me, Major Butt, Clarence Moore and Frank Millet, but the fourth was a stranger, whom I therefore cannot identify. All four seemed perfectly oblivious of what was going on on the decks outside. It is impossible to suppose that they did not know of the collision with an iceberg and that the room they were in had been deserted by all others, who had hastened away. It occurred to me at the time that these men desired to show their entire indifference to the danger and that if I advised them as to how seriously I regarded it, they would laugh at me. This was the last I ever saw of any of them, and I know of no one who testifies to seeing them later, except a lady who mentions having seen Major Butt on the bridge five

minutes before the last boat left the ship. There
is no authentic story of what they did when the
water reached this deck, and their ultimate fate is
only a matter of conjecture. That they went
down in the ship on this Deck A, when the steerage passengers (as described later) blocked the
way to the deck above, is my personal belief,
founded on the following facts, to wit: First, that
neither I nor anyone else, so far as I know,
ever saw any of them on the Boat Deck,
and second, that the bodies of none of them
were ever recovered, indicating the possibility
that all went down inside the ship or the enclosed
deck.

I next find myself forward on the port side,
part of the time on the Boat Deck, and part on
the deck below it, called Deck A, where I rejoined Clinch Smith, who reported that Mrs.
Candee had departed on one of the boats. We
remained together until the ship went down. I
was on the Boat Deck when I saw and heard the
first rocket, and then successive ones sent up at intervals thereafter. These were followed by the
Morse red and blue lights, which were signalled
near by us on the deck where we were; but we
looked in vain for any response. These signals
of distress indicated to every one of us that the

ship's fate was sealed, and that she might sink
before the lifeboats could be lowered.

And now I am on Deck A again, where I helped
in the loading of two boats lowered from the deck
above. There were twenty boats in all on the
ship: 14 wooden lifeboats, each thirty feet long
by nine feet one inch broad, constructed to carry
sixty-five persons each; 2 wooden cutters, emergency boats, twenty-five feet two inches long by
seven feet two inches broad, constructed to carry
forty persons each; and 4 Engelhardt "surf-
boats" with canvas collapsible sides extending
above the gunwales, twenty-five feet five inches
long by eight feet broad, constructed to carry
forty-seven persons each. The lifeboats were
ranged along the ship's rail, or its prolongation
forward and aft on the Boat Deck, the odd numbered on the starboard and the even numbered on
the port side. Two of the Engelhardt boats were
on the Boat Deck forward beneath the Emergency
boats suspended on davits above. The other
Engelhardt boats were on the roof of the officers'
house forward of the first funnel. They are
designated respectively by the letters, A. B. C. D;
A and C on the starboard, B and D on the port
sides. They have a rounded bottom like a canoe.
The name "collapsible boat" generally applied has
given rise to mistaken impressions in regard to

them, because of the adjustable canvas sides above-mentioned.

At this quarter I was no longer held back from approaching near the boats, but my assistance and work as one of the crew in the loading of boats and getting them away as quickly as possible were accepted, for there was now no time to spare. The Second Officer, Lightoller, was in command on the port side forward, where I was. One of his feet was planted in the lifeboat, and the other on the rail of Deck A, while we, through the wood frames of the lowered glass windows on this deck, passed women, children, and babies in rapid succession without any confusion whatsoever. Among this number was Mrs. Astor, whom I lifted over the four-feet high rail of the ship through the frame. Her husband held her left arm as we carefully passed her to Lightoller, who seated her in the boat. A dialogue now ensued between Colonel Astor and the officer, every word of which I listened to with intense interest. Astor was close to me in the adjoining window-frame, to the left of mine. Leaning out over the rail he asked permission of Lightoller to enter the boat to protect his wife, which, in view of her delicate condition, seems to have been a reasonable request, but the officer, intent upon his duty, and obeying orders, and not knowing the millionaire from the rest of us, replied: "No, sir, no men are allowed in these boats until women are loaded first." Colonel Astor did not demur, but bore the refusal bravely and resignedly, simply asking the number of the boat to help find his wife later in case he also was rescued. "Number 4," was Lightoller's reply. Nothing more was said. Colonel Astor moved away from this point and I never saw him again. I do not for a moment believe the report that he attempted to enter, or did enter, a boat and it is evident that if any such thought occurred to him at all it must have been at this present time and in this boat with his wife. Second Officer Lightoller recalled the incident perfectly when I reminded him of it. It was only through me that Colonel Astor's identity was established in his mind. "I assumed," said he, "that I was asked to give the number of the lifeboat as the passenger intended, for some unknown cause, to make complaint about me." From the fact that I never saw Colonel Astor on the Boat Deck later, and also because his body, when found, was crushed (according to the statement of one who saw it at Halifax, Mr. Harry K. White, of Boston, Mr. Edward A. Kent's brother-in-law, my schoolmate and friend from boyhood), I am of the opinion that he met his fate on the ship when the boilers tore through it, as described later.

One of the incidents I recall when loading the boats at this point was my seeing a young woman clinging tightly to a baby in her arms as she approached near the ship's high rail, but unwilling even for a moment to allow anyone else to hold the little one while assisting her to board the lifeboat. As she drew back sorrowfully to the outer edge of the crowd on the deck, I followed and persuaded her to accompany me to the rail again, promising if she would entrust the baby to me I would see that the officer passed it to her after she got aboard. I remember her trepidation as she acceded to my suggestion and the happy expression of relief when the mother was safely seated with the baby restored to her. "Where is my baby?" was her anxious wail. "I have your baby," I cried, as it was tenderly handed along. I remember this incident well because of my feeling at the time, when I had the babe in my care; though the interval was short, I wondered how I should manage with it in my arms if the lifeboats got away and I should be plunged into the water with it as the ship sank.

According to Lightoller's testimony before the Senate Committee he put twenty to twenty five women, with two seamen to row, in the first boat and thirty, with two seamen, in the second.

Our labors in loading the boats were now

shifted to the Boat Deck above, where Clinch
Smith and I, with others, followed Lightoller and
the crew. On this deck some difficulty was experienced in getting the boats ready to lower. Several causes may have contributed to this, viz., lack
of drill and insufficient number of seamen for such
emergency, or because of the new tackle not working smoothly. We had the hardest time with the
Engelhardt boat, lifting and pushing it towards
and over the rail. My shoulders and the whole
weight of my body were used in assisting the crew
at this work. Lightoller's testimony tells us that
as the situation grew more serious he began to
take chances and in loading the third boat he filled
it up as full as he dared to, with about thirty-five
persons. By this time he was short of seamen,
and in the fourth boat he put the first man passenger. "Are you a sailor?" Lightoller asked, and
received the reply from the gentleman addressed
that he was "a yachtsman." Lightoller told him
if he was "sailor enough to get out over the bul-
warks to the lifeboat, to go ahead." This passenger was Major Arthur Peuchen, of Toronto,
who acquitted himself as a brave man should. My
energies were so concentrated upon this work of
loading the boats at this quarter that lapse of
time, sense of sight and sense of hearing recorded
no impressions during this interval until the last

boat was loaded; but there is one fact of which I am positive, and that is that every man, woman, officer and member of the crew did their full duty without a sign of fear or confusion. Lightoller's strong and steady voice rang out his orders in clear firm tones, inspiring confidence and obedience. There was not one woman who shed tears or gave any sign of fear or distress. There was not a man at this quarter of the ship who indicated a desire to get into the boats and escape with the women. There was not a member of the crew who shirked, or left his post. The coolness, courage, and sense of duty that I here witnessed made me thankful to God and proud of my Anglo-Saxon race that gave this perfect and superb exhibition of self-control at this hour of severest trial. "The boat's deck was only ten feet from the water when I lowered the sixth boat," testified Lightoller, "and when we lowered the first, the distance to the water was seventy feet. We had now loaded all the women who were in sight at that quarter of the ship, and I ran along the deck with Clinch Smith on the port side some distance aft shouting, "Are there any more women?" "Are there any more women?" On my return there was a very palpable list to port as if the ship was about to topple over. The deck was on a corresponding slant. "All passengers to the starboard side," was Lightoller's loud command, heard by all of us. Here I thought the final crisis had come, with the boats all gone, and when we were to be precipitated into the sea.

Prayerful thoughts now began to rise in me that my life might be preserved and I be restored to my loved ones at home. I weighed myself in the balance, doubtful whether I was thus deserving of God's mercy and protection. I questioned myself as to the performance of my religious duties according to the instructions of my earliest Preceptor, the Rev. Henry A. Coit, whose St. Paul's School at Concord, N. H., I had attended. My West Point training in the matter of recognition of constituted authority and maintenance of composure stood me in good stead.

My friend, Clinch Smith, urged immediate obedience to Lightoller's orders, and, with other men passengers, we crossed over to the starboard quarter of the ship, forward on the same Boat Deck where, as I afterwards learned, the officer in command was First Officer Murdoch, who had also done noble work, and was soon thereafter to lose his life. Though the deck here was not so noticeably aslant as on the port side, the conditions appeared fully as desperate. All the lifeboats had been lowered and had departed. There was somewhat of a crowd congregated along the rail. The

light was sufficient for me to recognize distinctly
many of those with whom I was well acquainted.
Here, pale and determined, was Mr. John B.
Thayer, Second Vice-President of the Pennsylvania Railroad, and Mr. George D. Widener.
They were looking over the ship's gunwale, talking
earnestly as if debating what to do. Next to them
it pained me to discover Mrs. J. M. Brown and
Miss Evans, the two ladies whom more than an
hour previous I had, as related, consigned to the
care of Sixth Officer Moody on Deck A, where he,
as previously described, blocked my purpose of accompanying these ladies and personally assisting
them into the boat. They showed no signs of
perturbation whatever as they conversed quietly
with me. Mrs. Brown quickly related how they
became separated, in the crowd, from her sisters,
Mrs. Appleton and Mrs. Cornell. Alas! that they
had not remained on the same port side of the
ship, or moved forward on Deck A, or the Boat
Deck! Instead, they had wandered in some un-
explained way to the very furthest point diag-
onally from where they were at first. At the time
of introduction I had not caught Miss Evans'
name, and when we were here together at this crit-
ical moment I thought it important to ask, and
she gave me her name. Meantime the crew were
working on the roof of the officers' quarters to

cut loose one of the Engelhardt boats. All this took place more quickly than it takes to write it.

Meantime, I will describe what was going on at the quarter where I left Lightoller loading the last boat on the port side. The information was obtained personally from him, in answer to my careful questioning during the next few days on board the *Carpathia,* when I made notes thereof, which were confirmed again the next week in Washington, where we were both summoned before the Senate Investigating Committee. "Men from the steerage," he said, "rushed the boat." "Rush" is the word he used, meaning they got in without his permission. He drew his pistol and ordered them out, threatening to shoot if they attempted to enter the boat again. I presume it was in consequence of this incident that the crew established the line which I encountered, presently referred to, which blocked the men passengers from approaching the last boat loaded on the port side forward, where we had been, and the last one that was safely loaded from the ship.

During this very short interval I was on the starboard side, as described, next to the rail, with Mrs. Brown and Miss Evans, when I heard a member of the crew, coming from the quarter where the last boat was loaded, say that there was room for more ladies in it. I immediately seized each lady by the arm, and, with Miss Evans on my right and Mrs. Brown on my left, hurried, with three other ladies following us, toward the port side; but I had not proceeded half-way, and near amidship, when I was stopped by the aforesaid line of the crew barring my progress, and one of the officers told me that only the women could pass.

The story of what now happened to Mrs. Brown and Miss Evans after they left me must be told by Mrs. Brown, as related to me by herself when I rejoined her next on board the *Carpathia*. Miss Evans led the way, she said, as they neared the rail where what proved to be the last lifeboat was being loaded, but in a spirit of most heroic self-sacrifice Miss Evans insisted upon Mrs. Brown's taking precedence in being assisted aboard the boat. "You go first," she said. "You are married and have children." But when Miss Evans attempted to follow after, she was unable to do so for some unknown cause. The women in the boat were not able, it would appear, to pull Miss Evans in. It was necessary for her first to clear the four feet high ship's gunwale, and no man or member of the crew was at this particular point to lift her over. I have questioned Mr. Lightoller several times about this, but he has not been able to give any satisfactory explanation and cannot understand it, for when he gave orders to lower away, there was no woman in sight. I have further questioned him as to whether there was an interval between the ship's rail and the lifeboat he was loading, but he says, "No," for until the very last boat he stood, as has already been described, with one foot planted on the ship's gunwale and the other in the lifeboat. I had thought that the list of the ship might have caused too much of an interval for him to have done this. Perhaps what I have read in a letter of Mrs. Brown may furnish some reason why Miss Evans' efforts to board the lifeboat, in which there was plenty of room for her, were unavailing. "Never mind," she is said to have called out, "I will go on a later boat." She then ran away and was not seen again; but there was no later boat, and it would seem that after a momentary impulse, being disappointed and being unable to get into the boat, she went aft on the port side, and no one saw her again. Neither the second officer nor I saw any women on the deck during the interval thereafter of fifteen or twenty minutes before the great ship sank.

An inspection of the American and British Reports shows that all women and children of the first cabin were saved except five. Out of the one hundred and fifty these were the five lost: (1)

Miss Evans; (2) Mrs. Straus; (3) Mrs. H. J. Allison, of Montreal; (4) her daughter, Miss Allison, and (5) Miss A. E. Isham, of New York. The first two have already been accounted for. Mrs. Allison and Miss Allison could have been saved had they not chosen to remain on the ship. They refused to enter the lifeboat unless Mr. Allison was allowed to go with them. This statement was made in my presence by Mrs. H. A. Cassobeer, of New York, who related it to Mrs. Allison's brother, Mr. G. F. Johnston, and myself. Those of us who survived among the first cabin passengers will remember this beautiful Mrs. Allison, and will be glad to know of the heroic mould in which she was cast, as exemplified by her fate, which was similar to that of another, Mrs. Straus, who has been memorialized the world over. The fifth lady lost was Miss A. E. Isham, and she is the only one of whom no survivor, so far as I can learn, is able to give any information whatever as to where she was or what she did on that fateful Sunday night. Her relatives, learning that her stateroom, No. C, 49, adjoined mine, wrote me in the hope that I might be able to furnish some information to their sorrowing hearts about her last hours on the shipwrecked *Titanic*. It was with much regret that I replied that I had not seen my neighbor at any time, and, not having the pleasure of her acquaintance, identification was impossible. I was, however, glad to be able to assure her family of one point, viz., that she did not meet with the horrible fate which they feared. in being locked in her stateroom and drowned. I had revisited my stateroom twice after being aroused by the collision, and am sure that she was fully warned of what had happened, and after she left her stateroom it was locked behind her, as was mine.

The simple statement of fact that all of the first cabin women were sent off in the lifeboats and saved, except five—three of whom met heroic death through choice and two by some mischance —is in itself the most sublime tribute that could be paid to the self-sacrifice and the gallantry of the first cabin men, including all the grand heroes who sank with the ship and those of us who survived their fate. All authentic testimony of both first and second cabin passengers is also in evidence that the Captain's order for women and children to be loaded first met with the unanimous approval of us all, and in every instance was carried out both in letter and in spirit. In Second Officer Lightoller's testimony before the Senate Committee, when asked whether the Captain's order was a rule of the sea, he answered that it was "the rule of human nature." There is no doubt in my mind that the men at that quarter where we were would have adopted the same rule spontaneously whether ordered by the Captain, or not. Speaking from my own personal observation, which by comparison with that of the second officer I find in accord with his, all six boat loads, including the last, departed with women and children only, with not a man passenger except Major Peuchen, whose services were enlisted to replace the lack of crew. I may say further that with the single exception of Colonel Astor's plea for the protection of his wife, in delicate condition, there was not one who made a move or a suggestion to enter a boat.

While the light was dim on the decks it was always sufficient for me to recognize anyone with whom I was acquainted, and I am happy in being able to record the names of those I know beyond any doubt whatever, as with me in these last terrible scenes when Lightoller's boats were being lowered and after the last lifeboat had left the ship. The names of these were: James Clinch Smith, Colonel John Jacob Astor, Mr. John B. Thayer and Mr. George D. Widener. So far as I know, and my research has been exhaustive, I am the sole surviving passenger who was with or assisted Lightoller in the loading of the last boats. When I first saw and realized that every lifeboat had left the ship, the sensation felt was not an agreeable one. No thought of fear entered my head, but I experienced a feeling which others may recall when holding the breath in the face of some frightful emergency and when "vox faucibus hæsit," as frequently happened to the old Trojan hero of our school days. This was the nearest approach to fear, if it can be so characterized, that is discernible in an analysis of my actions or feelings while in the midst of the many dangers which beset me during that night of terror. Though still worse and seemingly many hopeless conditions soon prevailed, and unexpected ones, too, when I felt that "any moment might be my last," I had no time to contemplate danger when there was continuous need of quick thought, action and composure withal. Had I become rattled for a moment, or in the slightest degree been undecided during the several emergencies presently cited, I am certain that I never should have lived to tell the tale of my miraculous escape. For it is eminently fitting, in gratitude to my Maker, that I should make the acknowledgment that I know of no recorded instance of Providential deliverance more directly attributable to cause and effect, illustrating the efficacy of prayer and how "God helps those who help themselves." I should have only courted the fate of many hundreds of others had I supinely made no effort to supplement my prayers with all the strength and power which He has granted to me. While I said to myself, "Good-bye to all at home," I hoped and prayed for escape. My mind was nerved to do the duty of the moment, and my muscles seemed to be hardened in preparation for any struggle that might come. When I learned that there was still another boat, the Engelhardt, on the roof of the officers' quarters, I felt encouraged with the thought that here was a chance of getting away before the ship sank; but what was one boat among so many eager to board her?

During my short absence in conducting the ladies to a position of safety, Mr. Thayer and Mr. Widener had disappeared, but I know not whither. Mr. Widener's son, Harry, was probably with them, but Mr. Thayer supposed that his young son, Jack, had left the ship in the same boat with his mother. Messrs. Thayer and Widener must have gone toward the stern during the short interval of my absence. No one at this point had jumped into the sea. If there had been any, both Clinch Smith and I would have known it. After the water struck the bridge forward there were many who rushed aft, climbed over the rail and jumped, but I never saw one of them.

I was now working with the crew at the davits on the starboard side forward, adjusting them, ready for lowering the Engelhardt boat from the roof of the officers' house to the Boat Deck below. Some one of the crew on the roof, where it was, sang out, "Has any passenger a knife?"   I took mine out of my pocket and tossed it to him, saying, "Here is a small penknife, if that will do any good."   It appeared to me then that there was more trouble than there ought to have been in removing the canvas cover and cutting the boat loose, and that some means should have been available for doing this without any delay.   Meantime, four or five long oars were placed aslant against the walls of the officers' house to break the fall of the boat, which was pushed from the roof and slipped with a crash down on the Boat Deck, smashing several of the oars.   Clinch Smith and I scurried out of the way and stood leaning with our backs against the rail, watching this procedure and feeling anxious lest the boat might have been stove in, or otherwise injured so as to cause her to leak in the water.   The account of the junior Marconi operator, Harold S. Bride, supplements mine.   "I saw a collapsible boat," he said, "near a funnel, and went over to it.   Twelve men were trying to boost it down to the Boat Deck.   They were having an awful time.   It was the last boat left.   I looked at it longingly a few minutes; then I gave a hand and over she went."

About this time I recall that an officer on the roof of the house called down to the crew at this quarter, "Are there any seamen down there among you?" "Aye, aye, sir," was the response, and quite a number left the Boat Deck to assist in what I supposed to have been the cutting loose of the other Engelhardt boat up there on the roof. Again I heard an inquiry for another knife. I thought I recognized the voice of the second officer working up there with the crew. Lightoller has told me, and has written me as well, that "boat A on the starboard side did not leave the ship," * while "B was thrown down to the Boat Deck," and was the one on which he and I eventually climbed. The crew had thrown the Engelhardt boat to the deck, but I did not understand why they were so long about launching it, unless they were waiting to cut the other one loose and launch them both at the same time. Two young men of the crew, nice looking, dressed in white, one tall and the other smaller, were coolly debating as to whether the compartments would hold the ship afloat. They were standing with their backs to the rail looking on at the rest of the crew, and I recall asking one of them why he did not assist.

---

* With the evidence on the subject presented later he recognizes that Boat A floated away and was afterwards utilized.

At this time there were other passengers
around, but Clinch Smith was the only one associated with me here to the last. It was about this
time, fifteen minutes after the launching of the last
lifeboat on the port side, that I heard a noise that
spread consternation among us all. This was no
less than the water striking the bridge and gur-
gling up the hatchway forward. It seemed momentarily as if it would reach the Boat Deck. It
appeared as if it would take the crew a long time
to turn the Engelhardt boat right side up and lift
it over the rail, and there were so many ready to
board her that she would have been swamped.
Probably taking these points into consideration,
Clinch Smith made the proposition that we should
leave and go toward the stern, still on the starboard side, so he started and I followed immediately after him. We had taken but a few steps
in the direction indicated when there arose before
us from the decks below, a mass of humanity several lines deep, covering the Boat Deck, facing us,
and completely blocking our passage toward the
stern.

There were women in the crowd, as well
as men, and they seemed to be steerage passengers
who had just come up from the decks below. Instantly, when they saw us and the water on the
deck chasing us from behind, they turned in the

opposite direction towards the stern. This brought them at that point plumb against the iron fence and railing which divide the first and second cabin passengers. Even among these people there was no hysterical cry, or evidence of panic, but oh, the agony of it! Clinch Smith and I instantly saw that we could make no progress ahead, and with the water following us behind over the deck, we were in a desperate place. I can never forget the exact point on the ship where he and I were located, viz., at the opening of the angle made by the walls of the officers' house and only a short distance abaft the *Titanic's* forward "expansion joint." Clinch Smith was immediately on my left, nearer the apex of the angle, and our backs were turned toward the ship's rail and the sea. Looking up toward the roof of the officers' house I saw a man to the right of me and above lying on his stomach on the roof, with his legs dangling over. Clinch Smith jumped to reach this roof, and I promptly followed. The efforts of both of us failed. I was loaded down with heavy long-skirted overcoat and Norfolk coat beneath, with clumsy life-preserver over all, which made my jump fall short. As I came down, the water struck my right side. I crouched down into it preparatory to jumping with it, and rose as if on the crest of a wave on the seashore. This expedient brought the attainment of the object I had in view. I was able to reach the roof and the iron railing that is along the edge of it, and pulled myself over on top of the officers' house on my stomach near the base of the second funnel. The feat which I instinctively accomplished was the simple one, familiar to all bathers in the surf at the seashore. I had no time to advise Clinch Smith to adopt it. To my utter dismay, a hasty glance to my left and right showed that he had not followed my example, and that the wave, if I may call it such, which had mounted me to the roof, had completely covered him, as well as all people on both sides of me, including the man I had first seen athwart the roof.

I was thus parted forever from my friend, Clinch Smith, with whom I had agreed to remain to the last struggle. I felt almost a pang of responsibility for our separation; but he was not in sight and there was no chance of rendering assistance. His ultimate fate is a matter of conjecture. Hemmed in by the mass of people toward the stern, and cornered in the locality previously described, it seems certain that as the ship keeled over and sank, his body was caught in the angle or in the coils of rope and other appurtenances on the deck and borne down to the depths below. There could not be a braver man than James Clinch Smith. He was the embodiment of coolness and courage during the whole period of the disaster. While in constant touch and communication with him at the various points on the ship when we were together on this tragic night, he never showed the slightest sign of fear, but manifested the same quiet imperturbable manner so well known to all of his friends, who join with his family in mourning his loss. His conduct should be an inspiration to us all, and an appropriate epitaph to his memory taken from the words of Christ would be: "Greater love hath no man than this, that a man lay down his life for his friend."

CHAPTER III

THE FOUNDERING OF THE "TITANIC"

"There is sorrow on the sea; it cannot be quiet."
—Jeremiah 49:23.

BEFORE I resume the story of my personal escape it is pertinent that I should, at this juncture, discuss certain points wherein the statements of survivors are strangely at variance.

First: Was there an explosion of the ship's boilers?

I am of opinion that there was none, because I should have been conscious of it. When aboard ship I should have heard it and felt it, but I did not. As my senses were on the lookout for every danger, I cannot conceive it possible that an explosion occurred without my being made aware of it. When I went down holding on to the ship and was under water, I heard no sound indicating anything of the sort, and when I came to the surface there was no ship in sight. Furthermore, there was no perceptible wave which such a disturbance would have created.

The two ranking surviving officers of the *Ti-*

tanic, viz., Second Officer Lightoller and Third Officer Pitman, with whom I had a discussion on this and other points in almost daily conversation in my cabin on the *Carpathia,* agreed with me that there was no explosion of the boilers. The second officer and myself had various similar experiences, and, as will be noticed in the course of this narrative, we were very near together during all the perils of that awful night. The only material difference worth noting was the manner in which each parted company with the ship, and finally reached the bottom-up Engelhardt boat on top of which we made our escape. According to his testimony before the Senate Committee, he stood on the roof of the officers' quarters in front of the first funnel, facing forward, and as the ship dived, he dived also, while I held on to the iron railing on the same roof, near the second funnel, as has been described, and as the ship sank I was pulled down with it. The distance between us on the ship was then about fifteen yards.

There are so many newspaper and other published reports citing the statements of certain survivors as authority for this story of an explosion of the boilers that the reading world generally has been made to believe it. Among the names of passengers whose alleged statements (I have received letters repudiating some of these interviews) are thus given credence, I have read those of Miss Cornelia Andrews, of Hudson, N. Y.; Mrs. W. E. Carter, of Philadelphia, Pa.; Mr. John Pillsbury Snyder, of Minneapolis, Minn.; Miss Minahan, of Fond du Lac, Wis., and Lady Duff Gordon, of England, all of whom, according to the newspaper reports, describe their position in the lifeboats around the ship and how they heard, or saw, the "ship blow up," or "the boilers explode" with one or two explosions just before the ship sank out of their sight. On the other hand, Mr. Hugh Woolner told me on the *Carpathia* that from his position in the lifeboat, which he claims was the nearest one to the *Titanic* when she sank some seventy-five yards away, there was a terrific noise on the ship, as she slanted towards the head before the final plunge, which sounded like the crashing of millions of dishes of crockery. Woolner and I when on board the *Carpathia,* as presently described, had our cabin together, where we were visited by Officers Lightoller and Pitman. This was one of the points we discussed together, and the conclusion was at once reached as to the cause of this tremendous crash. Since then, Lightoller has been subjected to rigid examination before this country's and England's Investigating Committees, and has been a party to discussions with experts, including the designers and builders of the *Titanic*. His conclusion expressed on the *Carpathia* is now strengthened, and he says that there was no explosion of the boilers and that the great noise which was mistaken for it was due to "the boilers leaving their beds" on E Deck when the ship was aslant and, with their great weight, sliding along the deck, crushing and tearing through the doomed vessel forward toward the bow. Third Officer Pitman also gave his testimony on this, as well as the next point considered. Before the Senate Committee he said: "Then she turned right on end and made a big plunge forward. The *Titanic* did not break asunder. I heard reports like big guns in the distance. I assumed the great bulkheads had gone to pieces." Cabin-steward Samuel Rule said: "I think the noise we heard was that of the boilers and engines breaking away from their seatings and falling down through the forward bulkhead. At the time it occurred, the ship was standing nearly upright in the water."

The peculiar way in which the *Titanic* is described as hesitating and assuming a vertical position before her final dive to the depths below can be accounted for only on this hypothesis of the sliding of the boilers from their beds. A second cabin passenger, Mr. Lawrence Beesley, a Cambridge University man, has written an excellent book about the *Titanic* disaster, dwelling especially upon the lessons to be learned from it. His account given to the newspapers also contains the most graphic description from the viewpoint of those in the lifeboats, telling how the great ship looked before her final plunge. He "was a mile or two miles away," he writes, "when the oarsmen lay on their oars and all in the lifeboat were motionless as we watched the ship in absolute silence—save some who would not look and buried their heads on each others' shoulders. . . . As we gazed awe-struck, she tilted slightly up, revolving apparently about a centre of gravity just astern of amidships until she attained a vertical upright position, and there she remained—motionless! As she swung up, her lights, which had shown without a flicker all night, went out suddenly, then came on again for a single flash and then went out altogether; and as they did so there came a noise which many people, wrongly, I think, have described as an explosion. It has always seemed to me that it was nothing but the engines and machinery coming loose from their place and bearings and falling through the compartments, smashing everything in their way. It was partly a roar, partly a groan, partly a rattle and partly a smash, and it was not a sudden roar as an explosion would be; it went on successively for some seconds, possibly fifteen or twenty, as the heavy machinery dropped down to the bottom (now the bows) of the ship; I suppose it fell through the end and sank first before the ship. (For evidence of shattered timbers, see Hagan's testimony, page 85.) But it was a noise no one had heard before and no one wishes to hear again. It was stupefying, stupendous, as it came to us along the water. It was as if all the heavy things one could think of had been thrown downstairs from the top of a house, smashing each other, and the stairs and everything in the way.

"Several apparently authentic accounts have been given in which definite stories of explosions have been related—in some cases even with wreckage blown up and the ship broken in two; but I think such accounts will not stand close analysis. In the first place, the fires had been withdrawn and the steam allowed to escape some time before she sank, and the possibility from explosion from this cause seems very remote."

Second: Did the ship break in two?

I was on the *Carpathia* when I first heard any one make reference to this point. The seventeen-year-old son of Mr. John B. Thayer, "Jack" Thayer, Jr., and his young friend from Philadelphia, R. N. Williams, Jr., the tennis expert, in describing their experiences to me were positive that they saw the ship split in two. This was from their position in the water on the starboard quarter. "Jack" Thayer gave this same description to an artist, who reproduced it in an illustration in the New York *Herald,* which many of us have seen. Some of the passengers, whose names I have just mentioned, are also cited by the newspapers as authority for the statements that the ship "broke in two," that she "buckled amidships," that she "was literally torn to pieces," etc. On the other hand, there is much testimony available which is at variance with this much-advertised sensational newspaper account. Summing up its investigation of this point the Senate Committee's Report reads: "There have been many conflicting statements as to whether the ship broke in two, but the preponderance of evidence is to the effect that she assumed an almost end-on position and sank intact." This was as Lightoller testified before the Committee, that the *Titanic's* decks were "absolutely intact" when she went down. On this point, too, Beesley is in accord, from his viewpoint in the lifeboat some distance away out of danger, whence, more composedly than others, he could see the last of the ill-fated ship as the men lay on their oars watching until she disappeared. "No phenomenon," he continues, "like that pictured in some American and English papers occurred—

that of the ship breaking in two, and the two ends being raised above the surface. When the noise was over, the *Titanic* was still upright like a column; we could see her now only as the stern and some 150 feet of her stood outlined against the star-specked sky, looming black in the darkness, and in this position she continued for some minutes—I think as much as five minutes—but it may have been less. Then, as sinking back a little at the stern, I thought she slid slowly forwards through the water and dived slantingly down."

From my personal viewpoint I also know that the *Titanic's* decks were intact at the time she sank, and when I sank with her, there was over seven-sixteenths of the ship already under water, and there was no indication then of any impending break of the deck or ship. I recently visited the sister ship of the *Titanic,* viz., the *Olympic,* at her dock in New York harbor. This was for the purpose of still further familiarizing myself with the corresponding localities which were the scene of my personal experiences on the *Titanic,* and which are referred to in this narrative. The only difference in the deck plan of the sister ship which I noted, and which the courteous officers of the *Olympic* mentioned, is that the latter ship's Deck A is not glass-enclosed like the *Titanic's;* but one of the principal points of

discovery that I made during my investigation con-
cerns this matter of the alleged breaking in two
of this magnificent ship. The White Star Line
officers pointed out to me what they called the
ship's "forward expansion joint," and they
claimed the *Titanic* was so constructed that she
must have split in two at this point, if she did so
at all. I was interested in observing that this "expansion joint" was less than twelve feet forward
from that point on the Boat Deck whence I
jumped, as described (to the iron railing on the
roof of the officers' quarters). It is indicated by
a black streak of leather-covering running trans-
versely across the deck and then up the vertical
white wall of the officers' house. This "joint" ex-
tends, however, only through the Boat Deck and
Decks A and B, which are superimposed on Deck
C. If there was any splitting in two, it seems to
me also that this superstructure, weakly joined,
would have been the part to split; but it certainly
did not. It was only a few seconds before the
time of the alleged break that I stepped across this
dividing line of the two sections and went down
with the after section about twelve feet from this
"expansion joint."

One explanation which I offer of what must
be a delusion on the part of the advocates of the
"break-in-two" theory is that when the forward

funnel fell, as hereafter described, it may have looked as if the ship itself was splitting in two, particularly to the young men who are cited as authority.

Third: Did either the Captain or the First Officer shoot himself?

Notwithstanding all the current rumors and newspaper statements answering this question affirmatively, I have been unable to find any passenger or member of the crew cited as authority for the statement that either Captain Smith or First Officer Murdoch did anything of the sort. On the contrary, so far as relates to Captain Smith, there are several witnesses, including Harold S. Bride, the junior Marconi operator, who saw him at the last on the bridge of his ship, and later, when sinking and struggling in the water. Neither can I discover any authentic testimony about First Officer Murdoch's shooting himself. On the contrary, I find fully sufficient evidence that he did not. He was a brave and efficient officer and no sufficient motive for self-destruction can be advanced. He performed his full duty under difficult circumstances, and was entitled to praise and honor. During the last fifteen minutes before the ship sank, I was located at that quarter forward on the Boat Deck, starboard side, where Murdoch was in command and where the crew under him were engaged in the vain attempt of launching the Engelhardt boat. The report of a pistol shot during this interval ringing in my ears within a few feet of me would certainly have attracted my attention, and later, when I moved astern, the distance between us was not so great as to prevent my hearing it. The "big wave" or "giant wave," described by Harold Bride, swept away Murdoch and the crew from the Boat Deck first before it struck me, and when I rose with it to the roof of the officers' house, Bride's reported testimony fits in with mine so far as relates to time, place, and circumstance, and I quote his words as follows: "About ten minutes before the ship sank, Captain Smith gave word for every man to look to his own safety. I sprang to aid the men struggling to launch the life raft (Engelhardt boat), and we had succeeded in getting it to the edge of the ship when a giant wave carried it away." Lightoller also told me on board the *Carpathia* that he saw Murdoch when he was engulfed by the water and that if before this a pistol had been fired within the short distance that separated them, he also is confident that he would have heard it.

Fourth: On which side did the ship list?

The testimony on this point, which at first blush appears conflicting, proves on investigation not at all so, but just what was to be expected from the mechanical construction of the ship. We find the most authoritative testimony in evidence that the *Titanic* listed on the starboard side, and again, on equally authoritative testimony, that she listed on the port side. Quartermaster Hitchens, who was at the wheel when the iceberg struck the ship, testified on this point before the Senate Committee as follows: "The Captain came back to the wheel house and looked at the commutator (clinometer) in front of the compass, which is a little instrument like a clock to tell you how the ship is listing. The ship had a list of five degrees to the starboard about five or ten minutes after the impact. Mr. Karl Behr, the well-known tennis player, interviewed by the New York *Tribune* is quoted as saying: "We had just retired when the collision came. I pulled on my clothes and went down the deck to the Beckwith cabin and, after I had roused them, I noted that the ship listed to the starboard, and that was the first thing that made me think that we were in for serious trouble." On the other hand, the first time I noticed this list was, as already described in my narrative, when I met Clinch Smith in the companionway and we saw a slight list to port, which gave us the first warning of how serious the accident was. The next and last time, as has also been described, was when Second Officer Lightoller ordered all pasengers to

the starboard side because of the very palpable
list to port, when the great ship suddenly appeared
to be about to topple over. Lightoller also corroborates the statement as to this list on the port
side. Other witnesses might be quoted, some of
whom testify to the starboard list, and others to
the one to port. The conclusion, therefore, is
reached that the *Titanic* listed at one time to starboard and at another time to port. This is as it
should be because of the transverse water-tight
compartments which made the water, immediately
after the compact, rush from the starboard quarter to the port, and then back again, keeping the
ship balancing on her keel until she finally sank.
If she had been constructed otherwise, with longi-
tudinal compartments only, it is evident that after
the impact on the starboard side, the *Titanic* would
have listed only to the starboard side, and after a
very much shorter interval would have careened
over on that quarter, and a much smaller proportion of lives would have been saved.

CHAPTER IV

STRUGGLING IN THE WATER FOR LIFE

"Out of the deep have I called unto Thee, O Lord."
—Ps. 130:1.

I NOW resume the narrative description of my miraculous escape, and it is with considerable diffidence that I do so, for the personal equation monopolizes more attention than may be pleasing to my readers who are not relatives or intimate friends.

As may be noticed in Chapter II, it was Clinch Smith's suggestion and on his initiative that we left that point on the starboard side of the Boat Deck where the crew, under Chief Officer Wilde and First Officer Murdoch, were in vain trying to launch the Engelhardt boat B which had been thrown down from the roof of the officers' quarters forward of the first funnel. I say "Boat B" because I have the information to that effect in a letter from Second Officer Lightoller. Confirmation of this statement I also find in the reported interview of a Saloon Steward, Thomas Whitely, in the New York *Tribune* the day after the *Car-*

pathia's arrival. An analysis of his statement shows that Boat A became entangled and was abandoned, while he saw the other, bottom up and filled with people. It was on this boat that he also eventually climbed and was saved with the rest of us. Clinch Smith and I got away from this point just before the water reached it and drowned Chief Officer Wilde and First Officer Murdoch, and others who were not successful in effecting a lodgment on the boat as it was swept off the deck. This moment was the first fateful crisis of the many that immediately followed. As bearing upon it I quote the reported statement of Harold S. Bride, the junior Marconi operator. His account also helps to determine the fate of Captain Smith. He says: "Then came the Captain's voice [from the bridge to the Marconi operators], 'Men, you have done your full duty. You can do no more. Abandon your cabin. Now, it is every man for himself.'" "Phillips continued to work," he says, "for about ten minutes or about fifteen minutes after the Captain had released him. The water was then coming into our cabin. . . . I went to the place where I had seen the collapsible boat on the Boat Deck and to my surprise I saw the boat, and the men still trying to push it off. They could not do it. I went up to them and was just lending a hand when a large wave came awash of the deck. The big wave carried the boat off. I had hold of an oarlock and I went off with it. The next I knew I was in the boat. But that was not all. I was in the boat and the boat was upside down and I was under it. . . . How I got out from under the boat I do not know, but I felt a breath at last."

From this it appears evident that, so far as Clinch Smith is concerned, it would have been better to have stayed by this Engelhardt boat to the last, for here he had a chance of escape like Bride and others of the crew who clung to it, but which I only reached again after an incredibly long swim under water. The next crisis, which was the fatal one to Clinch Smith and to the great mass of people that suddenly arose before us as I followed him astern, has already been described. The simple expedient of jumping with the "big wave" as demonstrated above carried me to safety, away from a dangerous position to the highest part of the ship; but I was the only one who adopted it successfully. The force of the wave that struck Clinch Smith and the others undoubtedly knocked most of them there unconscious against the walls of the officers' quarters and other appurtenances of the ship on the Boat Deck. As the ship keeled over forward, I believe that their bodies were caught in the angles of this deck, or entangled in the ropes, and in these other appurtenances thereon, and sank with the ship.

My holding on to the iron railing just when I did prevented my being knocked unconscious. I pulled myself over on the roof on my stomach, but before I could get to my feet I was in a whirlpool of water, swirling round and round, as I still tried to cling to the railing as the ship plunged to the depths below. Down, down, I went: it seemed a great distance. There was a very noticeable pressure upon my ears, though there must have been plenty of air that the ship carried down with it. When under water I retained, as it appears, a sense of general direction, and, as soon as I could do so, swam away from the starboard side of the ship, as I knew my life depended upon it. I swam with all my strength, and I seemed endowed with an extra supply for the occasion. I was incited to desperate effort by the thought of boiling water, or steam, from the expected explosion of the ship's boilers, and that I would be scalded to death, like the sailors of whom I had read in the account of the British battle-ship *Victoria* sunk in collision with the *Camperdown* in the Mediterranean in 1893. Second Officer Lightoller told me he also had the same idea, and that if the fires had not been drawn the boilers would explode and the water become boiling hot. As a consequence, the plunge in the icy water produced no sense of coldness whatever, and I had no thought of cold until later on when I climbed on the bottom of the upturned boat. My being drawn down by suction to a greater depth was undoubtedly checked to some degree by the life-preserver which I wore, but it is to the buoyancy of the water, caused by the volume of air rising from the sinking ship, that I attributed the assistance which enabled me to strike out and swim faster and further under water than I ever did before. I held my breath for what seemed an interminable time until I could scarcely stand it any longer, but I congratulated myself then and there that not one drop of sea-water was allowed to enter my mouth. With renewed determination and set jaws, I swam on. Just at the moment I thought that for lack of breath I would have to give in, I seemed to have been provided with a second wind, and it was just then that the thought that this was my last moment came upon me. I wanted to convey the news of how I died to my loved ones at home. As I swam beneath the surface of the ocean, I prayed that my spirit could go to them and say, "Good-bye, until we meet again in heaven." In this connection, the thought was in my mind of a well authenticated experience of mental telepathy that occurred to a member of my wife's family. Here in my case was a similar experience of a ship-wrecked loved one, and I thought if I prayed hard enough that this, my last wish to communicate with my wife and daughter, might be granted.

To what extent my prayer was answered let Mrs. Gracie describe in her own written words, as follows: "I was in my room at my sister's house, where I was visiting, in New York. After retiring, being unable to rest I questioned myself several times over, wondering what it was that prevented the customary long and peaceful slumber, lately enjoyed. 'What is the matter?' I uttered. A voice in reply seemed to say, 'On your knees and pray.' Instantly, I literally obeyed with my prayer book in my hand, which by chance opened at the prayer 'For those at Sea.' The thought then flashed through my mind, 'Archie is praying for me.' I continued wide awake until a little before five o'clock a. m., by the watch that lay beside me. About 7 a. m. I dozed a while and then got up to dress for breakfast. At 8 o'clock my sister, Mrs. Dalliba Dutton, came softly to the door, newspaper in hand, to gently break the tragic news that the *Titanic* had sunk, and showed me the list of only twenty names saved, headed with '*Colonel* Archibald Butt'; but my husband's name was not included. My head sank in her protecting arms as I murmured helplessly, 'He is all I have in the whole world.' I could only pray for strength, and later in the day, believing myself a widow, I wrote to my daughter, who was in the care of our housekeeper and servants in our Washington home, 'Cannot you see your father in his tenderness for women and children, helping them all, and then going down with the ship? If he has gone, I will not live long, but I would not have him take a boat.' "

But let me now resume my personal narrative. With this second wind under water there came to me a new lease of life and strength, until finally I noticed by the increase of light that I was drawing near to the surface. Though it was not daylight, the clear star-lit night made a noticeable difference in the degree of light immediately below the surface of the water. As I was rising, I came in contact with ascending wreckage, but the only thing I struck of material size was a small plank, which I tucked under my right arm. This circumstance brought with it the reflection that it was advisable for me to secure what best I could to keep me afloat on the surface until succor arrived. When my head at last rose above the water, I detected a piece of wreckage like a wooden crate, and I eagerly seized it as a nucleus of the projected raft to be constructed from what flotsam and jetsam I might collect. Looking about me, I could see no *Titanic* in sight. She had entirely disappeared beneath the calm surface of the ocean and without a sign of any wave. That the sea had swallowed her up with all her precious belongings was indicated by the slight sound of a gulp behind me as the water closed over her. The length of time that I was under water can be estimated by the fact that I sank with her, and when I came up there was no ship in sight. The accounts of others as to the length of time it took the *Titanic* to sink afford the best measure of the interval I was below the surface.

What impressed me at the time that my eyes beheld the horrible scene was a thin light-gray smoky vapor that hung like a pall a few feet above the broad expanse of sea that was covered with a mass of tangled wreckage. That it was a tangible vapor, and not a product of imagination, I feel well assured. It may have been caused by smoke or steam rising to the surface around the area where the ship had sunk. At any rate it produced a supernatural effect, and the pictures I had seen by Dante and the description I had read in my Virgil of the infernal regions, of Charon, and the River Lethe, were then uppermost in my thoughts. Add to this, within the area described, which was as far as my eyes could reach, there arose to the sky the most horrible sounds ever heard by mortal man except by those of us who survived this terrible tragedy. The agonizing cries of death from over a thousand throats, the wails and groans of the suffering, the shrieks of the terror-stricken and the awful gaspings for breath of those in the last throes of drowning, none of us will ever forget to our dying day. "Help! Help! Boat ahoy! Boat ahoy!" and "My God! My God!" were the heart-rending cries and shrieks of men, which floated to us over the surface of the dark waters continuously for the next hour, but as time went on, growing weaker and weaker until they died out entirely.

As I clung to my wreckage, I noticed just in front of me, a few yards away, a group of three bodies with heads in the water, face downwards, and just behind me to my right another body, all giving unmistakable evidence of being drowned. Possibly these had gone down to the depths as I had done, but did not have the lung power that I had to hold the breath and swim under water, an accomplishment which I had practised from my school days. There was no one alive or struggling in the water or calling for aid within the immediate vicinity of where I arose to the surface. I threw my right leg over the wooden crate in an attempt to straddle and balance myself on top of it, but I turned over in a somersault with it under water, and up to the surface again. What may be of interest is the thought that then occurred to me of the accounts and pictures of a wreck, indelibly impressed upon my memory when a boy, because of my acquaintance with some of the victims, of a frightful disaster of that day, namely the wreck of the *Ville de Havre* in the English Channel in 1873, and I had in mind Mrs. Bulkley's description, and the picture of her clinging to some wreckage as a rescue boat caught sight of her, bringing the comforting words over the water, "We are English sailors coming to save you." I looked around, praying for a similar interposition of Fate, but I knew the thought of a rescuing boat was a vain one—for had not all the lifeboats, loaded with women and children, departed from the ship fifteen or twenty minutes before I sank with it? And had I not seen the procession of them on the port side fading away from our sight?

But my prayerful thought and hope were answered in an unexpected direction. I espied to my left, a considerable distance away, a better vehicle of escape than the wooden crate on which my attempt to ride had resulted in a second ducking. What I saw was no less than the same Engelhardt, or "surf-boat," to whose launching I had lent my efforts, until the water broke upon the ship's Boat Deck where we were. On top of this upturned boat, half reclining on her bottom, were now more than a dozen men, whom, by their dress, I took to be all members of the crew of the ship. Thank God, I did not hesitate a moment in discarding the friendly crate that had been my first aid. I struck out through the wreckage and after a considerable swim reached the port side amidships of this Engelhardt boat, which with her companions, wherever utilized, did good service in saving the lives of many others. All honor to the Dane, Captain Engelhardt of Copenhagen, who built them. I say "port side" because this boat as it was propelled through the water had Lightoller in the bow and Bride at the stern, and I believe an analysis of the testimony shows that the actual bow of the boat was turned about by the wave that struck it on the Boat Deck and the splash of the funnel thereafter, so that its bow pointed in an opposite direction to that of the ship. There was one member of the crew on this craft at the bow and another at the stern who had "pieces of boarding," improvised paddles, which were used effectually for propulsion.

When I reached the side of the boat I met with

a doubtful reception, and, as no extending hand was held out to me, I grabbed, by the muscle of the left arm, a young member of the crew nearest and facing me. At the same time I threw my right leg over the boat astraddle, pulling myself aboard, with a friendly lift to my foot given by someone astern as I assumed a reclining position with them on the bottom of the capsized boat. Then after me came a dozen other swimmers who clambered around and whom we helped aboard. Among them was one completely exhausted, who came on the same port side as myself. I pulled him in and he lay face downward in front of me for several hours, until just before dawn he was able to stand up with the rest of us. The journey of our craft from the scene of the disaster will be described in the following chapter. The moment of getting aboard this upturned boat was one of supreme mental relief, more so than any other until I reached the deck of the hospitable *Carpathia* on the next morning. I now felt for the first time after the lifeboats left us aboard ship that I had some chance of escape from the horrible fate of drowning in the icy waters of the middle Atlantic. Every moment of time during the many experiences of that night, it seemed as if I had all the God-given physical strength and courage needed for each emergency, and never suffered an instant from any exhaustion, or required the need of a helping hand. The only time of any stress whatever was during the swim, just described, under water, at the moment when I gained my second wind which brought me to the surface gasping somewhat, but full of vigor. I was all the time on the lookout for the next danger that was to be overcome. I kept my presence of mind and courage throughout it all. Had I lost either for one moment, I never could have escaped to tell the tale. This is in answer to many questions as to my personal sensations during these scenes and the successive dangers which I encountered. From a psychological viewpoint also, it may be a study of interest illustrating the power of mind over matter. The sensation of fear has a visible effect upon one. It palsies one's thoughts and actions. One becomes thereby short of breath; the heart actually beats quicker and as one loses one's head one grows desperate and is gone. I have questioned those who have been near drowning and who know this statement to be a fact. It is the same in other emergencies, and the lesson to be learned is that we should—

"Let courage rise with danger,
    And strength to strength oppose."

To attain this courage in the hour of danger is very much a matter of physical, mental and religious training. But courage and strength would have availed me little had I not providentially escaped from being knocked senseless, or maimed, as so many other strong swimmers undoubtedly were. The narrow escapes that I had from being thus knocked unconscious could be recapitulated, and I still bear the scars on my body of wounds received at the moment, or moments, when I was struck by some undefined object. I received a blow on the top of my head, but I did not notice it or the other wounds until I arrived on board the *Carpathia*, when I found inflamed cuts on both my legs and bruises on my knees, which soon became black and blue, and I was sore to the touch all over my body for several days.

It is necessary for me to turn to the accounts of others for a description of what happened during the interval that I was under water. My information about it is derived from many sources and includes various points of general interest, showing how the *Titanic* looked when she foundered, the undisputed facts that there was very little suction and that the forward funnel broke from the ship, falling on the starboard side into the sea. Various points of personal interest are also derived from the same source which the reader can analyze, for estimating the interval that I was below the surface of the ocean and the distance covered in my swim under water; for after I rose to the surface it appears that I had passed under both the falling funnel and then under the upturned boat, and a considerable distance beyond. Had I gone but a short distance under water and arisen straight up, I should have met the horrible fate of being struck by the falling funnel which, according to the evidence submitted, must have killed or drowned a number of unfortunates struggling in the water. I select these accounts of my shipwrecked companions, which supplement my personal experience, particularly the accounts of the same reliable and authoritative witnesses already cited, and from those who were rescued, as I was, on the bottom of the upset Engelhardt boat.

The following is from the account of Mr. Beesley: "The water was by now up to the last row of portholes. We were about two miles from her, and the crew insisted that such a tremendous wave would be formed by suction as she went down, that we ought to get as far as possible away. The 'Captain' (as he calls Stoker Fred Barrett), and all, lay on their oars. Presently, about 2 a. m. (2.15 a. m. per book account),

as near as I can remember, we observed her
settling very rapidly, with the bow and bridge
completely under water, and concluded it was now
only a question of minutes before she went; and
so it proved. She slowly tilted, straight on end,
with the stern vertically upward. . . . To
our amazement, she remained in that upright position for a time which I estimate as five minutes."
On a previous page of my narrative, I have already quoted from his book account how "the
stern and some 150 feet of the ship stood outlined against the star-specked sky, looming black
in the darkness, and in this position she continued
for some minutes—I think as much as five minutes,
but it may have been less." Now, when I disappeared under the sea, sinking with the ship, there
is nothing more surely established in my testimony
than that about nine-sixteenths of the *Titanic*
was still out of the water, and when my head
reached the surface she had entirely disappeared.

The New York *Times*, of April 19, 1912, contained the story of Mr. and Mrs. D. H. Bishop,
first cabin passengers from Dowagiac, Michigan.
Their short account is one of the best I have read.
As they wrote it independently of Beesley's account, and from a different point of view, being
in another lifeboat (No. 7, the first to leave the
ship), the following corroborative testimony,

taken from their story, helps to establish the truth:

"We did not begin to understand the situation till we were perhaps a mile away from the *Titanic.* Then we could see the row of lights along the deck begin to slant gradually upward from the bow. Very slowly the lines of light began to point downward at a greater and greater angle. The sinking was so slow that you could not perceive the lights of the deck changing their position. The slant seemed to be greater about every quarter of an hour. That was the only difference.

"In a couple of hours she began to go down more rapidly. . . . Suddenly the ship seemed to shoot up out of the water and stand there perpendicularly. It seemed to us that it stood *upright in the water for four full minutes.** Then it began to slide gently downwards. Its speed increased as it went down head first, so that the stern shot down with a rush."

Harold Bride, who was swept from the Boat Deck, held on to an oarlock of the Engelhardt boat (which Clinch Smith and I had left a few moments before, as has already been described). I have cited his account of coming up under the boat and then clambering upon it. He testifies to there being no suction and adds the following:

* Italics are mine.—AUTHOR.

"I suppose I was 150 feet away when the *Titanic*, on her nose with her after-quarter sticking straight up into the air, began to settle—slowly. When at last the waves washed over her rudder, there was not the least bit of suction I could feel. She must have kept going just so slowly as she had been." Second Officer Lightoller too, in his conversation with me, verified his testimony before the Senate Committee that, "The last boat, a flat collapsible (the Engelhardt) to put off was the *one on top of the officers'* quarters. Men jumped upon it on deck and waited for the water to float it off. The forward funnel fell into the water, just missing the raft (as he calls our upset boat). The funnel probably killed persons in the water. This was the boat I eventually got on. About thirty men clambered out of the water on to it."

Seventeen year old "Jack" Thayer was also on the starboard side of the ship, and jumped from the rail before the Engelhardt boat was swept from the Boat Deck by the "giant wave." Young Thayer's reported description of this is as follows:

"I jumped out, feet first, went down, and as I came up I was pushed away from the ship by some force. I was sucked down again, and as I came up I was pushed out again and twisted around by a large wave, coming up in the midst of a great deal of small wreckage. My hand

touched the canvas fender of an overturned lifeboat. I looked up and saw some men on the top.
One of them helped me up. In a short time the
bottom was covered with twenty-five or thirty men.
The assistant wireless operator (Bride) was right
next to me holding on to me and kneeling in the
water."

In my conversations with Thayer, Lightoller
and others, it appears that the funnel fell in the
water between the Engelhardt boat and the ship,
washing the former further away from the
Titanic's starboard side.

Since the foregoing was written, the testimony
before the United States Senate Committee has
been printed in pamphlet form, from which I have
been able to obtain other evidence, and particularly that of Second Officer Lightoller in regard
to the last quarter of an hour or so on board
the ship and up to the time we reached the upset
boat. I have also obtained and substantiated
other evidence bearing upon the same period.
Mr. Lightoller testified as follows: "Half an
hour, or three quarters of an hour before I left
the ship, when it was taking a heavy list—not a
heavy list—a list over to port, the order was
called, I think by the chief officer, "Everyone on
the starboard side to straighten her up," which
I repeated. When I left the ship I saw no women

or children aboard whatever. All the boats on
the port side were lowered with the exception of
one—the last boat, which was stowed on top of
the officers' quarters. We had not time to launch
it, nor yet to open it. When all the other boats
were away, I called for men to go up there; told
them to cut her adrift and throw her down. It
floated off the ship, and I understand the men
standing on top, who assisted to launch it down,
jumped on to it as it was on the deck and floated
off with it. It was the collapsible type of boat,
and the bottom-up boat we eventually got on.
When this lifeboat floated off the ship, we were
thrown off a couple of times. When I came to it,
it was bottom-up and there was no one on it. Immediately after finding that overturned lifeboat,
and when I came alongside of it, there were quite
a lot of us in the water around it preparatory to
getting up on it. Then the forward funnel fell
down. It fell alongside of the lifeboat about four
inches clear of it on all the people there alongside
of the boat. Eventually, about thirty of us got
on it: Mr. Thayer, Bride, the second Marconi
operator, and Col. Gracie. I think all the rest
were firemen taken out of the water."

Compare this with the description given by J.
Hagan in correspondence which he began with
me last May. J. Hagan is a poor chap, who

described himself in this correspondence as one who "was working my passage to get to America for the first time," and I am convinced that he certainly earned it, and, moreover, was one of us on that upset boat that night. His name does not appear on the list of the crew and must not be confounded with "John Hagan, booked as fireman on the steamer, who sailed for England April 20th on the *Lapland*," whereas our John Hagan was admitted to St. Vincent's hospital on April 22nd. In describing this period John Hagan says it was by the Captain's orders, when the ship was listing to port, that passengers were sent to the starboard side to straighten the ship. He went half-way and returned to where Lightoller was loading the last boat lowered. Lightoller told him there was another boat on the roof of the officers' house if he cared to get it down. This was the Engelhardt Boat B which, with three others, he could not open until assisted by three more, and then they pushed it, upside down, on the Boat Deck below. Hagan cut the string of the oars and was passing the first oar down to the others, who had left him, when the boat floated into the water, upside down. He jumped to the Boat Deck and into the water after the boat and "clung to the tail end of the keel." The ship was shaking very much, part of it being under water. "On looking up at it, I could see death in a minute for us as the forward funnel was falling and it looked a certainty it would strike our boat and smash it to pieces; but the funnel missed us about a yard, splashing our boat thirty yards outward from the ship, and washing off several who had got on when the boat first floated." Hagan managed to cling to it but got a severe soaking. The cries of distress that he heard near by were an experience he can never forget. It appeared to him that the flooring of the ship forward had broken away and was floating all around. Some of the men on the upset boat made use of some pieces of boarding for paddles with which to help keep clear of the ship.

John Collins, assistant cook on the *Titanic,* also gave his interesting testimony before the Senate Committee. He appears to have come on deck at the last moment on the starboard side and witnessed the Engelhardt boat when it floated off into the sea, he being carried off by the same wave when he was amidships on the bow as the ship sank, and kept down under water for at least two or three minutes. When he came up, he saw this boat again—the same boat on which he had seen men working when the waves washed it off the deck, and the men clinging to it. He was only about four or five yards off and swam over to it and got on to it. He says he is sure there were probably fifteen thereon at the time he got on. Those who were on the boat did not help him to get on. They were watching the ship. After he got on the boat, he did not see any lights on the *Titanic*, though the stern of the ship was still afloat when he first reached the surface. He accounts for the wave that washed him off amidships as due to the suction which took place when the bow went down in the water and the waves washed the decks clear. He saw a mass of people in the wreckage, hundreds in number, and heard their awful cries.

—*Indianapolis Star*

THE TOLL OF THE SEA

CHAPTER V

ALL NIGHT ON BOTTOM OF HALF SUBMERGED UP-TURNED BOAT

"O God of our salvation, Thou who art the hope of them that remain in the broad sea . . ."—Ps. 65:5, 7.

A LL my companions in shipwreck who made their escape with me on top of the bottom-side-up Engelhardt boat, must recall the anxious moment after the limit was reached when "about 30 men had clambered out of the water on to the boat." The weight of each additional body submerged our lifecraft more and more beneath the surface. There were men swimming in the water all about us. One more clambering aboard would have swamped our already crowded craft. The situation was a desperate one, and was only saved by the refusal of the crew, especially those at the stern of the boat, to take aboard another passenger. After pulling aboard the man who lay exhausted, face downward in front of me, I turned my head away from the sights in the water lest I should be called upon to refuse the pleading cries of those who were struggling for their lives. What happened at this juncture, therefore, my fellow companions in shipwreck can better describe. Steward Thomas Whiteley, interviewed by the New York *Tribune,* said: "I drifted near a boat wrong-side-up. About 30 men were clinging to it. They refused to let me get on. Somebody tried to hit me with an oar, but I scrambled on to her." Harry Senior, a fireman on the *Titanic,* as interviewed in the London *Illustrated News* of May 4th, and in the New York *Times* of April 19th, is reported as follows: "On the overturned boat in question were, amongst others, Charles Lightoller, Second Officer of the *Titanic;* Col. Archibald Gracie, and Mr. J. B. Thayer, Jr., all of whom had gone down with the liner and had come to the surface again"; and "I tried to get aboard of her, but some chap hit me over the head with an oar. There were too many on her. I got around to the other side of the boat and climbed on. There were thirty-five of us, including the second officer, and no women. I saw any amount of drowning and dead around us." Bride's story in the same issue of the New York *Times* says: "It was a terrible sight all around—men swimming and sinking. Others came near. Nobody gave them a hand. The bottom-up boat already had more men than it would hold and was sinking. At first the large waves splashed over my clothing; then they began to splash over my head and I had to breathe when I could."

Though I did not see, I could not avoid hearing what took place at this most tragic crisis in all my life. The men with the paddles, forward and aft, so steered the boat as to avoid contact with the unfortunate swimmers pointed out struggling in the water. I heard the constant explanation made as we passed men swimming in the wreckage, "Hold on to what you have, old boy; one more of you aboard would sink us all." In no instance, I am happy to say, did I hear any word of rebuke uttered by a swimmer because of refusal to grant assistance. There was no case of cruel violence. But there was one transcendent piece of heroism that will remain fixed in my memory as the most sublime and coolest exhibition of courage and cheerful resignation to fate and fearlessness of death. This was when a reluctant refusal of assistance met with the ringing response in the deep manly voice of a powerful man, who, in his extremity, replied: "All right, boys; good luck and God bless you." I have often wished that the identity of this hero might be established and an individual tribute to his memory preserved. He was not an acquaintance of mine, for the tones of his voice would have enabled me to recognize him.

Collins in his testimony and Hagan in his letter to me refer to the same incident, the former before the Senate Committee, saying: "All those who wanted to get on and tried to get on got on with the exception of only one. This man was not pushed off by anyone, but those on the boat asked him not to try to get on. We were all on the boat running [shifting our weight] from one side to the other to keep her steady. If this man had caught hold of her he would have tumbled the whole lot of us off. He acquiesced and said, 'that is all right, boys; keep cool; God bless you,' and he bade us good-bye."

Hagan refers to the same man who "swam close to us saying, 'Hello boys, keep calm, boys,' asking to be helped up, and was told he could not get on as it might turn the boat over. He asked for a plank and was told to cling to what he had. It was very hard to see so brave a man swim away saying, 'God bless you.' "

All this time our nearly submerged boat was amidst the wreckage and fast being paddled out of the danger zone whence arose the heart-rending cries already described of the struggling swimmers. It was at this juncture that expressions were used by some of the uncouth members of

the ship's crew, which grated upon my sensibilities.
The hearts of these men, as I presently discovered,
were all right and they were far from meaning
any offence when they adopted their usual slang,
sounding harsh to my ears, and referred to our
less fortunate shipwrecked companions as "the
blokes swimming in the water." What I thus
heard made me feel like an alien among my fellow
boatmates, and I did them the injustice of believing that I, as the only passenger aboard, would, in
case of diversity of interest, receive short shrift
at their hands and for this reason I thought it
best to have as little to say as possible. During
all these struggles I had been uttering silent
prayers for deliverance, and it occurred to me that
this was the occasion of all others when we should
join in an appeal to the Almighty as our last and
only hope in life, and so it remained for one of
these men, whom I had regarded as uncouth, a
Roman Catholic seaman, to take precedence in
suggesting the thought in the heart of everyone
of us. He was astern and in arm's length of me.
He first made inquiry as to the religion of each
of us and found Episcopalians, Roman Catholics
and Presbyterians. The suggestion that we should
say the Lord's Prayer together met with instant
approval, and our voices with one accord burst
forth in repeating that great appeal to the Creator

and Preserver of all mankind, and the only prayer that everyone of us knew and could unite in, thereby manifesting that we were all sons of God and brothers to each other whatever our sphere in life or creed might be. Recollections of this incident are embodied in my account as well as those of Bride and Thayer, independently reported in the New York papers on the morning after our arrival. This is what Bride recalls: "Somebody said 'don't the rest of you think we ought to pray?' The man who made the suggestion asked what the religion of the others was. Each man called out his religion. One was a Catholic, one a Methodist, one a Presbyterian. It was decided the most appropriate prayer for all of us was the Lord's Prayer. We spoke it over in chorus, with the man who first suggested that we pray as the leader."

Referring to this incident in his sermon on "The Lessons of the Great Disaster," the Rev. Dr. Newell Dwight Hillis, of Plymouth Church, says: "When Col. Gracie came up, after the sinking of the *Titanic*, he says that he made his way to a sunken raft. The submerged little raft was under water often, but every man, without regard to nationality, broke into instant prayer. There were many voices, but they all had one signification—their sole hope was in God. There were no millionaires, for millions fell away like leaves; there were no poor; men were neither wise nor ignorant; they were simply human souls on the sinking raft; the night was black and the waves yeasty with foam, and the grave where the *Titanic* lay was silent under them, and the stars were silent over them! But as they prayed, each man by that inner light saw an invisible Friend walking across the waves. Henceforth, these need no books on Apologetics to prove there is a God. This man who has written his story tells us that God heard the prayers of some by giving them death, and heard the prayers of others equally by keeping them in life; but God alone is great!"

The lesson thus drawn from the incident described must be well appreciated by all my boatmates who realized the utter helplessness of our position, and that the only hope we then had in life was in our God, and as the Rev. Dr. Hillis says: "In that moment the evanescent, transient, temporary things dissolved like smoke, and the big, permanent things stood out—God, Truth, Purity, Love, and Oh! how happy those who were good friends with God, their conscience and their record."

We all recognize the fact that our escape from a watery grave was due to the conditions of wind and weather. All night long we prayed that the calm might last. Towards morning the sea became rougher, and it was for the two-fold purpose of avoiding the ice-cold water,* and also to attract attention, that we all stood up in column, two abreast, facing the bow. The waves at this time broke over the keel, and we maintained a balance to prevent the escape of the small volume of air confined between sea and upset boat by shifting the weight of our bodies first to port and then to starboard. I believe that the life of everyone of us depended upon the preservation of this confined air-bubble, and our anxious thought was lest some of this air might escape and deeper down our overloaded boat would sink. Had the boat been completely turned over, compelling us to cling to the submerged gunwale, it could not have supported our weight, and we should have been frozen to death in the ice-cold water before rescue could reach us. My exertions had been so continuous and so strenuous before I got aboard this capsized boat that I had taken no notice of the icy temperature of the water. We all suffered severely from cold and exposure. The boat was so loaded down with the heavy weight

* Temperature of water 28 degrees, of air 27 degrees Fahrenheit, at midnight, April 14th (American Inquiry, page 1142).

it carried that it became partly submerged, and the water washed up to our waists as we lay in our reclining position. Several of our companions near the stern of the boat, unable to stand the exposure and strain, gave up the struggle and fell off.

After we had left the danger zone in the vicinity of the wreck, conversation between us first developed, and I heard the men aft of me discussing the fate of the Captain. At least two of them, according to their statements made at the time, had seen him on this craft of ours shortly after it was floated from the ship. In the interviews already referred to, Harry Senior the fireman, referring to the same overturned boat, said: "The Captain had been able to reach this boat. They had pulled him on, but he slipped off again." Still another witness, the entrée cook of the *Titanic*, J. Maynard, who was on our boat, corroborates what I heard said at the time about the inability of the Captain to keep his hold on the boat. From several sources I have the information about the falling of the funnel, the splash of which swept from the upturned boat several who were first clinging thereto, and among the number possibly was the Captain. From the following account of Bride, it would appear he was swept off himself and regained his hold later.

"I saw a boat of some kind near me and put all
my strength into an effort to swim to it. It was
hard work. I was all done when a hand reached
out from the boat and pulled me aboard. It was
our same collapsible. The same crew was on
it. There was just room for me to roll on the
edge. I lay there, not caring what happened."
Fortunately for us all, the majority of us were
not thus exhausted or desperate. On the contrary, these men on this upset boat had plenty of
strength and the purpose to battle for their lives.
There were no beacon torches on crag and cliff;
no shouts in the pauses of the storm to tell them
there was hope; nor deep-toned bell with its
loudest peal sending cheerily, o'er the deep, comfort to these wretched souls in their extremity.
There were, however, lights forward and on the
port side to be seen all the time until the *Carpathia* appeared. These lights were only those of
the *Titanic's* other lifeboats, and thus it was, as
they gazed with eager, anxious eyes that

"Fresh hope did give them strength and strength
  deliverance." *

The suffering on the boat from cold was intense.
My neighbor in front, whom I had pulled aboard,

* Maturin's *Bertram.*

must also have been suffering from exhaustion, but it was astern of us whence came later the reports about fellow boatmates who gave up the struggle and fell off from exhaustion, or died, unable to stand the exposure and strain. Among the number, we are told by Bride and Whiteley, was the senior Marconi operator, Phillips, but their statement that it was Phillips' lifeless body which we transferred first to a lifeboat and thence to the *Carpathia* is a mistake, for the body referred to both Lightoller and myself know to have been that of a member of the crew, as described later. Bride himself suffered severely. "Somebody sat on my legs," he says. "They were wedged in between slats and were being wrenched." When he reached the *Carpathia* he was taken to the hospital and on our arrival in New York was carried ashore with his "feet badly crushed and frostbitten."

The combination of cold and the awful scenes of suffering and death which he witnessed from our upturned boat deeply affected another first cabin survivor, an Englishman, Mr. R. H. Barkworth, whose tender heart is creditable to his character.

Another survivor of our upturned boat, James McGann, a fireman, interviewed by the New York *Tribune* on April 20th, says that he was one of the thirty of us, mostly firemen, clinging to it as she left the ship. As to the suffering endured that night he says: "All our legs were frost-bitten and we were all in the hospital for a day at least."

"Hagan" also adds his testimony as to the sufferings endured by our boatmates. He says: "One man on the upturned boat rolled off, into the water, at the stern, dead with fright and cold. Another died in the lifeboat." Here he refers to the lifeless body which we transferred, and finally put aboard the *Carpathia*, but which was not Phillips'.

Lightoller testified: "I think there were three or four who died during the night aboard our boat. The Marconi junior operator told me that the senior operator was on this boat and died, presumably from cold."

But the uncommunicative little member of the crew beside me did not seem to suffer much. He was like a number of others who were possessed of hats or caps—his was an outing cap; while those who sank under water had lost them. The upper part of his body appeared to be compara-tively dry; so I believe he and some others escaped being drawn under with the *Titanic* by clinging to the Engelhardt boat from the outset when it parted company with the ship and was washed

from the deck by the "giant wave." He seemed
so dry and comfortable while I felt so damp in
my waterlogged clothing, my teeth chattering and
my hair wet with the icy water, that I ventured to
request the loan of his dry cap to warm my head
for a short while. "And what wad oi do?" was
his curt reply. "Ah, never mind," said I, as I
thought it would make no difference a hundred
years hence. Poor chap, it would seem that all
his possessions were lost when his kit went down
with the ship. Not far from me and on the starboard side was a more loquacious member of the
crew. I was not near enough, however, to him
to indulge in any imaginary warmth from the
fumes of the O-be-joyful spirits which he gave
unmistakable evidence of having indulged in before leaving the ship. Most of the conversation,
as well as excitement, came from behind me,
astern. The names of other survivors who, besides those mentioned, escaped on the same nearly
submerged life craft with me are recorded in the
history of Boat B in chapter V, which contains the
results of my research work in regard thereto.

After we paddled away free from the wreckage
and swimmers in the water that surrounded us,
our undivided attention until the dawn of the next
day was concentrated upon scanning the horizon
in every direction for the lights of a ship that

might rescue us before the sea grew rougher,
for the abnormal conditions of wind and weather
that prevailed that night were the causes of the
salvation, as well as the destruction, of those
aboard this ill-fated vessel. The absolute calm
of the sea, while it militated against the detection
of the iceberg in our path, at the same time made
it possible for all of the lifeboats lowered from
the davits to make their long and dangerous descent to the water without being smashed against
the sides of the ship, or swamped by the waves
breaking against them, for, notwithstanding newspaper reports to the contrary, there appears no
authentic testimony of any survivor showing that
any loaded boat in the act of being lowered was
capsized or suffered injury. On the other hand,
we have the positive statements accounting for
each individual boatload, showing that every one
of them was thus lowered in safety. But it was
this very calm of the sea, as has been said, which
encompassed the destruction of the ship. The
beatings of the waves against the iceberg's sides
usually give audible warning miles away to the
approaching vessel, while the white foam at the
base, due to the same cause, is also discernible.
But in our case the beautiful star-lit night and
cloudless sky, combined with the glassy sea,
further facilitated the iceberg's approach with-

out detection, for no background was afforded against which to silhouette the deadly outline of this black appearing Protean monster which only looks white when the sun is shining upon it.

All experienced navigators of the northern seas, as I am informed on the highest authority, knowing the dangers attending such conditions, invariably take extra precautions to avoid disaster. The *Titanic's* officers were no novices, and were well trained in the knowledge of this and all other dangers of the sea. From the Captain down, they were the pick of the best that the White Star Line had in its employ. Our Captain, Edward J. Smith, was the one always selected to "try out" each new ship of the Line, and was regarded, with his thirty-eight years of service in the company, as both safe and competent. Did he take any precautions for safety, in view of the existing dangerous conditions? Alas! no! as appears from the testimony in regard thereto, taken before the Investigating Committee and Board in America and in England which we review in another chapter. And yet, warnings had been received on the *Titanic's* bridge from six different neighboring ships, one in fact definitely locating the latitude and longitude where the iceberg was encountered, and that too at a point of time calculated by one of the *Titanic's* officers. Who can satisfactorily explain this heedlessness of danger?

It was shortly after we had emerged from the horrible scene of men swimming in the water that I was glad to notice the presence among us on the upturned boat of the same officer with whom all my work that night and all my experience was connected in helping to load and lower the boats on the *Titanic's* Boat Deck and Deck "A." I identified him at once by his voice and his appearance, but his name was not learned until I met him again later in my cabin on board the *Carpathia* —Charles H. Lightoller. For what he did on the ship that night whereby six or more boatloads of women and children were saved and discipline maintained aboard ship, as well as on the Engelhardt upturned boat, he is entitled to honor and the thanks of his own countrymen and of us Americans as well. As soon as he was recognized, the loquacious member of the crew astern, already referred to, volunteered in our behalf and called out to him "We will all obey what the officer orders." The result was at once noticeable. The presence of a leader among us was now felt, and lent us purpose and courage. The excitement at the stern was demonstrated by the frequent suggestion of, "Now boys, all together"; and then in unison we shouted, "Boat ahoy! Boat ahoy!"

This was kept up for some time until it was seen to be a mere waste of strength. So it seemed to me, and I decided to husband mine and make provision for what the future, or the morrow, might require. After a while Lightoller, myself and others managed with success to discourage these continuous shouts regarded as a vain hope of attracting attention.

When the presence of the Marconi boy at the stern was made known, Lightoller called out, from his position in the bow, questions which all of us heard, as to the names of the steamships with which he had been in communication for assistance. We on the boat recall the names mentioned by Bride—the *Baltic*, *Olympic* and *Carpathia*. It was then that the *Carpathia's* name was heard by us for the first time, and it was to catch sight of this sturdy little Cunarder that we strained our eyes in the direction whence she finally appeared.

We had correctly judged that most of the lights seen by us belonged to our own *Titanic's* lifeboats, but Lightoller and all of us were badly fooled by the green-colored lights and rockets directly ahead of us, which loomed up especially bright at intervals. This, as will be noticed in a future chapter, was Third Officer Boxhall's Emergency Boat No. 2. We were assured that

these were the lights of a ship and were all glad
to believe it. There could be no mistake about it
and our craft was navigated toward it as fast as
its propelling conditions made possible; but it did
not take long for us to realize that this light, whatever it was, was receding instead of approaching
us.

Some of our boatmates on the *Titanic's* decks
had seen the same white light to which I have
already made reference in Chapter II, and the
argument was now advanced that it must have
been a sailing ship, for a steamer would have soon
come to our rescue; but a sailing ship would be
prevented by wind, or lack of facilities in coming
to our aid. I imagined that it was the lights of
such a ship that we again saw on our port side
astern in the direction where, when dawn broke,
we saw the icebergs far away on the horizon.

Some time before dawn a call came from the
stern of the boat, "There is a steamer coming behind us." At the same time a warning cry was
given that we should not all look back at once
lest the equilibrium of our precarious craft might
be disturbed. Lightoller took in the situation and
called out, "All you men stand steady and I will
be the one to look astern." He looked, but there
was no responsive chord that tickled our ears with
hope.

The incident just described happened when we were all standing up, facing forward in column, two abreast. Some time before this, for some undefined reason, Lightoller had asked the question, "How many are there of us on this boat?" and someone answered "thirty, sir." All testimony on the subject establishes this number. I may cite Lightoller, who testified: "I should roughly estimate about thirty. She was packed standing from stem to stern at daylight. We took all on board that we could. I did not see any effort made by others to get aboard. There were a great number of people in the water but not near us. They were some distance away from us."

Personally, I could not look around to count, but I know that forward of me there were eight and counting myself and the man abreast would make two more. As every bit of room on the Engelhardt bottom was occupied and as the weight aboard nearly submerged it, I believe that more than half our boatload was behind me. There is a circumstance that I recall which further establishes how closely packed we were. When standing up I held on once or twice to the life-preserver on the back of my boatmate in front in order to balance myself. At the same time and in the same way the man in my rear held on to me. This procedure, being objectionable to those concerned, was promptly discontinued.

It was at quite an early stage that I had seen far in the distance the unmistakable mast lights of a steamer about four or five points away on the port side, as our course was directed toward the green-colored lights of the imaginary ship which we hoped was coming to our rescue, but which, in fact, was the already-mentioned *Titanic* lifeboat of Officer Boxhall. I recall our anxiety, as we had no lights, that this imaginary ship might not see us and might run over our craft and swamp us. But my eyes were fixed for hours that night on the lights of that steamer, far away in the distance, which afterwards proved to be those of the *Carpathia*. To my great disappointment, they seemed to make no progress towards us to our rescue. This we were told later was due to meeting an iceberg as she was proceeding full speed toward the scene of the *Titanic's* wreck. She had come to a stop in sight of the lights of our lifeboats (or such as had them). The first boat to come to her sides was Boxhall's with its green lights. Finally dawn appeared and there on the port side of our upset boat where we had been looking with anxious eyes, glory be to God, we saw the steamer *Carpathia* about four or five miles away, with other *Titanic* lifeboats rowing towards her. But on our

starboard side, much to our surprise, for we had
seen no lights on that quarter, were four of the
Titanic's lifeboats strung together in line. These
were respectively Numbers 14, 10, 12 and 4, according to testimony submitted in our next chapter.

Meantime, the water had grown rougher, and,
as previously described, was washing over the keel
and we had to make shift to preserve the equilibrium. Right glad were all of us on our upturned boat when in that awful hour the break of
day brought this glorious sight to our eyes.
Lightoller put his whistle to his cold lips and blew
a shrill blast, attracting the attention of the boats
about half a mile away. "Come over and take
us off," he cried. "Aye, aye, sir," was the ready
response as two of the boats cast off from the
others and rowed directly towards us. Just before the bows of the two boats reached us,
Lightoller ordered us not to scramble, but each to
take his turn, so that the transfer might be made
in safety. When my turn came, in order not to
endanger the lives of the others, or plunge them
into the sea, I went carefully, hands first, into the
rescuing lifeboat. Lightoller remained to the last,
lifting a lifeless body into the boat beside me. I
worked over the body for some time, rubbing the
temples and the wrists, but when I turned the neck

it was perfectly stiff. Recognizing that rigor mortis had set in, I knew the man was dead. He was dressed like a member of the crew, and I recall that he wore gray woollen socks. His hair was dark. Our lifeboat was so crowded that I had to rest on this dead body until we reached the *Carpathia,* where he was taken aboard and buried. My efforts to obtain his name have been exhaustive, but futile. Lightoller was uncertain as to which one he was of two men he had in mind; but we both know that it was not the body of Phillips, the senior Marconi operator. In the lifeboat to which we were transferred were said to be sixty-five or seventy of us. The number was beyond the limit of safety. The boat sank low in the water, and the sea now became rougher. Lightoller assumed the command and steered at the stern. I was glad to recognize young Thayer amidships. There was a French woman in the bow near us actively ill but brave and considerate. She was very kind in loaning an extra steamer rug to Barkworth, by my side, who shared it with a member of the crew (a fireman perhaps) and myself. That steamer rug was a great comfort as we drew it over our heads and huddled close together to obtain some warmth. For a short time another *Titanic* lifeboat was towed by ours. My life-belt was wet and uncomfortable and I

threw it overboard. Fortunately there was no
further need of it for the use intended. I regret
I did not preserve it as a relic. When we were
first transferred and only two of the lifeboats
came to our rescue, some took it hard that the
other two did not also come to our relief, when we
saw how few these others had aboard; but the
officer in command of them, whom we afterwards
knew as Fifth Officer Lowe, had cleverly rigged
up a sail on his boat and, towing another astern,
made his way to the *Carpathia* a long time ahead
of us, but picked up on his way other unfortunates
in another Engelhardt boat, Boat A, which had
shipped considerable water.

My research, particularly the testimony taken
before the Senate Committee, establishes the
identity of the *Titanic* lifeboats to which, at daydawn, we of the upset boat were transferred.
These were Boats No. 12 and No. 4. The former was the one that Lightoller, Barkworth,
Thayer, Jr., and myself were in. Frederick
Clench, able seaman, was in charge of this boat,
and his testimony, as follows, is interesting:

"I looked along the water's edge and saw some
men on a raft. Then I heard two whistles blown.
I sang out, 'Aye, aye, I am coming over,' and
we pulled over and found it was not a raft exactly, but an overturned boat, and Mr. Lightoller

was there on that boat and I thought the wireless operator, too. We took them on board our boat and shared the amount of room. They were all standing on the bottom, wet through apparently. Mr. Lightoller took charge of us. Then we started ahead for the *Carpathia*. We had to row a tidy distance to the *Carpathia* because there were boats ahead of us and we had a boat in tow, with others besides all the people we had aboard. We were pretty well full up before, but the additional ones taken on made about seventy in our boat."

This corresponds with Lightoller's testimony on the same point. He says:

"I counted sixty-five heads, not including myself, and none that were in the bottom of the boat. I roughly estimated about seventy-five in the boat, which was dangerously full, and it was all I could do to nurse her up to the sea."

From Steward Cunningham's testimony I found a corroboration of my estimate of our distance, at daydawn, from the *Carpathia*. This he says "was about four or five miles."

Another seaman, Samuel S. Hemming, who was in Boat No. 4, commanded by Quartermaster Perkis, also gave his testimony as follows:

"As day broke we heard some hollering going

on and we saw some men standing on what we thought was ice about half a mile away, but we found them on the bottom of an upturned boat. Two boats cast off and we pulled to them and took them in our two boats. There were no women or children on this boat, and I heard there was one dead body. Second Officer Lightoller was on the overturned boat. He did not get into our boat. Only about four or five got into ours and the balance of them went into the other boat."

It seemed to me an interminable time before we reached the *Carpathia*. Ranged along her sides were others of the *Titanic's* lifeboats which had been rowed to the Cunarder and had been emptied of their loads of survivors. In one of these boats on the port side, standing up, I noticed my friend, Third Officer H. J. Pitman, with whom I had made my trip eastward on the Atlantic on board the *Oceanic*. All along the sides of the *Carpathia* were strung rope ladders. There were no persons about me needing my assistance, so I mounted the ladder, and, for the purpose of testing my strength, I ran up as fast as I could and experienced no difficulty or feeling of exhaustion. I entered the first hatchway I came to and felt like falling down on my knees and kissing the deck in gratitude for the preservation of my life. I

made my way to the second cabin dispensary, where
I was handed a hot drink. I then went to the
deck above and was met with a warm reception in
the dining saloon. Nothing could exceed the kindness of the ladies, who did everything possible for
my comfort. All my wet clothing, overcoat and
shoes, were sent down to the bake-oven to be dried.
Being thus in lack of clothing, I lay down on the
lounge in the dining saloon corner to the right of
the entrance under rugs and blankets, waiting for
a complete outfit of dry clothing.

I am particularly grateful to a number of kind
people on the *Carpathia* who helped replenish my
wardrobe, but especially to Mr. Louis M. Ogden,
a family connection and old friend. To Mrs.
Ogden and to Mr. and Mrs. Spedden, who were
on the *Titanic,* and to their boy's trained nurse,
I am also most grateful. They gave me hot
cordials and hot coffee which soon warmed me
up and dispersed the cold. Among the *Carpathia's*
passengers, bound for the Mediterranean, I discovered a number of friends of Mrs. Gracie's
and mine—Miss K. Steele, sister of Charles
Steele, of New York, Mr. and Mrs. Charles H.
Marshall and Miss Marshall, of New York.
Leaning over the rail of the port side I saw
anxiously gazing down upon us many familiar
faces of fellow survivors, and, among them,

friends and acquaintances to whom I waved my hand as I stood up in the bow of my boat.   This boat No. 12 was the last to reach the *Carpathia* and her passengers transferred about 8.30 a. m.

—*Columbus Evening Despatch*

CHAPTER VI

THE PORT SIDE: WOMEN AND CHILDREN FIRST

Foreword

THE previous chapters, describing my personal experience on board the *Titanic* and remarkable escape from death in the icy waters of the middle Atlantic, were written some months ago. In the interim I have received the pamphlets, printed in convenient form, containing the hearings of both the American and British Courts of Inquiry, and have given them considerable study.

These official sources of information have added materially to my store of knowledge concerning the shipwreck, and corroborate to a marked degree the description from my personal viewpoint, all the salient points of which were written before our arrival in New York, and on the S. S. *Carpathia,* under circumstances which will be related in a future chapter.

During the same interval, by correspondence with survivors and by reading all available printed

matter in books, magazine articles and newspapers, I have become still more conversant with
the story of this, the greatest of maritime disasters, which caused more excitement in our country
than any other single event that has occurred in
its history within a generation.

The adopted standard by which I propose to
measure the truth of all statements in this book
is the evidence obtained from these Courts of Inquiry, after it has been subjected to careful and
impartial analysis. All accounts of the disaster,
from newspapers and individual sources, for which
no basis can be found after submission to this re-
fining process, will find no place or mention herein.
In the discussion of points of historical interest
or of individual conduct, where such are matters
of public record, I shall endeavor to present them
fairly before the reader, who can pass thereon
his or her own opinion after a study of the testimony bearing on both sides of any controversy.
In connection with such discussion where the re-
flections cast upon individuals in the sworn testimony of witnesses have already gained publicity,
I claim immunity from any real or imaginary ani-
madversions which may be provoked by my impartial reference thereto.

I have already recorded my personal observation of how strictly the rule of human nature,

"Women and Children First," was enforced on the port side of the great steamship, whence no man escaped alive who made his station on this quarter and bade good-bye to wife, mother or sister.

I have done my best, during the limited time allowed, to exhaust all the above-defined sources of information, in an effort to preserve as complete a list as possible of those comrades of mine who, from first to last, on this port side of the ship, helped to preserve order and discipline, upholding the courage of women and children, until all the boats had left the *Titanic,* and who then sank with the ship when she went down.

I shall now present the record and story of each lifeboat, on both port and starboard sides of the ship, giving so far as I have been able to obtain them the names of persons loaded aboard each boat, passengers and crew; those picked up out of the water; the stowaways found concealed beneath the thwarts, and those men who, without orders, jumped from the deck into boats being lowered, injuring the occupants and endangering the lives of women and children. At the same time will be described the conditions existing when each boat was loaded and lowered, and whatever incidents occurred in the transfer of passengers to the rescuing steamer *Carpathia.*

The general testimony of record, covering the conduct which was exhibited on the port side of the ship, is contained in the careful statements of that splendid officer, Charles H. Lightoller, before the United States Senate Committee: (Am. Inq., p. 88.)

SENATOR SMITH: From what you have said, you discriminated entirely in the interest of the passengers—first women and children—in filling these lifeboats?

MR. LIGHTOLLER: Yes, sir.

SENATOR SMITH: Why did you do that? Because of the captain's orders, or because of the rule of the sea?

MR. LIGHTOLLER: The rule of human nature.

And also in his testimony before the British Inquiry (p. 71):

"I asked the captain on the Boat Deck, 'Shall I get women and children in the boats?' The captain replied, 'Yes, and lower away.' I was carrying out his orders. I am speaking of the port side of the ship. I was running the port side only. All the boats on this side were lowered except the last, which was stowed on top of the officers' quarters. This was the surf boat—the Engelhardt boat (A). We had not time to launch it, nor yet to open it."

(Br. Inq.) "I had no difficulty in filling the boat. The people were perfectly ready and quiet. There was no jostling or pushing or crowding whatever. The men all refrained from asserting their strength and from crowding back the women and children. They could not have stood quieter if they had been in church."

And referring to the last boats that left the ship (Br. Inq., p. 83):

"When we were lowering the women, there were any amount of Americans standing near who gave me every assistance they could."

The crow's nest on the foremast was just about level with the water when the bridge was submerged. The people left on the ship, or that part which was not submerged, did not make any demonstration. There was not a sign of any lamentation.

On the port side on deck I can say, as far as my own observations went, from my own endeavor and that of others to obtain women, there were none left on the deck.

My testimony on the same point before the United States Senate Committee (Am. Inq., p. 992) was as follows:

"I want to say that there was nothing but the

most heroic conduct on the part of all men and women at that time where I was at the bow on the port side.   There was no man who asked to get in a boat with the single exception that I have already mentioned.   (Referring to Col. Astor's request to go aboard to protect his wife.   Am. Inq., p. 991.)   No women even sobbed or wrung their hands, and everything appeared perfectly orderly.   Lightoller was splendid in his conduct with the crew, and the crew did their duty.   It seemed to me it was a little bit more difficult than it should have been to launch the boats alongside the ship.   I do not know the cause of that.   I know I had to use my muscle as best I could in trying to push those boats so as to get them over the gunwale.   I refer to these in a general way as to its being difficult in trying to lift them and push them over.   (As was the case with the Engelhardt "D.")   The crew, at first, sort of resented my working with them, but they were very glad when I worked with them later on. Every opportunity I got to help, I helped."

How these statements are corroborated by the testimony of others is recorded in the detailed description of each boat that left the ship on the port side as follows:

BOAT No. 6.*

No male passengers.

Passengers: Miss Bowerman, Mrs. J. J. Brown, Mrs. Candee, Mrs. Cavendish and her maid (Miss Barber), Mrs. Meyer, Miss Norton, Mrs. Rothschild, Mrs. L. P. Smith, Mrs. Stone and her maid (Miss Icard).

Ordered in to supply lack of crew: Major A. G. Peuchen.

Said good-bye to wives and sank with ship: Messrs. Cavendish, Meyer, Rothschild and L. P. Smith.

Crew: Hitchens, Q. M. (in charge). Seaman Fleet. (One fireman transferred from No. 16 to row.) Also a boy with injured arm whom Captain Smith had ordered in.

Total: 28. (Br. Inq.)

INCIDENTS

Lightoller's testimony (Am. Inq., p. 79):
I was calling for seamen and one of the seamen jumped out of the boat and started to lower away.

---

* British Report (p. 38) puts this boat first to leave port side at 12.55. Lightoller's testimony shows it could not have been the first.

The boat was half way down when a woman called out that there was only one man in it. I had only two seamen and could not part with them, and was in rather a fix to know what to do when a passenger called out: "If you like, I will go." This was a first-class passenger, Major Peuchen, of Toronto. I said: "Are you a seaman?" and he said: "I am a yachtsman." I said: "If you are sailor enough to get out on that fall—that is a difficult thing to get to over the ship's side, eight *feet* away, and means a long swing, on a dark night—if you are sailor enough to get out there, you can go down"; and he proved he was, by going down.

F. Fleet, L. O. (Am. Inq., 363) and (Br. Inq.):
Witness says there were twenty-three women, Major Peuchen and Seamen Hitchens and himself. As he left the deck he heard Mr. Lightoller shouting: "Any more women?" No. 6 and one other cut adrift after reaching the *Carpathia*.

Major Arthur Godfrey Peuchen, Manufacturing Chemist, Toronto, Canada, and Major of Toronto's crack regiment, The Queen's Own Rifles (Am. Inq., p. 334), testified:
I was standing on the Boat Deck, port side,

near the second officer and the captain. One of
them said: "We must get these masts and sails
out of these boats; you might give us a hand."
I jumped in, and with a knife cut the lashings
of the mast and sail and moved the mast out of
the boat. Only women were allowed in, and the
men had to stand back. This was the order, and
the second officer stood there and carried it out
to the limit. He allowed no men, except sailors
who were manning the boat. I did not see one
single male passenger get in or attempt to get in.
I never saw such perfect order. The discipline
was perfect. I did not see a cowardly act by any
man.

When I first came on this upper deck there were
about 100 stokers coming up with their dunnage
bags and they seemed to crowd this whole deck
in front of the boats. One of the officers, I don't
know which one, a very powerful man, came along
and drove these men right off this deck like a lot
of sheep. They did not put up any resistance.
I admired him for it. Later, there were counted
20 women, one quartermaster, one sailor and one
stowaway, before I was ordered in.

In getting into the boat I went aft and said to
the quartermaster: "What do you want me to
do?" "Get down and put that plug in," he answered. I made a dive down for the plug. The

ladies were all sitting pretty well aft and I could
not see at all. It was dark down there. I felt
with my hands and then said it would be better
for him to do it and me do his work. I said,
"Now, you get down and put in the plug and I
will undo the shackles," that is, take the blocks
off, so he dropped the blocks and got down to
fix the plug, and then he came back to assist me
saying, "Hurry up." He said: "This boat is
going to founder." I thought he meant our lifeboat
was going to founder, but he meant the large boat,
and that we were to hurry up and get away from
it, so we got the rudder in and he told me to
go forward and take an oar. I did so, and got
an oar on the port side. Sailor Fleet was on my
left on the starboard side. The quartermaster
told us to row as hard as we could to get
away from the suction. We got a short
distance away when an Italian, a stowaway,
made his appearance. He had a broken wrist
or arm, and was of no use to row. He was
stowed away under the boat where we could not
see him.

Toward morning we tied up to another boat
(No. 16) for fifteen minutes. We said to those
in the other boat: "Surely you can spare us one
man if you have so many." One man, a fireman,
was accordingly transferred, who assisted in row-

ing on the starboard side. The women helped
with the oars, and very pluckily too.*

We were to the weather of the *Carpathia*, and
so she stayed there until we all came down on her.
I looked at my watch and it was something after
eight o'clock.

Mrs. Candee's account of her experience is as
follows:

She last saw Mr. Kent in the companionway
between Decks A and B. He took charge of an
ivory miniature of her mother, etc., which afterwards were found on his body when brought into
Halifax. He appeared at the time to hesitate
accepting her valuables, seeming to have a pre-
monition of his fate.

She witnessed the same incident described by
Major Peuchen, when a group of firemen came
up on deck and were ordered by the officer to return below. She, however, gives praise to these
men. They obeyed like soldiers, and without a
murmur or a protest, though they knew better
than anyone else on the ship that they were going
straight to their death. No boats had been
lowered when these firemen first appeared upon

* "An English girl (Miss Norton) and I rowed for four
hours and a half."—Mrs. Meyer in New York *Times,* April
14th, 1912.

the Boat Deck, and it would have been an easy matter for them to have "rushed" the boats.

Her stateroom steward also gave an exhibition of courage. After he had tied on her life preserver and had locked her room as a precaution against looters, which she believed was done all through the deck, she said to this brave man: "It is time for you to look out for yourself," to which the steward replied, "Oh, plenty of time for that, Madam, plenty of time for that." He was lost.

As she got into boat No. 6, it being dark and not seeing where she stepped, her foot encountered the oars lying lengthwise in the boat and her ankle was thus twisted and broken.

Just before her boat was lowered away a man's voice said: "Captain, we have no seaman." Captain Smith then seized a boy by the arm and said: "Here's one." The boy went into the boat as ordered by the captain, but afterwards he was found to be disabled. She does not think he was an Italian.

Her impression is that there were other boats in the water which had been lowered before hers. There was a French woman about fifty years of age in the boat who was constantly calling for her son. Mrs. Candee sat near her. After arrival on the *Carpathia* this French woman became hysterical.

Notwithstanding Hitchens' statements, she says that there was absolutely no upset feeling on the women's part at any time, even when the boat, as it was being lowered, on several occasions hung at a dangerous angle—sometimes bow up and sometimes stern up. The lowering process seemed to be done by jerks. She herself called out to the men lowering the boat and gave instructions: otherwise they would have been swamped.

The Italian boy who was in the boat was not a stowaway, he was ordered in by the captain as already related. Neither did he refuse to row. When he tried to do so, it was futile, because of an injury to his arm or wrist.

Through the courtesy of another fellow passenger, Mrs. J. J. Brown, of Denver, Colorado, I am able to give her experiences in boat No. 6, told in a delightful, graphic manner; so much so that I would like to insert it all did not space prevent:

In telling of the people she conversed with, that Sunday evening, she refers to an exceedingly intellectual and much-travelled acquaintance, Mrs. Bucknell, whose husband had founded the Bucknell University of Philadelphia; also to another passenger from the same city, Dr. Brewe, who had done much in scientific research. During her conversation with Mrs. Bucknell, the latter reiterated a statement previously made on the tender at Cherbourg while waiting for the *Titanic*. She said she feared boarding the ship because she had evil forebodings that something might happen. Mrs. Brown laughed at her premonitions and shortly afterwards sought her quarters.

Instead of retiring to slumber, Mrs. Brown was absorbed in reading and gave little thought to the crash at her window overhead which threw her to the floor. Picking herself up she proceeded to see what the steamer had struck; but thinking nothing serious had occurred, though realizing that the engines had stopped immediately after the crash and the boat was at a standstill, she picked up her book and began reading again. Finally she saw her curtains moving while she was reading, but no one was visible. She again looked out and saw a man whose face was blanched, his eyes protruding, wearing the look of a haunted creature. He was gasping for breath and in an undertone gasped, "Get your life preserver." He was one of the buyers for Gimbel Bros., of Paris and New York.

She got down her life preserver, snatched up her furs and hurriedly mounted the stairs to A

Deck, where she found passengers putting on life-belts like hers. Mrs. Bucknell approached and whispered, "Didn't I tell you something was going to happen?" She found the lifeboats lowered from the falls and made flush with the deck. Madame de Villiers appeared from below in a nightdress and evening slippers, with no stockings. She wore a long woollen motorcoat. Touching Mrs. Brown's arm, in a terrified. voice she said she was going below for her money and valuables. After much persuasion Mrs. Brown prevailed upon her not to do so, but to get into the boat. She hesitated and became very much excited, but was finally prevailed upon to enter the lifeboat. Mrs. Brown was walking away, eager to see what was being done elsewhere. Suddenly she saw a shadow and a few seconds later someone seized her, saying: "You are going, too," and she was dropped fully four feet into the lowering lifeboat. There was but one man in charge of the boat. As it was lowered by jerks by an officer above, she discovered that a great gush of water was spouting through the porthole from D Deck, and the lifeboat was in grave danger of being submerged. She immediately grasped an oar and held the lifeboat away from the ship.

When the sea was reached, smooth as glass, she looked up and saw the benign, resigned countenance, the venerable white hair and the Chester-fieldian bearing of the beloved Captain Smith with whom she had crossed twice before, and only three months previous on the *Olympic*. He peered down upon those in the boat, like a solicitous father, and directed them to row to the light in the distance—all boats keeping together.

Because of the fewness of men in the boat she found it necessary for someone to bend to the oars. She placed her oar in an oarlock and asked a young woman nearby to hold one while she placed the other on the further side. To Mrs. Brown's surprise, the young lady (who must have been Miss Norton, spoken of elsewhere), immediately began to row like a galley slave, every stroke counting. Together they managed to pull away from the steamer.

By this time E and C Decks were completely submerged. Those ladies who had husbands, sons or fathers on the doomed steamer buried their heads on the shoulders of those near them and moaned and groaned. Mrs. Brown's eyes were glued on the fast-disappearing ship. Suddenly there was a rift in the water, the sea opened up and the surface foamed like giant arms and spread around the ship and the vessel disappeared from sight, and not a sound was heard.

Then follows Mrs. Brown's account of the

conduct of the quartermaster in the boat which will be found under the heading presently given, and it will be noticed that her statements correspond with those of all others in the boat.

The dawn disclosed the awful situation. There were fields of ice on which, like points on the landscape, rested innumerable pyramids of ice. Seemingly a half hour later, the sun, like a ball of molten lead, appeared in the background. The hand of nature portrayed a scenic effect beyond the ken of the human mind. The heretofore smooth sea became choppy and retarded their progress. All the while the people in boat No. 6 saw the other small lifeboats being hauled aboard the *Carpathia*. By the time their boat reached the *Carpathia* a heavy sea was running, and, No. 6 boat being among the last to approach, it was found difficult to get close to the ship. Three or four unsuccessful attempts were made. Each time they were dashed against the keel, and bounded off like a rubber ball. A rope was then thrown down, which was spliced in four at the bottom, and a Jacob's ladder was made. Catching hold, they were hoisted up, where a dozen of the crew and officers and doctors were waiting. They were caught and handled as tenderly as though they were children.

HITCHENS' CONDUCT

Major Peuchen (Am. Inq., p. 334) continued:
There was an officers' call, sort of a whistle,
calling us to come back to the boat. The quartermaster told us to stop rowing. We all thought we
ought to go back to the ship, but the quartermaster said "No, we are not going back to the boat;
it is our lives now, not theirs." It was the women
who rebelled against this action. I asked him to
assist us in rowing and let some of the women
steer the boat, as it was a perfectly calm night and
no skill was required. He refused, and told me
he was in command of that boat and that I was
to row.

He imagined he saw a light. I have done a
great deal of yachting in my life. I have owned
a yacht for six years. I saw a reflection. He
thought it was a boat of some kind; probably it
might be a buoy, and he called out to the next boat
asking them if they knew any buoys were around
there. This struck me as being perfectly absurd.

I heard what seemed to be one, two, three
rumbling sounds; then the lights of the ship went
out. Then the terrible cries and calls for help—
moaning and crying. It affected all the women in
our boat whose husbands were among those in
the water. This went on for some time, grad-

ually getting fainter and fainter. At first it was horrible to listen to. We must have been five-eighths of a mile away when this took place. There were only two of us rowing a very heavy boat with a good many people in it, and I do not think we covered very much ground. Some of the women in the boat urged the quartermaster to return. He said there was no use going back,— that there were only a "lot of stiffs there." The women resented it very much.

Seaman Fleet (Am. Inq., p. 363) :
All the women asked us to pull to the place where the *Titanic* went down, but the quarter-master, who was at the tiller all the time, would not allow it. They asked him, but he would not hear of it.

Mrs. Candee continues :
Hitchens was cowardly and almost crazed with fear all the time. After we left the ship he thought he heard the captain say: "Come along-side," and was for turning back until reminded by the passengers that the captain's final orders were: "Keep boats together and row away from the ship." She heard this order given.

After that he constantly reminded us who were at the oars that if we did not make better speed with our rowing we would all be sucked under the water by the foundering of the ship. This he repeated whenever our muscles flagged.

Directly the *Titanic* had foundered a discussion arose as to whether we should return. Hitchens said our boat would immediately be swamped if we went into the confusion. The reason for this was that our boat was not manned with enough oars.

Then after the sinking of the *Titanic* Hitchens reminded us frequently that we were hundreds of miles from land, without water, without food, without protection against cold, and if a storm should come up that we would be helpless. Therefore, we faced death by starvation or by drowning. He said we did not even know the direction in which we were rowing. I corrected him by pointing to the north star immediately over our bow.

When our boat came alongside No. 16, Hitchens immediately ordered the boats lashed together. He resigned the helm and settled down to rest. When the *Carpathia* hove in sight he ordered that we drift. Addressing the people in both boats Mrs. Candee said: "Where those lights are lies our salvation; shall we not go towards them?" The reply was a murmur of approval and immediate recourse to the oars.

Hitchens was requested to assist in the toilsome rowing. Women tried to taunt and provoke him into activity. When it was suggested that he permit the injured boy to take the tiller and that Hitchens should row, he declined, and in every case he refused labor. He spoke with such uncivility to one of the ladies that a man's voice was heard in rebuke: "You are speaking to a lady," to which he replied: "I know whom I am speaking to, and I am commanding this boat."

When asked if the *Carpathia* would come and pick us up he replied: "No, she is not going to pick us up; she is to pick up bodies." This when said to wives and mothers of the dead men was needlessly brutal.

When we neared the *Carpathia* he refused to go round on the smooth side because it necessitated keeping longer in the rough sea, so we made a difficult landing.

In Mrs. Brown's account of her experience she relates the following about the conduct of the quartermaster in charge of the boat in which she was:

He, Quartermaster Hitchens, was at the rudder and standing much higher than we were, shivering like an aspen. As they rowed away from the ship he burst out in a frightened voice and warned them of the fate that awaited them, saying that the task in rowing away from the sinking ship was futile, as she was so large that in sinking she would draw everything for miles around down with her suction, and, if they escaped that, the boilers would burst and rip up the bottom of the sea, tearing the icebergs asunder and completely submerging them. They were truly doomed either way. He dwelt upon the dire fate awaiting them, describing the accident that happened to the S. S. *New York* when the *Titanic* left the docks at Southampton.

After the ship had sunk and none of the calamities that were predicted by the terrified quartermaster were experienced, he was asked to return and pick up those in the water. Again the people in the boat were admonished and told how the frantic drowning victims would grapple the sides of the boat and capsize it. He not yielding to the entreaties, those at the oars pulled away vigorously towards a faintly glimmering light on the horizon. After three hours of pulling the light grew fainter, and then completely disappeared. Then this quartermaster, who stood on his pinnacle trembling, with an attitude like some one preaching to the multitude, fanning the air with his hands, recommenced his tirade of awful forebodings, telling those in the boat that they were likely to drift for days, all the while reminding them that they were surrounded by icebergs, as he pointed to a pyramid of ice looming up in the distance, possibly seventy feet high. He forcibly impressed upon them that there was no water in the casks in the lifeboats, and no bread, no compass and no chart. No one answered him. All seemed to be stricken dumb. One of the ladies in the boat had had the presence of mind to procure her silver brandy flask. As she held it in her hand the silver glittered and he being attracted to it implored her to give it to him, saying that he was frozen. She refused the brandy, but removed her steamer blanket and placed it around his shoulders, while another lady wrapped a second blanket around his waist and limbs, he looking "as snug as a bug in a rug."

The quartermaster was then asked to relieve one or the other of those struggling at the oars, as someone else could manage the rudder while he rowed. He flatly refused and continued to lampoon them, shouting: "Here, you fellow on the starboard side, your oar is not being put in the water at the right angle." No one made any protest to his outbursts, as he broke the monotony, but they continued to pull at the oars with no goal in sight. Presently he raised his voice and shouted to another lifeboat to pull near and lash alongside, commanding some of the other ladies to take the light and signal to the other life-boats. His command was immediately obeyed. He also gave another command to drop the oars and lay to. Some time later, after more shouts, a lifeboat hove to and obeyed his orders to throw a rope, and was tied alongside. On the cross-seat of that boat stood a man in white pajamas, looking like a snow man in that icy region. His teeth were chattering and he appeared quite numb. Seeing his predicament, Mrs. Brown told him he had better get to rowing and keep his blood in circulation. But the suggestion met with a forci-ble protest from the quartermaster in charge. Mrs. Brown and her companions at the oars, after their exercise, felt the blasts from the ice-fields and demanded that they should be allowed to row to keep warm.

Over into their boat jumped a half-frozen stoker, black and covered with dust. As he was dressed in thin jumpers, she picked up a large sable stole which she had dropped into the boat and wrapped it around his limbs from his waist down and tied the tails around his ankles. She handed him an oar and told the pajama man to cut loose. A howl arose from the quartermas-ter in charge. He moved to prevent it, and Mrs. Brown told him if he did he would be thrown overboard. Someone laid a hand on her shoulder to stay her threats, but she knew it would not be necessary to push him over, for had she only moved in the quartermaster's direction, he would have tumbled into the sea, so paralyzed was he with fright. By this time he had worked himself up to a pitch of sheer despair, fearing that a scramble of any kind would remove the plug from the bottom of the boat. He then became very impertinent, and our fur-enveloped stoker in as broad a cockney as one hears in the Haymarket shouted: "Oi sy, don't you know you are talkin' to a lidy?" For the time being the seaman was silenced and we resumed our task at the oars. Two other ladies came to the rescue.

While glancing around watching the edge of the horizon, the beautifully modulated voice of the young Englishwoman at the oar (Miss Norton) exclaimed, "There is a flash of lightning." "It is a falling star," replied our pessimistic seaman. As it became brighter he was then convinced that it was a ship. However, the distance, as we rowed, seemed interminable. We saw the ship was anchored. Again the declaration was made that we, regardless of what our quartermaster said, would row toward her, and the young Englishwoman from the Thames got to work, accompanying her strokes with cheerful words to the wilted occupants of the boat.

Mrs. Brown finishes the quartermaster in her final account of him. On entering the dining-room on the *Carpathia*, she saw him in one corner—this brave and heroic seaman! A cluster of people were around him as he wildly gesticulated, trying to impress upon them what difficulty he had in maintaining discipline among the occupants of his boat; but on seeing Mrs. Brown and a few others of the boat nearby he did not tarry long, but made a hasty retreat.

R. Hitchens, Q. M. (Am. Inq., p. 451. Br. Inq.) explains his conduct:

I was put in charge of No. 6 by the Second Officer, Mr. Lightoller. We lowered away from the ship. I told them in the boat somebody would have to pull. There was no use stopping alongside the ship, which was gradually going by the head. We were in a dangerous place, so I told them to man the oars—ladies and all. "All of you do your best." I relieved one of the young ladies with an oar and told her to take the tiller. She immediately let the boat come athwart, and the ladies in the boat got very nervous; so I took the tiller back again and told them to manage the best way they could. The lady I refer to, Mrs. Meyer, was rather vexed with me in the boat and I spoke rather straight to her. She accused me of wrapping myself up in the blankets in the boat, using bad language and drinking all the whisky, which I deny, sir. I was standing to attention, exposed, steering the boat all night, which is a very cold billet. I would rather be pulling the boat than be steering, but I saw no one there to steer, so I thought, being in charge of the boat, it was the best way to steer myself, especially when I saw the ladies get very nervous.

I do not remember that the women urged me to go toward the *Titanic.* I did not row toward the scene of the *Titanic* because the suction of the ship would draw the boat, with all its occupants, under water. I did not know which way to go back to the *Titanic.* I was looking at all the other boats. We were looking at each other's lights. After the lights disappeared and went out, we did hear cries of distress—a lot of crying, moaning and screaming, for two or three minutes. We made fast to another boat—that of the master-at-arms. It was No. 16. I had thirty-eight women in my boat. I counted them, sir. One seaman, Fleet; the Canadian Major, who testified here yesterday, myself and the Italian boy.

We got down to the *Carpathia* and I saw every lady and everybody out of the boat, and I saw them carefully hoisted on board the *Carpathia,* and I was the last man to leave the boat.

BOAT NO. 8 *

No male passengers in this boat.

Passengers: Mrs. Bucknell and her maid (Albina Bazzani); Miss Cherry, Mrs. Kenyon, Miss Leader, Mrs. Pears, Mrs. Penasco and her maid (Mlle. Olivia); Countess Rothes and her maid (Miss Maloney); Mrs. Swift, Mrs. Taussig, Miss Taussig, Mrs. White and her maid (Amelia Bessetti); Mrs. Wick, Miss Wick, Miss Young and Mrs. Straus' maid (Ellen Bird).

Women: 24.

Said good-bye to wives and sank with the ship: Messrs. Kenyon, Pears, Penasco, Taussig and Wick.

Crew: Seaman T. Jones, Stewards Crawford and Hart, and a cook.

Total: 28.

INCIDENTS

T. Jones, seaman (Am. Inq., p. 570).

The captain asked me if the plug was in the boat and I answered, "Yes, sir." "All right," he

---

* British Report (p. 38) puts this boat second on port side at 1.10. Notwithstanding Seaman Fleet's testimony (Am. Inq., p. 363), I think she must have preceded No. 6.

said, "any more ladies?" He shouted twice again, "Any more ladies?"

I pulled for the light, but I found that I could not get to it; so I stood by for a while. I wanted to return to the ship, but the ladies were frightened. In all, I had thirty-five ladies and three stewards, Crawford, Hart and another. There were no men who offered to get in the boat. I did not see any children, and very few women when we left the ship. There was one old lady there and an old gentleman, her husband. She wanted him to enter the boat with her but he backed away. She never said anything; if she did, we could not hear it, because the steam was blowing so and making such a noise.*

Senator Newlands: Can you give me the names of any passengers on this boat?

Witness: One lady—she had a lot to say and I put her to steering the boat.

Senator Newlands: What was her name?

Witness: Lady Rothes; she was a countess, or something.

A. Crawford, steward (Am. Inq., pp. 111, 827, 842).

* By the testimony of the witness and Steward Crawford it appears that Mr. and Mrs. Straus approached this boat and their maid got in, but Mr. Straus would not follow his wife and she refused to leave him.

After we struck I went out and saw the iceberg, a large black object, much higher than B Deck, passing along the starboard side. We filled No. 8 with women. Captain Smith and a steward lowered the forward falls. Captain Smith told me to get in. He gave orders to row for the light and to land the people there and come back to the ship. The Countess Rothes was at the tiller all night. There were two lights not further than ten miles—stationary masthead lights. Everybody saw them—all the ladies in the boat. They asked if we were drawing nearer to the steamer, but we could not seem to make any headway, and near daybreak we saw another steamer coming up, which proved to be the *Carpathia,* and then we turned around and came back. We were the furthest boat away. I am sure it was a steamer, because a sailing vessel would not have had two masthead lights.

Mrs. J. Stuart White (Am. Inq., p. 1008).

Senator Smith: Did you see anything after the accident bearing on the discipline of the officers or crew, or their conduct which you desire to speak of?

Mrs. White: Before we cut loose from the ship these stewards took out cigarettes and lighted them. On an occasion like that! That is one thing I saw. All of these men escaped under the pretence of being oarsmen. The man who rowed near me took his oar and rowed all over the boat in every direction. I said to him: "Why don't you put the oar in the oarlock?" He said: "Do you put it in that hole?" I said: "Certainly." He said: "I never had an oar in my hand before." I spoke to the other man and he said: "I have never had an oar in my hand before, but I think I can row." These were the men we were put to sea with, that night—with all those magnificent fellows left on board who would have been such a protection to us—those were the kind of men with whom we were put to sea that night! There were twenty-two women and four men in my boat. None of the men seemed to understand the management of a boat except one who was at the end of our boat and gave the orders. The officer who put us in the boat gave strict orders to make for the light opposite, land passengers and then get back just as soon as possible. That was the light everybody saw in the distance. I saw it distinctly. It was ten miles away, but we rowed, and rowed, and rowed, and then we all decided that it was impossible for us to get to it, and the thing to do was to go back and see what we could do for the others. We had only twenty-two in our boat. We turned and went back and lingered around for a long time. We could not locate the other boats except by hearing them. The only way to look was by my electric light. I had an electric cane with an electric light in it. The lamp in the boat was worth absolutely nothing. There was no excitement whatever on the ship. Nobody seemed frightened. Nobody was panic-stricken. There was a lot of pathos when husbands and wives kissed each other good-bye.

We were the second boat (No. 8) that got away from the ship and we saw nothing that happened after that. We were not near enough. We heard the yells of the passengers as they went down, but we saw none of the harrowing part of it. The women in our boat all rowed—every one of them. Miss Young rowed every minute. The men (the stewards) did not know the first thing about it and could not row. Mrs. Swift rowed all the way to the *Carpathia.* Countess Rothes stood at the tiller. Where would we have been if it had not been for the women, with such men as were put in charge of the boat? Our head seaman was giving orders and these men knew nothing about a boat. They would say: "If you don't stop talking through that hole in your face there will be one less in the boat." We were in the hands of men of that kind. I settled two or three fights between them and quieted them down. Imagine getting right out there and taking out a pipe and smoking it, which was most dangerous. We had woollen rugs all around us. There was another thing which I thought a disgraceful point. The men were asked when they got in if they could row. Imagine asking men who are supposed to be at the head of lifeboats if they can row!

Senator Smith: There were no male passengers in your boat?

Mrs. White: Not one. I never saw a finer body of men in my life than the men passengers on this ship—athletes and men of sense—and if they had been permitted to enter these lifeboats with their families, the boats would have been properly manned and many more lives saved, instead of allowing stewards to get in the boats and save their lives under the pretence that they could row when they knew nothing about it.

BOAT NO. 10.*

No male passengers in this boat.

Passengers: First cabin, Miss Andrews, Miss Longley, Mrs. Hogeboom. Second cabin, Mrs. Parrish, Mrs. Shelley. 41 women, 7 children.

* British Report (p. 38) says third at 1.20. I think No. 6 went later, though Buley (Am. Inq., p. 604) claims No. 10 as the last lifeboat lowered.

Crew: Seamen: Buley (in charge), Evans; Fireman Rice; Stewards Burke and one other.

Stowaway: 1 Japanese.

Jumped from A Deck into boat being lowered: 1 Armenian.

Total: 55.

INCIDENTS

Edward J. Buley, A. B. (Am. Inq., p. 604).

Chief Officer Wilde said: "See if you can find another seaman to give you a hand, and jump in." I found Evans, my mate, the able-bodied seaman, and we both got in the boat.

Much of Seaman Buley's and of Steward Burke's testimony is a repetition of that of Seaman Evans, so I cite the latter only:

F. O. Evans, A. B. (Am. Inq., p. 675).

I went up (on the Boat Deck) with the remainder of the crew and uncovered all of the port boats. Then to the starboard side and lowered the boats there with the assistance of the Boatswain of the ship, A. Nichol. I went next (after No. 12) to No. 10. Mr. Murdoch was standing there. I lowered the boat with the assistance of a steward. The chief officer said: "Get into that boat." I got into the bows. A young ship's baker (J. Joughin) was getting the children and chucking them into the boat. Mr. Murdoch and the baker made the women jump across into the boat about two feet and a half. "He threw them on to the women and he was catching children by their dresses and chucking them in." One woman in a black dress slipped and fell. She seemed nervous and did not like to jump at first. When she did jump she did not go far enough, but fell between the ship and the boat. She was pulled in by some men on the deck below, went up to the Boat Deck again, took another jump, and landed safely in the boat. There were none of the children hurt. The only accident was with this woman. The only man passenger was a foreigner, up forward. He, as the boat was being lowered, jumped from A Deck into the boat—deliberately jumped across and saved himself.

When we got to the water it was impossible to get to the tripper underneath the thwart on account of women being packed so tight. We had to lift the fall up off the hook by hand to release the spring to get the block and fall away from it. We pushed off from the ship and rowed away about 200 yards. We tied up to three other boats. We gave the man our painter and made fast to No. 12. We stopped there about an hour, and Officer Lowe came over with his boat No. 14

and said: "You seamen will have to distribute these passengers among these boats. Tie them together and come into my boat to go over to the wreckage and pick up anyone that is alive there."

Witness testified that the larger lifeboats would hold sixty people.

Senator Smith: Do you wish to be understood that each lifeboat like Nos. 12 and 14 and 10 could be filled to its fullest capacity and lowered to the water with safety?

Mr. Evans: Yes, because we did it then, sir.

Senator Smith: That is a pretty good answer.

Mr. Evans: It was my first experience in seeing a boat loaded like that, sir.

The stern of the ship, after plunging forward, remained floating in a perpendicular position about four or five minutes.

W. Burke, dining-room steward (Am. Inq., p. 822).

I went to my station and found that my boat, No. 1, had gone. Then to the port side and assisted with No. 8 boat and saw her lowered. Then I passed to No. 10. The officer said, "Get right in there," and pushed me toward the boat, and I got in. When there were no women to be had around the deck the officer gave the order for the boat to be lowered.

After the two seamen (Buley and Evans) were transferred to boat No. 14, some of the women forward said to me: "There are two men down here in the bottom of the boat." I got hold of them and pulled one out. He apparently was a Japanese and could not speak English. I put him at an oar. The other appeared to be an Italian. I tried to speak to him but he said: "Armenian." I also put him at an oar. I afterwards made fast to an officer's boat—I think it was Mr. Lightoller's (i. e., No. 12).

Mrs. Imanita Shelley's affidavit (Am. Inq., p. 1146).

Mrs. Shelley with her mother, Mrs. L. D. Parrish, were second cabin passengers. Mrs. Shelley had been sick and it was with difficulty that she reached the deck, where she was assisted to a chair. After some time a sailor ran to her and implored her to get in the lifeboat that was then being launched—one of the last on the ship. Pushing her mother toward the sailor, Mrs. Shelley made for the davits where the boat hung.

There was a space of between four or five feet between the edge of the deck and the suspended boat. The sailor picked up Mrs. Parrish and threw her bodily into the boat. Mrs. Shelley jumped and landed safely. There were a fireman and a ship's baker among the crew at the time of launching. The boat was filled with women and children, as many as could get in without overcrowding. There was trouble with the tackle and the ropes had to be cut.

Just as they reached the water, a crazed Italian jumped from the deck into the lifeboat, landing on Mrs. Parrish, severely bruising her right side and leg.

Orders had been given to keep in sight of the ship's boat which had been sent out ahead to look for help. Throughout the entire period, from the time of the collision and taking to the boats, the ship's crew behaved in an ideal manner. Not a man tried to get into a boat unless ordered to, and many were seen to strip off their clothing and wrap it around the women and children, who came up half-clad from their beds. Mrs. Shelley says that no crew could have behaved in a more perfect manner.

J. Joughin, head baker (Br. Inq.)
Chief Officer Wilde shouted to the stewards to keep the men passengers back, but there was no necessity for the order as they were keeping back. The order was splendid. The stewards, firemen and sailors got in line and passed the ladies in; and then we had difficulty to find ladies to go into

the boat. No distinction at all as to class was made. I saw a number of third-class women with their bags, which they would not let go.

The boat was let down and the women were forcibly drawn into it. The boat was a yard and a half from the ship's side. There was a slight list and we had to drop them in. The officer ordered two sailors and a steward to get in.

BOAT NO. 12.*

No male passenger in this boat.

Passengers: Miss Phillips.

Bade good-bye to his daughter and sank with the ship: Mr. Phillips. Women and children, 40.

Crew: Seamen Poigndestre (in charge), F. Clench. Later, Lucas and two firemen were transferred from boat "D."

Jumped from deck below as boat was lowered: 1 Frenchman.

Total: 43.

Transfers were made to this boat *first* from Engelhardt "D" and *second,* from Engelhardt upset boat "B," so that it reached the *Carpathia's* side with seventy, or more.

---

* British Report (p. 38) says this was the fourth boat lowered on port side at 1.25 A. M.

INCIDENTS

F. Clench, A. B. (Am. Inq., p. 636).

The second officer and myself stood on the gunwale and helped load women and children. The chief officer passed them along to us and we filled three boats, No. 12 first. In each there were about forty or fifty people. After finishing No. 16 boat, I went back to No. 12. "How many men (crew) have you in this boat?" the chief officer said, and I said, "Only one, sir." He looked up and said: "Jump into that boat," and that made a complement of two seamen. An able seaman was in charge of this boat. (Poigndestre.) We had instructions to keep our eye on No. 14 and keep together.

There was only one male passenger in our boat, and that was a Frenchman who jumped in and we could not find him. He got under the thwart, mixed up with the women, just as we dropped into the water before the boat was lowered and without our knowledge. Officer Lowe transferred some of his people into our boat and others, making close on to sixty, and pretty full up. When Mr. Lowe was gone I heard shouts. I looked around and saw a boat in the way that appeared to be like a funnel; we thought it was the top of a funnel. (It was Engelhardt overturned boat

"B.")   There were about twenty on this, and we took off approximately ten, making seventy in my boat.

John Poigndestre, A. B. (Br. Inq., p. 82).

Lightoller ordered us to lay off and stand by close to the ship.   Boat "D" and three lifeboats made fast to No. 12.   Stood off about 100 yards after ship sank.   Not enough sailors to help pick up swimmers.   No light.   Transfer of about a dozen women passengers from No. 14 to No. 12.   About 150 yards off when *Titanic* sank.   No compass.

BOAT NO. 14.*

No male passenger in this boat.

Passengers: Mrs. Compton, Miss Compton, Mrs. Minahan, Miss Minahan, Mrs. Collyer, Miss Collyer.

Picked up out of sea: W. F. Hoyt (who died), Steward J. Stewart, and a plucky Japanese.

Women: 50.

Volunteer when crew was short: C. Williams.

Crew: Fifth Officer Lowe, Seaman Scarrot, 2 firemen, Stewards Crowe and Morris.

* British Report (p. 38) says this was the fifth boat on the port side, lowered at 1.30.

Stowaway: 1 Italian.
Bade good-bye and sank with ship: Dr. Minahan, Mr. Compton, Mr. Collyer.
Total: 60.

INCIDENTS

H. G. Lowe, Fifth Officer (Am. Inq., 116).
Nos. 12, 14 and 16 were down about the same time. I told Mr. Moody that three boats had gone away and that an officer ought to go with them. He said: "You go." There was difficulty in lowering when I got near the water. I dropped her about five feet, because I was not going to take the chance of being dropped down upon by somebody. While I was on the Boat Deck, two men tried to jump into the boat. I chased them out.

We filled boats 14 and 16 with women and children. Moody filled No. 16 and I filled No. 14. Lightoller was there part of the time. They were all women and children, barring one passenger, who was an Italian, and he sneaked in dressed like a woman. He had a shawl over his head. There was another passenger, a chap by the name of C. Williams, whom I took for rowing. He gave me his name and address (referring to book), "C. Williams, Racket Champion of the

World, 2 Drury Road, Harrow-on-the-Hill, Middlesex, England."

As I was being lowered, I expected every moment that my boat would be doubled up under my feet. I had overcrowded her, but I knew that I had to take a certain amount of risk. I thought if one additional body was to fall into that boat, that slight additional weight might part the hooks, or carry away something; so as we were coming down past the open decks, I saw a lot of Latin people all along the ship's rails. They were glaring more or less like wild beasts, ready to spring. That is why I yelled out to "look out," and let go, bang! right along the ship's side. There was a space I should say of about three feet between the side of the boat and the ship's side, and as I went down I fired these shots without any intention of hurting anybody and with the positive knowledge that I did not hurt anybody. I fired, I think, three times.

Later, 150 yards away, I herded five boats together. I was in No. 14; then I had 10, 12, collapsible "D" and one other boat (No. 4), and made them tie up. I waited until the yells and shrieks had subsided for the people to thin out, and then I deemed it safe for me to go amongst the wreckage; so I transferred all my passengers, somewhere about fifty-three, from my boat and equally distributed them among my other four boats. Then I asked for volunteers to go with me to the wreck, and it was at this time that I found the Italian. He came aft and had a shawl over his head, and I suppose he had skirts. Anyhow, I pulled the shawl off his face and saw he was a man. He was in a great hurry to get into the other boat and I got hold of him and pitched him in.

Senator Smith: Pitched him in?

Mr. Lowe: Yes; because he was not worth being handled better.

Senator Smith: You pitched him in among the women?

Mr. Lowe: No, sir; in the forepart of the lifeboat in which I transferred my passengers.

Senator Smith: Did you use some pretty emphatic language when you did this?

Mr. Lowe: No, sir; I did not say a word to him.

Then I went off and rowed to the wreckage and around the wreckage and picked up four people alive. I do not know who these live persons were. They never came near me afterwards either to say this or that or the other. But one died, Mr. W. F. Hoyt, of New York. After we got him in the boat we took his collar off so as to give him more chance to breathe, but unfortunately, he died. He was too far gone when we picked him up. I then left the wreck. I went right around, and, strange to say, I did not see a single female body around the wreckage. I did not have a light in my boat. Then I could see the *Carpathia* coming up and I thought: "Well, I am the fastest boat of the lot," as I was sailing, you see. I was going through the water four or five knots, bowling along very nicely.

By and by, I noticed a collapsible boat, Engelhardt "D." It looked rather sorry, so I thought: "Well, I will go down and pick her up and make sure of her." This was Quartermaster Bright's boat. Mrs. H. B. Harris, of New York, was in it. She had a broken arm. I had taken this first collapsible ("D") in tow and I noticed that there was another collapsible ("A") in a worse plight than this one that I had in tow. I got to her just in time and took off, I suppose, about twenty men and one lady. I left three male bodies in it. I may have been a bit hard-hearted in doing this. I thought: "I am not here to worry about bodies; I am here to save life and not bother about bodies." The people on the raft told me these had been dead for some time. I do not know whether any one endeavored to find anything on their persons that would identify them, because they were all up to their ankles in water when I took them off.

Joseph Scarrot, A. B. (Br. Inq., pp. 29, 30) : I myself took charge of No. 14 as the only sailorman there. The Chief Officer ordered women and children to be taken in. Some men came and tried to rush the boat. They were foreigners and could not understand the orders I gave them, but I managed to keep them away. I had to use some persuasion with a boat tiller. One man jumped in twice and I had to throw him out the third time. I got all the women and children into the boat. There were fifty-four women and four children—one of them a baby in arms. There were myself, two firemen, three or four stewards and Mr. Lowe, who got into the boat. I told him the trouble I had with the men and he brought out his revolver and fired two shots and said: "If there is any more trouble I will fire at them." The shots fired were fired between the boat and the ship's side. The after fall got twisted and we dropped the boat by the releasing gear and got clear of the ship. There were four men rowing. There was a man in the boat who we thought was a sailor, but he was not. He was a window cleaner. The *Titanic* was then about fifty yards off, and we lay there with the other boats. Mr. Lowe was at the helm. We went in the direction of the cries and came among hundreds of dead bodies and life belts. We got one man, who died shortly after he got into the boat. One of the stewards tried to restore him, but without avail. There was another man who was calling for help, but among the bodies and wreckage it was too late for us to reach him. It took half an hour to get to that man. Cannot say exactly, but think we got about twenty off of the Engelhardt boat ("A").

E. J. Buley, A. B. (Am. Inq., p. 605) :
(After his transfer from No. 10 to No. 14.) Then, with Lowe in his boat No. 14, I went back to where the *Titanic* sank and picked up the remaining live bodies. We got four; all the others were dead. We turned over several to see if they were alive. It looked as if none of them were drowned. They looked as if frozen. The life belts they had on were that much (indicating) out of the water, and their heads lay back with their faces on the water. They were head and shoulders out of water, with their heads thrown back. In the morning, after we had picked up all that were alive, there was a collapsible boat ("A") swamped, which we saw with a lot of people up to their knees in water. We sailed over to them. We then picked up another boat ("D") and took her in tow. I think we were about the seventh or eighth boat alongside the *Carpathia*.

F. O. Evans, A. B. (Am. Inq., p. 677):

So from No. 10 we got into his (Lowe's) boat,
No. 14, and went straight over towards the wreckage with eight or nine men and picked up four
persons alive, one of whom died on the way to the
Carpathia. Another picked up was named J.
Stewart, a steward. You could not hardly count
the number of dead bodies. I was afraid to look
over the sides because it might break my nerves
down. We saw no other people in the water or
heard their cries, other than these four picked
up. The officer said: "Hoist a sail forward."
I did so and made sail in the direction of the
collapsible boat "A" about a mile and a half
away, which had been swamped. There were in
it one woman and about ten or eleven men. Then
we picked up another collapsible boat ("D") and
took her in tow to the *Carpathia.* There were
then about twenty-five people in our boat No. 14,
including the one who died.

One of the ladies there passed over a flask of
whisky to the people who were all wet through.
She asked if anybody needed the spirits, and these
people were all soaking wet and nearly perished
and they passed it around among these men and
women. It took about twenty minutes after we
sighted the *Carpathia* to get alongside of her.
We saw five or six icebergs—some of them tre-

mendous, about the height of the *Titanic*—and field ice. After we got on the *Carpathia* we saw, at a rough estimate, a twenty-five mile floe, sir, flat like the floor.

F. Crowe, steward (Am. Inq., p. 615):

I assisted in handing the women and children into boat No. 12, and was asked if I could take an oar. I said: "Yes," and was told to man the boat, I believe, by Mr. Murdoch. After getting the women and children in we lowered down to within four or five feet of the water, and then the block and tackle got twisted in some way, causing us to have to cut the ropes to allow the boat to get into the water. This officer, Lowe, told us to do this. He was in the boat with us. I stood by the lever—the lever releasing the blocks from the hooks in the boat. He told me to wait, to get away and cut the line to raise the lever, thereby causing the hooks to open and allow the boat to drop in the water.

There was some shooting that occurred at the time the boat was lowered. There were various men passengers, probably Italians or some foreign nationality other than English or American, who attempted to "rush" the boats. The officers threatened to shoot any man who put his foot into the boat. An officer fired a revolver, but

either downward or upward, not shooting at any
one of the passengers at all and not injuring anybody. He fired perfectly clear upward and downward and stopped the rush. There was no disorder after that. One woman cried, but that
was all. There was no panic or anything in the
boat.

After getting into the water I pushed out to
the other boats. In No. 14 there were fifty-seven
women and children and about six men, including
one officer, and I may have been seven. I am
not quite sure. I know how many, because when
we got out a distance the officer asked me how
many people were in the boat.

When the boat was released and fell I think
she must have sprung a leak. A lady stated that
there was some water coming up over her ankles.
Two men and this lady assisted in bailing it out
with bails that were kept in the boat for that
purpose. We transferred our people to other
boats so as to return to the wreck and see if we
could pick up anybody else. Returning to the
wreck, we heard various cries and endeavored
to get among them, and we were successful in
doing so, and picked up one body that was floating around in the water. It was that of a man
and he expired shortly afterwards. Going further into the wreckage we came across a steward

(J. Stewart) and got him into the boat. He was very cold and his hands were kind of stiff. He recovered by the time that we got back to the *Carpathia*.

A Japanese or Chinese young fellow that we picked up on top of some wreckage, which may have been a sideboard or a table that was floating around, also survived.* We stopped (in the wreckage) until daybreak, and we saw in the distance an Engelhardt collapsible boat ("A") with a crew of men in it. We went over to the boat and found twenty men and one woman; also three dead bodies, which we left. Returning under sail we took another collapsible boat in tow (boat "D") containing fully sixty people, women and children.

I did not see the iceberg that struck the ship. When it came daylight and we could see, there were two or three bergs around, and one man pointed out that that must have been the berg, and another man pointed out another berg. Really, I do not think anybody knew which one struck the ship.

Mrs. Charlotte Collyer, third-class passenger,

* Undoubtedly reference is here made to the same Japanese described in an account attributed to a second-class passenger, Mrs. Collyer, and which follows Crowe's testimony.

in The Semi-Monthly Magazine, May, 1912:

A little further on we saw a floating door that must have been torn loose when the ship went down. Lying upon it, face downward, was a small Japanese. He had lashed himself with a rope to his frail raft, using the broken hinges to make the knots secure. As far as we could see, he was dead. The sea washed over him every time the door bobbed up and down, and he was frozen stiff. He did not answer when he was hailed, and the officer hesitated about trying to save him.

"What's the use?" said Mr. Lowe. "He's dead, likely, and if he isn't there's others better worth saving than a Jap!"

He had actually turned our boat around, but he changed his mind and went back. The Japanese was hauled on board, and one of the women rubbed his chest, while others chafed his hands and feet. In less time than it takes to tell, he opened his eyes. He spoke to us in his own tongue; then, seeing that we did not understand, he struggled to his feet, stretched his arms above his head, stamped his feet and in five minutes or so had almost recovered his strength. One of the sailors near to him was so tired that he could hardly pull his oar. The Japanese bustled over, pushed him from his seat, took his

oar and worked like a hero until we were finally
picked up. I saw Mr. Lowe watching him in
open-mouthed surprise.

"By Jove!" muttered the officer, "I'm ashamed
of what I said about the little blighter. I'd
save the likes o' him six times over if I got the
chance."

Miss Minahan's affidavit (Am. Inq., p. 1109):
After the *Titanic* went down the cries were
horrible. Some of the women implored Officer
Lowe of No. 10 to divide his passengers among
the three other boats and go back to rescue them.
His first answer to these requests was: "You
ought to be d—— glad you are here and have
got your own life." After some time he was
persuaded to do as he was asked. As I came up
to him to be transferred to the other boat, he
said: "Jump, G—d d—n you, jump." I had
shown no hesitancy and was waiting until my turn.
He had been so blasphemous during the hours
we were in his boat that the women in my end of
the boat all thought he was under the influence
of liquor. (Testimony elsewhere shows that
Officer Lowe is a teetotaler.) Then he took all
the men who had rowed No. 14, together with
the men from other boats, and went back to the
scene of the wreck. We were left with a steward

and a stoker to row our boat, which was crowded. The steward did his best, but the stoker refused at first to row, but finally helped two men who were the only ones pulling on that side. It was just four o'clock when we sighted the *Carpathia,* and we were three hours getting to her. On the *Carpathia* we were treated with every kindness and given every comfort possible.

The above affidavit being of record shows Officer Lowe in an unfortunate, bad light. There is no doubt of it that he was intemperate in his language only. In all other respects he was a first-class officer, as proven by what he accomplished. But I am glad that I have the account of another lady passenger in the same boat, which is a tribute to what he did. I met Officer Lowe in Washington the time that both of us were summoned before the U. S. Court of Inquiry, and I am quite sure that the only point against him is that he was a little hasty in speech in the accomplishment of his work.

Miss Compton, who lost her brother, I had the pleasure of meeting on the *Carpathia.* She is still a sufferer from injuries received in the wreck, and yet has been very kind in sending me an account of her experience, from which I cite the following:

As she stood on the rail to step into boat **No.
14** it was impossible to see whether she would
step into the boat or into the water. She was
pushed into the boat with such violence that she
found herself on her hands and knees, but fortunately landed on a coil of rope. This seemed
to be the general experience of the women. All
the passengers entered the lifeboat at the same
point and were told to move along to make place
for those who followed. This was difficult, as
the thwarts were so high that it was difficult to
climb over them, encumbered as the ladies were
with lifebelts. It was a case of throwing one's
self over rather than climbing over.

Miss Compton from her place in the stern of
the lifeboat overheard the conversation between
Officer Lowe and another officer, which the former gave in his testimony.

Just before the boat was lowered a man jumped
in. He was immediately hauled out. Mr. Lowe
then pulled his revolver and said: "If anyone
else tries that this is what he will get." He then
fired his revolver in the air.

She mentions the same difficulties, elsewhere
recorded, about the difficulties in lowering the
boat, first the stern very high, and then the bow;
also how the ropes were cut and **No. 14** struck
the water hard. At this time the count showed

58 in the boat, and a later one made the number 60. A child near her answered in neither of the counts.

"Mr. Lowe's manly bearing," she says, "gave us all confidence. As I look back now he seems to me to personify the best traditions of the British sailor. He asked us all to try and find a lantern, but none was to be found. Mr. Lowe had with him, however, an electric light which he flashed from time to time. Almost at once the boat began to leak and in a few moments the women in the forward part of the boat were standing in water. There was nothing to bail with and I believe the men used their hats.

"Officer Lowe insisted on having the mast put up. He crawled forward and in a few moments the mast was raised and ready. He said this was necessary as no doubt with dawn there would be a breeze. He returned to his place and asked the stewards and firemen, who were acting as crew, if they had any matches, and insisted on having them passed to him. He then asked if they had any tobacco and said: 'Keep it in your pockets, for tobacco makes you thirsty.' Mr. Lowe wished to remain near the ship that he might have a chance to help someone after she sank. Some of the women protested and he replied: 'I don't like to leave her, but if you feel that way about it we will pull away a little distance.' "

Miss Compton's account corroborates other information about boat No. 14, which we have elsewhere. She was among the number transferred to Engelhardt boat "D." "I now found myself," she said, "in the stern of a collapsible boat. In spite of Mr. Lowe's warning the four small boats began to separate, each going its own way. Soon it seemed as though our boat was the only one on the sea. We went through a great deal of wreckage. The men who were supposed to be rowing—one was a fireman—made no effort to keep away from it. They were all the time looking towards the horizon. With daylight we saw the *Carpathia,* and not so very long afterwards Officer Lowe, sailing towards us, for, as he had predicted, quite a strong breeze had sprung up. We caught the rope which he threw us from the stern of his boat. Someone in ours succeeded in catching it and we were taken in tow to the *Carpathia.*"

No. 16.*

No male passenger.

Passengers: Fifty women and children—second and third-class.

* British Report (p. 38) gives this as the sixth boat lowered from the port side at 1.35 A. M.

Crew: Master-at-arms Bailey in charge. Seaman Archer, Steward Andrews, Stewardess Leather, and two others.

Total: 56.

INCIDENTS

E. Archer, A. B. (Am. Inq., p. 645):

I assisted in getting Nos. 12, 14 and 16 out—getting the falls and everything ready and passengers into No. 14. Then I went to No. 16. I saw that the plug was in tight. I never saw any man get in, only my mate. I heard the officer give orders to lower the boat and to allow nobody in it, having fifty passengers and only my mate and myself. The master-at-arms came down after us; he was the coxswain and took charge. When we were loading the boat there was no effort on the part of others to crowd into it; no confusion at all. No individual men, or others were repelled from getting in; everything was quiet and steady. One of the lady passengers suggested going back to see if there were any people in the water we could get, but I never heard any more of it after that. There was one lady in the boat, a stewardess (Mrs. Leather) who tried to assist in rowing. I told her it was not necessary, but she said she would like to do it to keep herself warm. There was one fireman found in the boat after we got clear. I do not know how he came there. He was transferred to another boat (No. 6) to help row.

C. E. Andrews, steward (Am. Inq., p. 623):
Besides these six men I should think there were about fifty passengers.

There was no effort on the part of the steerage men to get into our boat. I was told by the officer to allow none in it. When the officer started to fill the boat with passengers and the men to man it, there were no individuals who tried to get in, or that he permitted to get in. There was no confusion whatever. The officer asked me if I could take an oar. I said I could.

BOAT No. 2.*

Only one old man, third-class, a foreigner in this boat.

Passengers: Miss Allen (now Mrs. J. B. Mennell), Mrs. Appleton, Mrs. Cornell, Mrs. Douglas and maid (Miss Le Roy), Miss Madill, Mrs. Robert and maid (Amelia Kenchen). One old man, third-class, foreigner, and family:

* British Report (p. 38) gives this as the seventh boat lowered on the port side at 1.45 A. M.

Brahim Youssef, Hanne Youssef, and children
Marian and Georges. The rest second and third-
class.

Bade good-bye to wife and sank with ship:
Mr. Douglas.

Crew: Fourth Officer Boxhall, Seamen Osman
and Steward Johnston, cook.

Total: 25.

INCIDENTS

J. G. Boxhall, Fourth Officer (Am. Inq., p. 240,
and Br. Inq.) :

I was sent away in Emergency boat 2, the last
boat but one on the port side. There was one
of the lifeboats (No. 4) lowered away a few
minutes after I left. That was the next lifeboat
to me aft. Engelhardt boat "D" was being got
ready. There was no anxiety of people to get
into these boats. There were four men in this
boat—a sailorman (Osman), a steward (Johnston), a cook and myself, and one male passenger
who did not speak English—a middle-aged man
with a black beard. He had his wife there and
some children. When the order was given to
lower the boat, which seemed to be pretty full,
it was about twenty minutes to half an hour be-

fore the ship sank. Someone shouted through a megaphone: "Some of the boats come back and come around to the starboard side." All rowed except this male passenger. I handled one oar and a lady assisted me. She asked to do it. I got around to the starboard side intending to go alongside. I reckoned I could take about three more people off the ship with safety; and when about 22 yards off there was a little suction, as the boat seemed to be drawn closer, and I thought it would be dangerous to go nearer the ship. I suggested going back (after ship sank) to the sailorman in the boat, but decided it was unwise to do so. There was a lady there, Mrs. Douglas, whom I asked to steer the boat according to my orders. She assisted me greatly in it. They told me on board the *Carpathia* afterwards that it was about ten minutes after four when we went alongside.

After we left the *Titanic* I showed green lights most of the time. When within two or three ship lengths of the *Carpathia*, it was just breaking daylight, and I saw her engines were stopped. She had stopped within half a mile or a quarter of a mile of an iceberg. There were several other bergs, and I could see field ice as far as I could see. The bergs looked white in the sun, though when I first saw them at daylight they looked black. This was the first time I had seen field ice on the Grand Banks. I estimate about 25 in my boat.

F. Osman, A. B. (Am. Inq., p. 538):

All of us went up and cleared away the boats. After that we loaded all the boats there were. I went away in No. 2, the fourth from the last to leave the ship. Boxhall was in command. Murdoch directed the loading. All passengers were women and children, except one man, a third-class passenger, his wife and two children. After I got in the boat the officer found a bunch of rockets which was put in the boat by mistake for a box of biscuits. The officer fired some off, and the *Carpathia* came to us first and picked us up half an hour before anybody else. Not until morning did we see an iceberg about 100 feet out of the water with one big point sticking on one side of it, apparently dark, like dirty ice, 100 yards away. I knew that was the one we struck. It looked as if there was a piece broken off.

There was no panic at all. There was no suction whatever. When we were in the boat I shoved off from the ship and I said to the officer: "See if you can get alongside to see if you can get some more hands—squeeze some more hands in"; so the women started to get nervous after

I said that, and the officer said: "All right." The women disagreed to that. We pulled around to the starboard side of the ship and found that we could not get to the starboard side because it was listing too far. We pulled astern again that way, and after we lay astern we lay on our oars and saw the ship go down. It seemed to me as if all the engines and everything that was in the after part slid down into the forward part. We did not go back to the place where the ship had sunk because the women were all nervous, and we pulled around as far as we could get from it so that the women would not see and cause a panic. We got as close as we would dare to. We could not have taken any more hands into the boat. It was impossible. We might have gotten one in; that is all. There was no panic amongst the steerage passengers when we started manning the boats. I saw several people come up from the steerage and go straight up to the Boat Deck, and the men stood back while the women and children got into the boats—steerage passengers as well as others.

Senator Burton: So in your judgment it was safer to have gone on the boat than to have stayed on the *Titanic?*

Witness: Oh, yes, sir.

Senator Burton: That was when you left?

Witness: Yes, sir.

Senator Burton: What did you think when the first boat was launched?

Witness: I did not think she was going down then.

J. Johnston, steward (Br. Inq.):

Crew: Boxhall and four men, including perhaps McCullough. (None such on list.) Boxhall said: "Shall we go back in the direction of cries of distress?" which were a half or three-quarters of a mile off. Ladies said: "No." Officer Boxhall signalled the *Carpathia* with lamp. Soon after launching the swish of the water was heard against the icebergs. In the morning *Carpathia* on the edge of ice-field about 200 yards off.

Mrs. Walter D. Douglas's affidavit (Am. Inq., p. 1100):

Mr. Boxhall had difficulty in getting the boat loose and called for a knife. We finally were launched. Mrs. Appleton and a man from the steerage faced me. Mrs. Appleton's sister, Mrs. Cornell, was back of me and on the side of her the officer. I think there were eighteen or twenty in the boat. There were many who did not speak English. The rowing was very difficult, for no

one knew how. We tried to steer under Mr. Boxhall's orders, and he put an old lantern, with very
little oil in it, on a pole, which I held up for some
time. Mrs. Appleton and some other women had
been rowing, and did row all the time. Mr. Boxhall had put into the Emergency boat a tin box
of green lights like rockets. These he sent off
at intervals, and very quickly we saw the lights
of the *Carpathia,* whose captain said he saw our
green lights ten miles away and steered directly
towards us, so we were the first boat to arrive at
the *Carpathia.* When we pulled alongside, Mr.
Boxhall called out: "Slow down your engines
and take us aboard. I have only one seaman."

Mrs. J. B. Mennell (née Allen) :
My aunt, Mrs. Roberts' maid, came to the
door and asked if she could speak to me. I went
into the corridor and she said: "Miss Allen,
the baggage room is full of water." I replied she
needn't worry, that the water-tight compartments
would be shut and it would be all right for her
to go back to her cabin. She went back and returned to us immediately to say her cabin, which
was forward on Deck E, was flooded.
We were on the Boat Deck some minutes before being ordered into the lifeboat. Neither my
aunt, Mrs. Roberts, my cousin, Miss Madill, nor

myself ever saw or heard the band. As we stood
there we saw a line of men file by and get
into the boat—some sixteen or eighteen stokers. An officer* came along and shouted to
them: "Get out, you damned cowards; I'd
like to see everyone of you overboard." They
all got out and the officer said: "Women and
children into this boat," and we got in and were
lowered.

With the exception of two very harrowing
leave-takings, we saw nothing but perfect order
and quiet on board the *Titanic*. We were rowed
round the stern to the starboard side and away
from the ship, as our boat was a small one and
Boxhall feared the suction. Mrs. Cornell helped
to row all the time.

As the *Titanic* plunged deeper and deeper we
could see her stern rising higher and higher until
her lights began to go out. As the last lights
on the stern went out we saw her plunge dis-
tinctively, bow first and intact. Then the screams
began and seemed to last eternally. We rowed
back, after the *Titanic* was under water, toward
the place where she had gone down, but we saw
no one in the water, nor were we near enough to
any other lifeboats to see them. When Boxhall

* Probably the same officer, Murdoch, described by Maj.
Peuchen, p. 122, this chapter.

lit his first light the screams grew louder and then died down.

We could hear the lapping of the water on the icebergs, but saw none, even when Boxhall lit his green lights, which he did at regular intervals, till we sighted the *Carpathia*. Our boat was the first one picked up by the *Carpathia*. I happened to be the first one up the ladder, as the others seemed afraid to start up, and when the officer who received me asked where the *Titanic* was, I told him she had gone down.

Capt. A. H. Rostron, of the *Carpathia* (Am. Inq., p. 22):

We picked up the first boat, which was in charge of an officer who I saw was not under full control of his boat. He sang out that he had only one seaman in the boat, so I had to manœuvre the ship to get as close to the boat as possible, as I knew well it would be difficult to do the pulling. By the time we had the first boat's people it was breaking day, and then I could see the remaining boats all around within an area of about four miles. I also saw icebergs all around me. There were about twenty icebergs that would be anywhere from about 150 to 200 feet high, and numerous smaller bergs; also numerous ones we call "growlers" anywhere from 10 to 12 feet high and 10 to 15 feet long, above the water.

BOAT No. 4.*

No man passenger in this boat.

Passengers: Mrs. Astor and maid (Miss Bidois), Miss Bowen, Mrs. Carter and maid (Miss Serepeca), Mrs. Clark, Mrs. Cummings, Miss Eustis, Mrs. Ryerson and children, Miss S. R., Miss E. and Master J. B. and maid (Chandowson), Mrs. Stephenson, Mrs. Thayer and maid, Mrs. Widener and maid.

Women and children: 36. (Br. Rpt.)

Crew: Perkis, Q. M., in charge. Seamen: McCarthy, Hemmings,† Lyons;‡ Storekeeper Foley and Assistant Storekeeper Prentice;† Firemen: Smith and Dillon;† Greasers: Granger and Scott;† Stewards: Cunningham,† Siebert.‡

Bade good-bye to wives and sank with ship: Messrs. Astor, Clark, Cummings, Ryerson, Thayer, Widener and his son Harry.

Stowaway: One Frenchman.

Total: 40. (Br. Rpt.)

---

* British Report (p. 38) says this was the **eighth and last** *lifeboat* that left the ship and lowered at 1.55 A. M.
† Picked up from sea.
‡ Picked up from sea but died in boat.

INCIDENTS

C. H. Lightoller, Second Officer (Am. Inq.,
p. 81):

Previous to putting out Engelhardt Boat "D,"
Lightoller says, referring to boat No. 4: "We
had previously lowered a boat from A Deck, one
deck down below. That was through my fault.
It was the first boat I had lowered. I was intending to put the passengers in from A Deck.
On lowering the boat I found that the windows
were closed; so I sent someone down to open the
windows and carried on with the other boats, but
decided it was not worth while lowering them
down—that I could manage just as well from the
Boat Deck. When I came forward from the
other boats I loaded that boat from A Deck by
getting the women out through the windows. My
idea in filling the boats there was because there
was a wire hawser running along the side of the
ship for coaling purposes and it was handy to
tie the boat in to hold it so that nobody could
drop between the side of the boat and the ship.
No. 4 was the fifth boat or the sixth lowered on
the port side." *

* I agree with this statement though other testimony and
the British Report decide against us. The difference may
be reconciled by the fact that the loading of this boat began
early, but the final lowering was delayed.

W. J. Perkis, Quartermaster (Am. Inq., p. 581):

I lowered No. 4 into the water and left that boat and walked aft; and I came back and a man that was in the boat, one of the seamen, sang out to me: "We need another hand down here," so I slid down the lifeline there from the davit into the boat. I took charge of the boat after I got in, with two sailormen besides myself. There were forty-two, including all hands. We picked up eight people afterwards swimming with life-preservers when about a ship's length away from the ship. No. 4 was the last big boat on the port side to leave the ship. Two that were picked up died in the boat—a seaman (Lyons) and a steward (Siebert). All the others were passengers. After we picked up the men I could not hear any more cries anywhere. The discipline on board the ship was excellent. Every man knew his station and took it. There was no excitement whatever among the officers or crew, the firemen or stewards. They conducted themselves the same as they would if it were a minor, everyday occurrence.

Senator Perkins (addressing Perkis, Symon and Hogg:)

All three of you seem to be pretty capable young men and have had a great deal of experience at sea, and yet you have never been wrecked?

Mr. Perkis: Yes, sir.

Senator Perkins: Is there any other one of you who has been in a shipwreck?

Mr. Hogg: I have been in a collision, Senator, but with no loss of life.

Senator Perkins: Unless you have something more to state that you think will throw light on this subject, that will be all, and we thank you for what you have said.

Mr. Hogg: That is all I have to say except this: I think the women ought to have a gold medal on their breasts. God bless them. I will always raise my hat to a woman after what I saw.

Senator Perkins: What countrywomen were they?

Mr. Hogg: They were American women I had in mind. They were all Americans.

Senator Perkins: Did they man the oars? Did they take the oars and pull?

Mr. Hogg: Yes, sir; I took an oar all the time myself and also steered. Then I got one lady to steer; then another to assist me with an oar. She rowed to keep herself warm.

Senator Perkins: One of you stated that his boat picked up eight people, and the other that he did not pick up any. Could you not have picked up just as well as this other man?

Mr. Hogg: I wanted to assist in picking up people, but I had an order from somebody in the boat (No. 7)—I do not know who it was—not to take in any more; that we had done our best.

Senator Perkins: I merely ask the question because of the natural thought that if one boat picked up eight persons the other boat may have been able to do so.—You did not get any orders, Mr. Symon (boat No. 1), not to pick up any more people?

Mr. Symon: No, sir; there were no more around about where I was.

Senator Perkins: As I understand, one of the boats had more packed into it than the other. As I understand it, Mr. Symon pulled away from the ship and then when he came back there they picked up all the people that were around?

Mr. Symon made no reply.

S. S. Hemming, A. B. (Am. Inq.):
Everything was black over the starboard side. I could not see any boats. I went over to the port side and saw a boat off the port quarter and I went along the port side and got up the after boat davits and slid down the fall and swam to the boat about 200 yards. When I reached the

boat I tried to get hold of the grab-line on the bows. I pulled my head above the gunwale, and I said: "Give us a hand, Jack." Foley was in the boat; I saw him standing up. He said: "Is that you, Sam?" I said: "Yes" to him and the women and children pulled me in the boat.

After the ship sank we pulled back and picked up seven of the crew including a seaman, Lyons, a fireman, Dillon, and two stewards, Cunningham and Siebert. We made for the light of another lifeboat and kept in company with her. Then day broke and we saw two more lifeboats. We pulled toward them and we all made fast by the painter. Then we helped with boat No. 12 to take off the people on an overturned boat ("B"). From this boat ("B") we took about four or five, and the balance went into the other boat. There were about twenty altogether on this boat ("B").

A. Cunningham, Steward (Am. Inq., p. 794):
I first learned of the very serious character of the collision from my own knowledge when I saw the water on the post-office deck. I waited on the ship until all the boats had gone, and then threw myself into the water. This was about 2 o'clock. I was in the water about half an hour before the ship sank. I swam clear of the ship about three-quarters of a mile. I was afraid of

the suction. My mate, Siebert, left the ship with me. I heard a lifeboat and called to it and went toward it. I found Quartermaster Perkis in charge. Hemmings, the sailor, Foley (store-keeper) and a fireman (Dillon) were in this boat. I never saw any male passengers in the boat. We picked up Prentice, assistant storekeeper. I think No. 4 was the nearest to the scene of the accident because it picked up more persons in the water. About 7.30 we got aboard the *Carpathia*. When we sighted her she might have been four or five miles away.

R. P. Dillon, trimmer (Br. Inq.):
I went down with the ship and sank about two fathoms. Swam about twenty minutes in the water and was picked up by No. 4. About 1,000 others in the water in my estimation. Saw no women. Recovered consciousness and found Sailor Lyons and another lying on top of me dead.

Thomas Granger, greaser (Br. Inq.):
I went to the port side of the Boat Deck aft, climbed down a rope and got into a boat near the ship's side, No. 4, which had come back be-cause there were not enough men to pull her. She was full of women and children. F. Scott, greaser, also went down the falls and got into this

boat. Perkis, quartermaster, and Hemmings then in it. Afterwards picked up Dillon and another man (Prentice) out of the water.

F. Scott, greaser (Br. Inq.):
We went on deck on starboard side first as she had listed over to the port side, but we saw no boats. When I came up the engineers came up just after me on the Boat Deck. I saw only eight of them out of thirty-six on the deck. Then we went to the port side and saw boats. An officer fired a shot and I heard him say that if any man tried to get in that boat he would shoot him like a dog. At this time all the boats had gone from the starboard side. I saw one of the boats, No. 4, returning to the ship's side and I climbed on the davits and tried to get down the falls but fell in the water and was picked up. It was nearly two o'clock when I got on the davits and down the fall.

Mrs. E. B. Ryerson's affidavit (Am. Inq., p. 1107):
We were ordered down to A Deck, which was partly enclosed. We saw people getting into boats, but waited our turn. My boy, Jack, was with me. An officer at the window said: "That boy cannot go." My husband said: "Of course

that boy goes with his mother; he is only thirteen"; so they let him pass. I turned and kissed
my husband and as we left he and the other men
I knew, Mr. Thayer, Mr. Widener and others,
were standing together very quietly. There were
two men and an officer inside and a sailor outside
to help us. I fell on top of the women who were
already in the boat and scrambled to the bow
with my eldest daughter. Miss Bowen and my
boy were in the stern, and my second daughter
was in the middle of the boat with my maid.
Mrs. Thayer, Mrs. Widener, Mrs. Astor and
Miss Eustis were the only ones I knew in our
boat.

Presently an officer called out from the upper
deck: "How many women are there in that
boat?" Someone answered: "Twenty-four."
"That's enough; lower away."

The ropes seemed to stick at one end. Someone called for a knife, but it was not needed until
we got into the water as it was but a short distance; and then I realized for the first time how
far the ship had sunk. The deck we left was
only about twenty feet from the sea. I could
see all the portholes open and the water washing
in, and the decks still lighted. Then they called
out: "How many seamen have you?" and they
answered: "One." "That is not enough," said

the officer, "I will send you another"; and he sent a sailor down the rope. In a few minutes several other men, not sailors, came down the ropes over the davits and dropped into our boat. The order was given to pull away, and then they rowed off. Someone shouted something about a gangway, and no one seemed to know what to do. Barrels and chairs were being thrown overboard. As the bow of the ship went down the lights went out. The stern stood up for several minutes black against the stars and then the boat plunged down. Then began the cries for help of people drowning all around us, which seemed to go on forever. Someone called out: "Pull for your lives or you will be sucked under," and everyone that could rowed like mad. I could see my younger daughter and Mrs. Thayer and Mrs. Astor rowing, but there seemed to be no suction. Then we turned and picked up some of those in the water. Some of the women protested, but others persisted, and we dragged in six or seven men. The men rescued were stewards, stokers, sailors, etc., and were so chilled and frozen already that they could hardly move. Two of them died in the stern later and many of them were raving and moaning and delirious most of the time. We had no lights or compass. There were several babies in the boat.

Officer Lowe called out to tie together, and as soon as we could make out the other boats in the dark five were tied together. We could dimly see an overturned boat with about twenty men standing on it, back to back. As the sailors in our boat said we could still carry from eight to ten people, we called for another boat to volunteer and go and rescue them, so we cut loose our painters and between us got all the men off. Then when the sun rose we saw the *Carpathia* standing up about five miles away, and for the first time saw the icebergs all around us. We got on board about 8 o'clock.

Mrs. Thayer's affidavit:

The after part of the ship then reared in the air, with the stern upwards, until it assumed an almost vertical position. It seemed to remain stationary in this position for many seconds (perhaps twenty), then suddenly dove straight down out of sight. It was 2.20 a. m. when the *Titanic* disappeared, according to a wrist watch worn by one of the passengers in my boat.

We pulled back to where the vessel had sunk and on our way picked up six men who were swimming—two of whom were drunk and gave us much trouble all the time. The six men we picked up were hauled into the boat by the women. Two of these men died in the boat.

The boat we were in started to take in water; I do not know how. We had to bail. I was standing in ice cold water up to the top of my boots all the time, and rowing continuously for nearly five hours. We took off about fifteen more people who were standing on a capsized boat. In all, our boat had by that time sixty-five or sixty-six people. There was no room to sit down in our boat, so we all stood, except some sitting along the side.

I think the steerage passengers had as good a chance as any of the rest to be saved.

The boat I was in was picked up by the *Carpathia* at 7 a. m. on Monday, we having rowed three miles to her, as we could not wait for her to come up on account of our boat taking in so much water that we would not have stayed afloat much longer.

I never saw greater courage or efficiency than was displayed by the officers of the ship. They were calm, polite and perfectly splendid. They also worked hard. The bedroom stewards also behaved extremely well.

Mrs. Stephenson's and Miss Eustis's story

kindly handed me for publication in my book contains the following:

"We were in the companionway of A Deck
when order came for *women and children to Boat
Deck and men to starboard side.* Miss Eustis
and I took each other's hands, not to be separated in the crowd, and all went on deck, we
following close to Mrs. Thayer and her maid and
going up narrow iron stairs to the forward Boat
Deck which, on the *Titanic,* was the captain's
bridge.

"At the top of the stairs we found Captain
Smith looking much worried and anxiously waiting
to get down after we got up. The ship listed heav-
ily to port just then. As we leaned against the
walls of the officers' quarters rockets were being
fired over our heads, which was most alarming, as
we fully realized if the *Titanic* had used her wireless to ill effect and was sending rockets it must be
serious. Shortly after that the order came from
the head dining room steward (Dodd) to go
down to A Deck, when Mrs. Thayer remarked,
'Tell us where to go and we will follow. You
ordered us up here and now you are taking us
back,' and he said, 'Follow me.'

"On reaching the A Deck we could see, for the
decks were lighted by electricity, that a boat
was lowered parallel to the windows; these were

opened and a steamer chair put under the rail
for us to step on. The ship had listed badly by
that time and the boat hung far out from the side,
so that some of the men said, 'No woman could
step across that space.' A call was made for a
ladder on one of the lower decks, but before it
ever got there we were all in the boat. Whether
they had drawn the boat over with boathooks
nearer the side I do not know, but the space was
easily jumped with the help of two men in the
boat.

"I remember seeing Colonel Astor, who called
'Good-bye' and said he would follow in another
boat, asking the number of our boat, which they
said was 'No. 4.' In going through the window
I was obliged to throw back the steamer rug, for,
with my fur coat and huge cork life-preserver, I
was very clumsy. Later we found the stewards
or crew had thrown the steamer rugs into the
boat, and they did good service, Miss Eustis'
around a baby thinly clad, and mine for a poor
member of the crew pulled in from the sea.

"Our boat I think took off every woman on
the deck at that time and was the last on the port
side to be lowered.

"When we reached the sea we found the ship
badly listed, her nose well in so that there was
water on the D Deck, which we could plainly see

as the boat was lighted and the ports on D Deck were square instead of round. No lights could be found in our boat and the men had great difficulty in casting off the blocks as they did not know how they worked. My fear here was great, as she seemed to be going faster and faster and I dreaded lest we should be drawn in before we could cast off.

"When we finally were ready to move the order was called from the deck to go to the stern hatch and take off some men. There was no hatch open and we could see no men, but our crew obeyed orders, much to our alarm, for they were throwing wreckage over and we could hear a cracking noise resembling china breaking. We implored the men to pull away from the ship, but they refused, and we pulled three men into the boat who had dropped off the ship and were swimming toward us. One man was drunk and had a bottle of brandy in his pocket which the quartermaster promptly threw overboard and the drunken man was thrown into the bottom of the boat and a blanket thrown over him. After these three men were hauled in, they told how fast the ship was sinking and we all implored them to pull for our lives to get out from the suction when she should go down. The lights on the ship burned till just before she went. When the call came that she was going I covered my face and heard some one call, 'She's broken.' After what seemed a long time I turned my head only to see the stern almost perpendicular in the air so that the full outline of the blades of the propeller showed above the water. She then gave her final plunge and the air was filled with cries. We rowed back and pulled in five more men from the sea. Their suffering from the icy water was intense and two men who had been pulled into the stern afterwards died, but we kept their bodies with us until we reached the *Carpathia,* where they were taken aboard and Monday afternoon given a decent burial with three others.

"After rescuing our men we found several lifeboats near us and an order was given to tie together, which we obeyed. It did not seem as if we were together long when one boat said they could rescue more could they get rid of some of the women and children aboard and some of them were put into our boat. Soon after cries of 'Ship ahoy' and a long low moan came to us and an officer in command of one of the boats ordered us to follow him. We felt that we were already too crowded to go, but our men, with quartermaster and boatswain in command, followed the officer and we pulled over to what proved to be an overturned boat crowded with men. We had to approach it very cautiously, fearing our wash would sweep them off. We could take only a few and they had to come very cautiously. The other boat (No. 12) took most of them and we then rowed away."

This rescue, which Mrs. Stephenson so well describes, occurred at dawn. Her story now returns to the prior period of night time.

"The sea was smooth and the night brilliant with more stars than I had ever seen.

"Occasionally a green light showed which proved to be on the Emergency boat, and our men all recognized it as such. We all prayed for dawn, and there was no conversation, everyone being so awed by the disaster and bitterly cold.

"With the dawn came the wind, and before long quite a sea was running. Just before daylight on the horizon we saw what we felt sure must be the lights of a ship. The quartermaster was a long time in admitting that we were right, urging that it was the moon, but we insisted and they then said it might be the *Carpathia* as they had been told before leaving the *Titanic* that she was coming to us. For a long time after daylight we were in great wreckage from the *Titanic,* principally steamer chairs and a few white pilasters.

"We felt we could never reach the *Carpathia* when we found she had stopped, and afterwards when we asked why she didn't come closer we were told that some of the early boats which put off from the starboard side reached her a little after four, while it was after six when we drew under the side of the open hatch.

"It had been a long trying row in the heavy sea and impossible to keep bow on to reach the ship. We stood in great danger of being swamped many times and Captain Rostron, who watched us come up, said he doubted if we could have lived an hour longer in that high sea. Our boat had considerable water in the centre, due to the leakage and also the water brought in by the eight men from their clothing. They had bailed her constantly in order to relieve the weight. Two of the women near us were dying seasick, but the babies slept most of the night in their mothers' arms. The boatswain's chair was slung down the side and there were also rope ladders. Only few, however, of the men were able to go up the ladders. Mail bags were dropped down in which the babies and little children were placed and hoisted up. We were told to throw off our life-preservers and then placed in a boatswain's chair and hoisted to the open hatch where ready arms pulled us in; warm blankets waited those in need and brandy was offered to everybody. We were shown at once to the saloon, where hot coffee and sandwiches were being served."

ENGELHARDT BOAT "D." *

No male passenger in this boat.

Passengers: Mrs. J. M. Brown, Mrs. Harris, Mrs. Frederick Hoyt, the Navratil children.

Picked up from the sea: Frederick Hoyt.

Bade good-bye to wife and sank with ship: Mr. Harris.

Crew: Bright, Q. M., in charge; Seaman Lucas; Steward Hardy.

Stowaway: One steerage foreigner, Joseph Dugemin.

Jumped from deck below as boat was lowered: H. B. Steffanson (Swede), and H. Woolner (Englishman).

Total: 44. British Report (p. 38): Crew 2, men passengers 2, women and children 40.

INCIDENTS

C. H. Lightoller, Second Officer (Am. Inq., p. 81):

* British Report (p. 38) puts this as the last boat lowered at 2.05.

In the case of the last boat I got out, the very
last of all to leave the ship, I had the utmost
difficulty in finding women. After all the other
boats were put out we came forward to put out
the Engelhardt collapsible boats. In the meantime the forward Emergency boat (No. 2) had
been put out by one of the other officers, so we
rounded up the tackles and got the collapsible
boat to put that over. Then I called for women
and could not get any. Somebody said: "There
are no women." This was on the Boat Deck
where all the women were supposed to be because
the boats were there. There were between fifteen
and twenty people put into this boat—one seaman
and another seaman, or steward. This was the
very last boat lowered in the tackles. I noticed
plenty of Americans standing near me, who gave
me every assistance they could, regardless of
nationality.

And before the British Court of Inquiry the
same officer testified:

Someone shouted: "There are no more
women." Some of the men began climbing in.
Then someone said: "There are some more
women," and when they came forward the men
got out of the boat again. I saw no men in her,

but I believe a couple of Chinese stowed away in her.

When that boat went away there were no women whatever. I did not consider it advisable to wait, but to try to get at once away from the ship. I did not want the boat to be "rushed." Splendid order was maintained. No attempt was made to "rush" that boat by the men. When this boat was being loaded I could see the water coming up the stairway. There was splendid order on the boat until the last. As far as I know there were no male passengers in the boats I saw off except the one man I ordered in, Major Peuchen.

A. J. Bright, Q. M. (Am. Inq., p. 831):

Quartermaster Rowe, Mr. Boxhall and myself fired the distress signals, six rockets I think in all, at intervals. After we had finished firing the distress signals, there were two boats left (Engelhardt collapsibles "C" and "D"). All the lifeboats were away before the collapsible boats were lowered. They had to be, because the collapsible boats were on the deck and the other boats had to be lowered before they could be used. The same tackle with which the lifeboats and the Emergency boats were lowered was employed after they had gone in lowering the collapsible boats.

Witness says that both he and Rowe assisted in getting out the starboard collapsible boat "C" and then he went to the port side and filled up the other boat "D" with passengers, about twenty-five in all. There was a third-class passenger, a man, in the boat, who was on his way to Albion, N. Y. (The passenger list shows this man to have been Joseph Dugemin.)

We were told to pull clear and get out of the suction. When boat "D" was lowered the forecastle head was just going under water; that would be about twenty feet lower than the bridge, and the ship had then sunk about fifty feet—all of that, because when boat "D" was lowered the foremost fall was lower down and the after one seemed to hang and he called out to hang on to the foremost fall and to see what was the matter and let go the after fall. Boat "D" was fifty to a hundred yards away when the ship sank.* They had a lantern in the boat but no oil to light it. After leaving the boat, witness heard something but not an explosion. It was like a rattling of chains more than anything else.

---

* The interval of time can then be approximated as nearly a half hour, that we remained on the ship after the lifeboats left.

After "D" got away Mr. Lowe came along-side in another boat, No. 14, and told them to stick together and asked for the number in "D" boat. Steward Hardy counted and told him. Lowe then put about ten or a dozen men from some other boat into witness's boat because it was not filled up. One seaman was taken out. This would make thirty-seven in "D" boat. Just at daylight they saw one of the collapsible boats, "A," that was awash—just flush with the water. Officer Lowe came and took boat "D" in tow, because it had very few men to pull, and towed it to boat "A" and took twelve men and one woman off and put them into his boat No. 14. They were standing in water just about to their ankles when No. 14 and "D" came up to them. They turned the swamped boat adrift with two (three) dead bodies. They were then towed under sail by Mr. Lowe's boat to the *Carpathia,* about four miles away.

William Lucas, A. B. (Br. Inq.):
Got into Engelhardt "D." The water was then right up under the bridge. Had not gone more than 100 yards when there was an explosion and 150 yards when the *Titanic* sank. Had to get some of the women to take oars. There was no rudder in the boat. Changed oars from one

side to the other to get her away. Saw a faint
red light abaft the *Titanic's* beam about nine miles
away—the headlight also. The witness was
transferred to No. 12.

J. Hardy, Chief Steward, second-class (Am.
Inq., p. 587):
We launched this boat filled with passengers.
Mr. Lightoller and myself loaded it. I went away
in it with the quartermaster (Bright) and two
firemen. There were Syrians in the bottom of
the boat, third-class passengers, chattering the
whole night in their strange language. There
were about twenty-five women and children. We
lowered away and got to the water; the ship then
had a heavy list to port. We got clear of the
ship and rowed out some distance from her. Mr.
Lowe told us to tie up with other boats, that we
would be better seen and could keep better together. He, having a full complement of passengers in his boat, transferred about ten to ours,
making thirty-five in our boat. When we left
the ship, where we were lowered, there were no
women and children there in sight at all. There
was nobody to lower the boat. No men passengers when we were ready to lower it. They had
gone; where, I could not say. We were not more
than forty feet from the water when we were

lowered. We picked up the husband (Frederick W. Hoyt) of a wife that we had loaded in the boat. The gentleman took to the water and climbed in the boat after we had lowered it. He sat there wringing wet alongside me, helping to row.

I had great respect and great regret for Officer Murdoch. I was walking along the deck forward with him and he said: "I believe she is gone, Hardy." This was a good half hour before my boat was lowered.

Senator Fletcher: Where were all these passengers; these 1,600 people?

Mr. Hardy: They must have been between decks or on the deck below or on the other side of the ship. I cannot conceive where they were.

In his letter to me, Mr. Frederick M. Hoyt relates his experience as follows:

"I knew Captain Smith for over fifteen years. Our conversation that night amounted to little or nothing. I simply sympathized with him on the accident; but at that time, as I then never expected to be saved, I did not want to bother him with questions, as I knew he had all he wanted to think of. He did suggest that I go down to A Deck and see if there were not a boat alongside. This I did, and to my surprise saw the boat

"D" still hanging on the davits (there having been some delay in lowering her), and it occurred to me that if I swam out and waited for her to shove off they would pick me up, which was what happened."

Hugh Woolner, first-class passenger (Am. Inq., p. 887):

Then I said to Steffanson, "Let us go down on to A Deck." And we went down again, but there was nobody there. I looked on both sides of the deck and saw no people. It was absolutely deserted, and the electric lights along the ceiling of A Deck were beginning to turn red, just a glow, a red sort of glow. So I said to Steffanson, "This is getting to be rather a tight corner; let us go out through the door at the end." And as we went out *the sea came in onto the deck at our feet.* Then we hopped up onto the gunwale, preparing to jump into the sea, because if we had waited a minute longer we should have been boxed in against the ceiling. And as we looked out we saw this collapsible boat, the last boat on the port side, being lowered right in front of our faces.

Senator Smith: How far out?

Mr. Woolner: It was about nine feet out.

Senator Smith: Nine feet away from the side of A Deck?

Mr. Woolner: Yes.

Senator Smith: You saw a collapsible boat being lowered?

Mr. Woolner: Being lowered; yes.

Senator Smith: Was it filled with people?

Mr. Woolner: It was full up to the bow, and I said to Steffanson, "There is nobody in the bows. Let us make a jump for it. You go first." And he jumped out and tumbled in head over heels into the boat, and I jumped too and hit the gunwale with my chest, which had on the life-preserver, of course, and I sort of tumbled off the gunwale and caught the gunwale with my fingers and slipped off backwards.

Senator Smith: Into the water?

Mr. Woolner: As my legs dropped down I felt that they were in the sea.

Senator Smith: You are quite sure you jumped nine feet to get that boat?

Mr. Woolner: That is my estimate. By that time you see we were jumping slightly downward.

Senator Smith: Did you jump out or down?

Mr. Woolner: Both.

Senator Smith: Both out and down?

Mr. Woolner: Slightly down and out.

Senator Smith: It could not have been very

far down if the water was on A Deck; it must have been out.

Mr. Woolner: Chiefly out; but it was sufficiently down for us to see just over the edge of the gunwale of the boat.

Senator Smith: You pulled yourself up out of the water?

Mr. Woolner: Yes; and then I hooked my right heel over the gunwale, and by this time Steffanson was standing up and he caught hold of me and lifted me in.

One lady (Mrs. Harris) had a broken elbow bone. She was in a white woollen jacket. At dawn Officer Lowe transferred five or six from his boat No. 14 to ours, which brought us down very close to the water. At daylight we saw a great many icebergs of different colors, as the sun struck them. Some looked white, some looked blue, some looked mauve and others were dark gray. There was one double-toothed one that looked to be of good size; it must have been about one hundred feet high.

The *Carpathia* seemed to come up slowly, and then she stopped. We looked out and saw there was a boat alongside and then we realized she was waiting for us to come up to her instead of her coming to us, as we hoped. Then Mr. Lowe towed us with his boat, No. 14, under sail. After taking a group of people off of boat "A"—a dozen of them—including one woman, we sailed to the *Carpathia*.   There was a child in the boat —one of those little children whose parents everybody was looking for (the Navatil children).

The last of the *Titanic's* boats which were never launched, but floated off, were the two Engelhardt collapsibles "A" and "B" on the roof of the officers' house.   In my personal account I have already given the story of boat "B," the upset one on which Second Officer Lightoller, Jack Thayer, myself and others escaped.   Since I wrote the account of my personal experience I have had access to other sources of information, including some already referred to; and though at the expense of some repetition, I think it may be of interest to include the record of this boat in the present chapter, as follows:

ENGELHARDT BOAT "B"

[*The Upset Boat*]

Passengers: A. H. Barkworth, Archibald Gracie, John B. Thayer, Jr., first cabin.

Crew: Second Officer Lightoller, Junior Marconi Operator Bride, Firemen: McGann, Senior;

Chief Baker Joughin; Cooks: Collins, May-
nard; Steward Whiteley, "J. Hagan." Seaman J.
McGough (possibly). Two men died on boat.
Body of one transferred to No. 12 and finally to
Carpathia. He was a fireman probably, but
Cunard Co. preserved no record of him or his
burial.

INCIDENTS

C. H. Lightoller, Second Officer (Am. Inq.,
pp. 87, 91, 786):

I was on top of the officers' quarters and there
was nothing more to be done. The ship then took
a dive and I turned face forward and also took
a dive from on top, practically amidships a little
to the starboard, where I had got to. I was
driven back against the blower, which is a large
thing that shape (indicating) which faces forward to the wind and which then goes down to the
stoke hole; but there is a grating there and it was
against this grating that I was sucked by the
water, and held there under water. There was a
terrific blast of air and water and I was blown out
clear. I came up above the water, which barely
threw me away at all, because I went down again
against these fiddley gratings immediately abreast
of the funnel over the stoke hole to which this

fiddley leads. Colonel Gracie, I believe, was sucked down in identically the same manner on the fiddley gratings, caused by the water rushing down below as the ship was going down.

I next found myself alongside of that over-turned boat. This was before the *Titanic* sank. The funnel then fell down and if there was any-body on that side of the Engelhardt boat it fell on them. The ship was not then submerged by considerable. The stern was completely out of the water. I have heard some controversy as to the boilers exploding owing to coming in contact with salt water, by men who are capable of giving an opinion, but there seems to be an open ques-tion as to whether cold water actually does cause boilers to explode.

I hardly had any opportunity to swim. It was the action of the funnel falling that threw us out a considerable distance away from the ship. We had no oars or other effective means for propel-ling the overturned boat. We had little bits of wood, but they were practically ineffective.

On our boat, as I have said before, were Colonel Gracie and young Thayer. I think they were the only two passengers. There were no women on our overturned boat. These were all taken out of the water and they were firemen and others of the crew—roughly about thirty. I take that from my own estimate and from the estimate of someone who was looking down from the bridge of the *Carpathia*.

And from the same officer's testimony before the British Court as follows:

An order was given to cut the lashings of the other Engelhardt boats. It was then too late as the water was rushing up to the Boat Deck and there was not time to get them to the falls. He then went across to the officers' quarters on the starboard side to see what he could do. Then the vessel seemed to take a bit of a dive. He swam off and cleared the ship. The water was so intensely cold that he first tried to get out of it into the crow's nest, close at hand. Next he was pushed up against the blower on the forepart of the funnel, the water rushing down this blower, holding him against the grating for a while. Then there seemed to be a rush of air and he was blown away from the grating. He was dragged below the surface, but not for many moments. He came up near the Engelhardt boat "B" which was not launched, but had been thrown into the water. The forward funnel then fell down. Some little time after this he saw half a dozen men standing on the collapsible boat, and got on to it. The whole of the third funnel was still visible, the vessel gradually raising her stern out of the water. The ship did not break in two, and could not be broken in two. She actually attained the perpendicular before sinking. His impression was that no lights were then burning in the after part not submerged. It is true that the after part of the vessel settled level with the water. He watched the ship keenly all the time. After she reached an angle of 60 degrees there was a rumbling sound which he attributed to the boilers leaving their beds and crashing down. Finally she attained an absolute perpendicular position and then went slowly down. He heard no explosion whatever, but noticed about that time that the water became much warmer. There were about those on the Engelhardt boat "B," several people struggling in the water who came on it. Nearly twenty-eight or thirty were taken off in the morning at daybreak. In this rescuing boat (No. 12), after the transfer, there were seventy-five. It was the last boat to the *Carpathia*. The next morning (Monday) he saw some icebergs from fifty to sixty to two hundred feet high, but the nearest was about ten miles away.

After the boats had left the side of the ship he heard orders given by the commander through the megaphone. He heard him say: "Bring that boat alongside." Witness presumed allusion was made to bringing of boats to the gangway doors. Witness could not gather whether the orders were being obeyed. Said he had not been on the Engelhardt boat more than half an hour before a swell was distinctly visible. In the morning there was quite a breeze. It was when he was at No. 6 boat that he noticed the list. Though the ship struck on the starboard side, it was not an extraordinary thing that there should be a list to port. It does not necessarily follow that there should be a list to the side where the water was coming in.

Harold Bride, junior Marconi operator in his Report of April 27th to W. B. Cross, Traffic Manager, Marconi Co. (Am. Inq., p. 1053), says:

Just at this moment the captain said: "You cannot do any more; save yourselves." Leaving the captain we climbed on top of the house comprising the officers' quarters and our own. Here I saw the last of Mr. Phillips, for he disappeared, walking aft. I now assisted in pushing off the collapsible boat on to the Boat Deck. Just as the boat fell, I noticed Captain Smith dive from the bridge into the sea. Then followed a general scramble out on to the Boat Deck, but no sooner had we got there than the sea washed over. I managed to catch hold of the boat we had pre-

viously fixed up and was swept overboard with
her. I then experienced the most exciting three
or four hours anyone can reasonably wish for,
and was, in due course with the rest of the survivors, picked up by the *Carpathia*. As you probably heard, I got on the collapsible boat the second time, which was, as I had left it, upturned. I
called Phillips but got no response. I learned
later from several sources that he was on this
boat and expired even before we were picked up
by the *Titanic's* lifeboat (No. 12). I am told
that fright and exposure were the causes of his
death. So far as I can find out, he was taken on
board the *Carpathia* and buried at sea from her,
though for some reason the bodies of those who
died were not identified before burial from the
Carpathia, and so I cannot vouch for the truth of
this.

He also gave testimony before the American
Inquiry (pp. 110, 161):

This boat was over the officers' cabin at the
side of the forward funnel. It was pushed over on
to the Boat Deck. It went over the starboard
side and I went over with it. It was washed off
and over the side of the ship by a wave into the
water bottom side upward. I was inside the boat
and under it, as it fell bottom side upward. I

could not tell how long. It seemed a life time to me really. I got on top of the boat eventually. There was a big crowd on top when I got on. I should say that I remained under the boat three-quarters of an hour, or a half hour. I then got away from it as quickly as I could. I freed myself from it and cleared out of it but I do not know why, but swam back to it about three-quarters of an hour to an hour afterwards. I was upside down myself—I mean I was on my back.

It is estimated that there were between thirty and forty on the boat; no women. When it was pushed over on the Boat Deck we all scrambled down on to the Boat Deck again and were going to launch it properly when it was washed over before we had time to launch it. I happened to be nearest to it and I grabbed it and went down with it. There was a passenger on this boat; I could not see whether he was first, second or third class. I heard him say at the time that he was a passenger. I could not say whether it was Colonel Gracie. There were others who struggled to get on; dozens of them in the water. I should judge they were all part of the boat's crew.

I am twenty-two years old. Phillips was about twenty-four or twenty-five. My salary from the Marconi Co. is four pounds a month.

As to the attack made upon Mr. Phillips to

take away his life belt I should say the man was dressed like a stoker. We forced him away. I held him and Mr. Phillips hit him.

J. Collins, cook (Am. Inq., p. 628):
This was my first voyage. I ran back to the upper deck to the port side with another steward and a woman and two children. The steward had one of the children in his arms and the woman was crying. I took the child from the woman and made for one of the boats. Then the word came around from the starboard side that there was a collapsible boat getting launched on that side and that all women and children were to make for it, so the other steward and I and the two children and the woman came around to the starboard side. We saw the collapsible boat taken off the saloon deck, and then the sailors and the firemen who were forward saw the ship's bow in the water and that she was sinking by her bow. They shouted out for us to go aft. We were just turning round to make for the stern when a wave washed us off the deck—washed us clear of it, and the child was washed out of my arms. I was kept down for at least two or three minutes under water.

Senator Bourne: Two or three minutes?
Mr. Collins: Yes; I am sure.

Senator Bourne: Were you unconscious?

Mr. Collins: No; not at all. It did not affect me much—the salt water.

Senator Bourne: But you were under water? You cannot stay under water two or three minutes.

Mr. Collins: Well, it seemed so to me. I could not exactly state how long. When I came to the surface I saw this boat that had been taken off. I saw a man on it. They had been working on it taking it off the saloon deck, and when the wave washed it off the deck, they clung to it. Then I made for it when I came to the surface, swimming for it. I was only four or five yards off of it. I am sure there were more than fifteen or sixteen who were then on it. They did not help me to get on. They were all watching the ship. All I had to do was to give a spring and I got on to it. We were drifting about for two hours in the water.

Senator Bourne: When you came up from the water on this collapsible boat, did you see any evidence of the ship as she sank then?

Mr. Collins: I did, sir; I saw her stern end.

Senator Bourne: Where were you on the boat at the time you were washed off the ship?

Mr. Collins: Amidships, sir.

Senator Bourne: You say you saw the stern end after you got on the collapsible boat?

Mr. Collins: Yes, sir.

Senator Bourne: Did you see the bow?

Mr. Collins: No, sir.

Senator Bourne: How far were you from the stern end of the ship when you came up and got on to the collapsible boat?

Mr. Collins: I could not just exactly state how far I was away from the *Titanic* when I came up. I was not far, because her lights were out then. Her lights went out when the water got almost to amidships on her.

Senator Bourne: As I understand it, you were amidships of the bow as the ship sank?

Mr. Collins: Yes, sir.

Senator Bourne: You were washed off by a wave? You were under water as you think for two or three minutes and then swam five or six yards to the collapsible boat and got aboard the boat? The stern (of ship) was still afloat?

Mr. Collins: The stern was still afloat.

Senator Bourne: The lights were burning?

Mr. Collins: I came to the surface, sir, and I happened to look around and I saw the lights and nothing more, and I looked in front of me and saw the collapsible boat and I made for it.

Senator Bourne: How do you account for this wave that washed you off amidships?

Mr. Collins: By the suction which took place when the bow went down in the water. There were probably fifteen on the boat when I got on. There was some lifeboat that had a green light on it and we thought it was a ship, after the *Titanic* had sunk, and we commenced to shout. All we saw was the green light. We were drifting about two hours, and then we saw the topmast lights of the *Carpathia*. Then came daylight and we saw our own lifeboats and we were very close to them. When we spied them we shouted to them and they came over to us and they lifted a whole lot of us that were on the collapsible boat.

J. Joughin, head baker (Br. Inq.) :
I got on to the starboard side of the poop; found myself in the water. I do not believe my head went under the water at all. I thought I saw some wreckage. Swam towards it and found collapsible boat ("B") with Lightoller and about twenty-five men on it. There was no room for me. I tried to get on, but was pushed off, but I hung around. I got around to the opposite side and cook Maynard, who recognized me, helped me and held on to me.

The experience of my fellow passenger on this boat, John B. Thayer, Jr., is embodied in accounts written by him on April 20th and 23rd, just after landing from the *Carpathia*: the first given to the press as the only statement he had made, the second in a very pathetic letter written to Judge Charles L. Long, of Springfield, Mass., whose son, Milton C. Long, was a companion of young Thayer all that evening, April 14th, until at the very last both jumped into the sea and Long was lost, as described:

"Thinking that father and mother had managed to get off in a boat we, Long and myself, went to the starboard side of the Boat Deck where the boats were getting away quickly. Some were already off in the distance. We thought of getting into one of them, the last boat on the forward part of the starboard side, but there seemed to be such a crowd around that I thought it unwise to make any attempt to get into it. I thought it would never reach the water right side up, but it did.

Here I noticed nobody that I knew except Mr. Lingrey, whom I had met for the first time that evening. I lost sight of him in a few minutes. Long and I then stood by the rail just a little aft of the captain's bridge. There was such a big list to port that it seemed as if the ship would turn on her side.

About this time the people began jumping from

the stern. I thought of jumping myself, but was afraid of being stunned on hitting the water. Three times I made up my mind to jump out and slide down the davit ropes and try to swim to the boats that were lying off from the ship, but each time Long got hold of me and told me to wait a while. I got a sight on a rope between the davits and a star and noticed that the ship was gradually sinking. About this time she straightened up on an even keel again, and started to go down fairly fast at an angle of about thirty degrees. As she started to sink we left the davits and went back and stood by the rail aft, even with the second funnel. Long and myself stood by each other and jumped on the rail. We did not give each other any messages for home because neither of us thought we would ever get back. Long put his legs over the rail, while I straddled it. Hanging over the side and holding on to the rail with his hands he looked up at me and said: 'You are coming, boy, aren't you?' I replied: 'Go ahead, I'll be with you in a minute.' He let go and slid down the side and I never saw him again. Almost immediately after he jumped I jumped. All this last part took a very short time, and when we jumped we were about ten yards above the water. Long was perfectly calm all the time and kept his nerve to the very end."

How he sank and finally reached the upset boat is quoted accurately from the newspaper report from this same source given in my personal narrative. He continues as follows:

"As often as we saw other boats in the distance we would yell, 'Ship ahoy!' but they could not distinguish our cries from any of the others, so we all gave it up, thinking it useless. It was very cold, and the water washed over the upset boat almost all the time. Towards dawn the wind sprung up, roughening the water and making it difficult to keep the boat balanced. The wireless man raised our hopes a great deal by telling us that the *Carpathia* would be up in about three hours. About 3.30 or 4 o'clock some men at the bow of our boat sighted her mast lights. I could not see them as I was sitting down with a man kneeling on my leg. He finally got up, and I stood up. We had the Second Officer, Mr. Lightoller, on board. He had an officer's whistle and whistled for the boats in the distance to come up and take us off. Two of them came up. The first took half and the other took the balance, including myself. In the transfer we had difficulty in balancing our boat as the men would lean too far over, but we were all taken aboard the already crowded boats and taken to the *Carpathia* in safety."

One of these boats was No. 4, in which his mother was.

—*Indianapolis Star*

LEST WE FORGET

CHAPTER VII

STARBOARD SIDE: WOMEN FIRST, BUT MEN WHEN
THERE WERE NO WOMEN

I KNOW of the conditions existing on the port side of the ship from personal knowledge, as set forth in the first five chapters describing my personal experience, while the previous chapter VI is derived from an exhaustive study of official and of other authoritative information relating to the same side from experiences of others. I have devoted an equal amount of study to the history of what happened on the starboard side of the ship, and the tabulated statements in this chapter are the outcome of my research into the experiences of my fellow passengers on this side of the ship where I was located only during the last half hour before the ship foundered, after all passengers on the port side had been ordered to the starboard in consequence of the great list to port, and after the departure of the last boat "D," that left the ship on the port side. During this last half hour, though it seemed shorter, my attention was confined to the work of the crew, assisting them in their vain efforts to launch the Engelhardt boat "B" thrown down from the roof of the officers' house. All the starboard boats had left the ship before I came there.

Many misunderstandings arose in the public mind because of ignorance of the size of the ship and inability to understand that the same conditions did not prevail at every point and that the same scenes were not witnessed by every one of us. Consider the great length of the ship, 852 feet; its breadth of beam, 92.6 feet; and its many decks, eleven in number; counting the roof of the officers' house as the top deck, then the Boat Deck, and Decks A, B, C, D, E, F, G, and, in the hold, two more. Bearing this in mind I illustrated to my New York friends, in answer to their questions, how impossible it would be for a person standing at the corner of 50th Street and Fifth Avenue to know just what was going on at 52nd Street on the same Avenue, or what was going on at the corner of 52nd Street and Madison Avenue. Therefore, when one survivor's viewpoint differs from that of another, the explanation is easily found.

Consideration must also be taken of the fact that the accident occurred near midnight, and though it was a bright, starlit night, and the ship's electric lights shone almost to the last, it was possible to recognize only one's intimates at close quarters.

My research shows that there was no general order from the ship's officers on the starboard side for "Women and children first." On the other hand, I have the statements of Dr. Washington Dodge, John B. Thayer, Jr., and Mrs. Stephenson, also the same of a member of the crew testifying before the British Court of Inquiry, from which it appears that some sort of a command was issued ordering the women to the port side and the men to the starboard, indicating that no men would be allowed in the port boats, and only in the starboard side boats after the women had entered them first. If such were the orders, they were carried out to the letter. Another point of difference, especially conspicuous to myself, is the fact that on the starboard side there appears to have been an absence of women at the points where the boats were loaded, while on the port side all the boats loaded, from the first up to the last, found women at hand and ready to enter them. It was only at the time of the loading of the last boat "D," that my friend, Clinch Smith, and I ran up and down the port side shouting: "Are there any more women?" This too is the testimony of Officer Lightoller, in charge of loading boats on the port side.

BOAT NO. 7 *

No disorder in loading or lowering this boat.

Passengers: Mesdames Bishop, Earnshaw, Gibson, Greenfield, Potter, Snyder, and Misses Gibson and Hays, Messrs. Bishop, Chevré, Daniel, Greenfield, McGough, Maréchal, Seward, Sloper, Snyder, Tucker.

Transferred from Boat No. 5: Mrs. Dodge and her boy; Messrs. Calderhead and Flynn.

Crew: Seamen: Hogg (in charge), Jewell, Weller.

Total: 28.

INCIDENTS

Archie Jewell, L. O. (Br. Inq.) :
Was awakened by the crash and ran at once on deck where he saw a lot of ice. All went below again to get clothes on. The boatswain called all hands on deck. Went to No. 7 boat. The ship had stopped. All hands cleared the boats, cleared away the falls and got them all right. Mr. Mur-

* First to leave ship starboard side at 12.45 [Br. Rpt., p. 38.]

doch gave the order to lower boat No. 7 to the
rail with women and children in the boat. Three
or four Frenchmen, passengers, got into the boat.
No. 7 was lowered from the Boat Deck. The
orders were to stand by the gangway. This boat
was the first on the starboard side lowered into the
water. All the boats were down by the time it
was pulled away from the ship because it was
thought she was settling down.

Witness saw the ship go down by the head very
slowly. The other lifeboats were further off, his
being the nearest. No. 7 was then pulled further
off and about half an hour later, or about an hour
and a half after this boat was lowered, and when it
was about 200 yards away, the ship took the final
dip. He saw the stern straight up in the air with
the lights still burning. After a few moments she
then sank very quickly and he heard two or three
explosions just as the stern went up in the air.
No. 7 picked up no dead bodies. At daylight
they saw a lot of icebergs all around, and reached
the *Carpathia* about 9 o'clock. This boat had no
compass and no light. (The above, given in detail, represents the general testimony of the next
witness.)

G. A. Hogg, A. B. (Am. Inq., p. 577):
He had forty-two when the boat was shoved

from the ship's side. He asked a lady if she could steer who said she could. He pulled around in search of other people. One man said: "We have done our best; there are no more people around." He said: "Very good, we will get away now." There was not a ripple on the water; it was as smooth as glass.

Mrs. H. W. Bishop, first-class passenger (Am. Inq., p. 998):

The captain told Colonel Astor something in an undertone. He came back and told six of us who were standing with his wife that we had better put on our life belts. I had gotten down two flights of stairs to tell my husband, who had returned to the stateroom for the moment, before I heard the captain announce that the life belts should be put on. We came back upstairs and found very few people on deck. There was very little confusion—only the older women were a·little frightened. On the starboard side of the Boat Deck there were only two people—a young French bride and groom. By that time an old man had come upstairs and found Mr. and Mrs. Harder, of New York. He brought us all together and told us to be sure and stay together—that he would be back in a moment. We never saw him again.

About five minutes later the boats were lowered and we were pushed in. This was No. 7 lifeboat. My husband was pushed in with me and we were lowered with twenty-eight people in the boat. We counted off after we reached the water. There were only about twelve women and the rest were men—three crew and thirteen male passengers; several unmarried men—three or four of them foreigners. Somewhat later five people were put into our boat from another one, making thirty-three in ours. Then we rowed still further away as the women were nervous about suction. We had no compass and no light. We arrived at the *Carpathia* five or ten minutes after five. The conduct of the crew, as far as I could see, was absolutely beyond criticism. One of the crew in the boat was Jack Edmonds,(?) and there was another man, a Lookout (Hogg), of whom we all thought a great deal. He lost his brother.

D. H. Bishop, first-class passenger (Am. Inq., p. 1000):

There was an officer stationed at the side of the lifeboat. As witness's wife got in, he fell into the boat. The French aviator Maréchal was in the boat; also Mr. Greenfield and his mother. There was little confusion on the deck while the boat was being loaded; no rush to boats at all. Witness agrees with his wife in the matter of the counting of twenty-eight, but he knows that there were some who were missed. There was a woman with her baby transferred from another lifeboat. Witness knows of his own knowledge that No. 7 was the first boat lowered from the starboard side. They heard no order from any one for the men to stand back or "women first," or "women and children first." Witness also says that at the time his lifeboat was lowered that that order had not been given on the starboard side.

J. R. McGough's affidavit (Am. Inq., p. 1143):
After procuring life preservers we went back to the top deck and discovered that orders had been given to launch the lifeboats, which were already being launched. Women and children were called for to board the boats first. Both women and men hesitated and did not feel inclined to get into the small boats. He had his back turned, looking in an opposite direction, and was caught by the shoulder by one of the officers who gave him a push saying: "Here, you are a big fellow; get into that boat."

Our boat was launched with twenty-eight people in all. Five were transferred from one of the others. There were several of us who wanted drinking water. It was unknown to us that there was a tank of water and crackers also in our boat until we reached the *Carpathia*. There was no light in our boat.

Mrs. Thomas Potter, Jr. Letter:
There was no panic. Everyone seemed more stunned than anything else. . . . We watched for upwards of two hours the gradual sinking of the ship—first one row of light and then another disappearing at shorter and shorter intervals, with the bow well bent in the water as though ready for a dive. After the lights went out, some ten minutes before the end, she was like some great living thing who made a last superhuman effort to right herself and then, failing, dove bow forward to the unfathomable depths below.

We did not row except to get away from the suction of the sinking ship, but remained lashed to another boat until the *Carpathia* came in sight just before dawn.

BOAT NO. 5 *

No disorder in loading or lowering this boat.
Passengers: Mesdames Cassebeer, Chambers, Crosby, Dodge and her boy, Frauenthal, Golden-

* Second boat lowered on the starboard side at 12.55 [Br. Rpt., p. 38.]

berg, Harder, Kimball, Stehli, Stengel, Taylor, Warren, and Misses Crosby, Newson, Ostby and Frolicher Stehli.

Messrs: Beckwith, Behr, Calderhead, Chambers, Flynn, Goldenberg, Harder, Kimball, Stehli, Taylor.

Bade good-bye to wives and daughters and sank with ship: Captain Crosby, Mr. Ostby and Mr. Warren.

Jumped from deck into boat being lowered: German Doctor Frauenthal and brother Isaac, P. Maugé.

Crew: 3rd Officer Pitman. Seaman: Olliver, Q. M.; Fireman Shiers; Stewards, Etches, Guy. Stewardess ———.

Total: 41.

INCIDENTS

H. J. Pitman, 3rd Officer (Am. Inq., p. 277, and Br. Inq.) :

I lowered No. 5 boat to the level with the rail of the Boat Deck. A man in a dressing gown said that we had better get her loaded with women and children. I said: "I wait the commander's orders," to which he replied: "Very well," or something like that. It then dawned on me that it might be Mr. Ismay, judging by the description I had had given me. I went to the bridge and saw Captain Smith and told him that I thought it was Mr. Ismay that wanted me to get the boat away with women and children in it and he said: "Go ahead; carry on." I came along and brought in my boat. I stood in it and said: "Come along, ladies.". There was a big crowd. Mr. Ismay helped get them along. We got the boat nearly full and I shouted out for any more ladies. None were to be seen so I allowed a few men to get into it. Then I jumped on the ship again. Mr. Murdoch said: "You go in charge of this boat and hang around the after gangway." About thirty (Br. Inq.) to forty women were in the boat, two children, half a dozen male passengers, myself and four of the crew. There would not have been so many men had there been any women around, but there were none. Murdoch shook hands with me and said: "Good-bye; good luck," and I said: "Lower away." This boat was the second one lowered on the starboard side. No light in the boat.

The ship turned right on end and went down perpendicularly. She did not break in two. I heard a lot of people say that they heard boiler explosions, but I have my doubts about that. I do not see why the boilers would burst, because there was no steam there. They should have been stopped about two hours and a half. The fires had not been fed so there was very little steam there. From the distance I was from the ship, if it had occurred, I think I would have known it. As soon as the ship disappeared I said: "Now, men, we will pull toward the wreck." Everyone in my boat said it was a mad idea because we had far better save what few I had in my boat than go back to the scene of the wreck and be swamped by the crowds that were there. My boat would have accommodated a few more— about sixty in all. I turned No. 5 boat around to go in the direction from which these cries came but was dissuaded from my purpose by the passengers. My idea of lashing Nos. 5 and 7 together was to keep together so that if anything hove in sight before daylight we could steady ourselves and cause a far bigger show than one boat only. I transferred two men and a woman and a child from my boat to No. 7 to even them up a bit.

H. S. Etches, steward (Am. Inq., p. 810):
Witness assisted Mr. Murdoch, Mr. Ismay, Mr. Pitman and Quartermaster Olliver and two stewards in the loading and launching of No. 7, the gentlemen being asked to keep back and the ladies in first. There were more ladies to go in No. 7 because No. 5 boat, which we went to next,

took in over thirty-six ladies. In No. 7 boat I saw one child, a baby boy, with a small woollen cap. After getting all the women that were there they called out three times—Mr. Ismay twice—in a loud voice: "Are there any more women before this boat goes?" and there was no answer. Mr. Murdoch called out, and at that moment a female came up whom he did not recognize. Mr. Ismay said: "Come along; jump in." She said: "I am only a stewardess." He said: "Never mind —you are a woman; take your place." That was the last woman I saw get into boat No. 5. There were two firemen in the bow; Olliver, the sailor, and myself; and Officer Pitman ordered us into the boat and lowered under Murdoch's order.

Senator Smith: What other men got into that boat?

Mr. Etches: There was a stout gentleman, sir, stepped forward then. He had assisted to put his wife in the boat. He leaned forward and she stood up in the boat and put her arms around his neck and kissed him, and I heard her say: "I cannot leave you," and with that I turned my head. The next moment I saw him sitting beside her in the bottom of the boat, and some voice said: "Throw that man out of the boat," but at that moment they started lowering away and the man remained.

Senator Smith: Who was he?

Mr. Etches: I do not know his name, sir, but he was a very stout gentleman. (Dr. H. W. Frauenthal.)

We laid off about 100 yards from the ship and waited. She seemed to be going down at the head and we pulled away about a quarter of a mile and laid on our oars until the *Titanic* sank. She seemed to rise once as though she was going to take a final dive, but sort of checked as though she had scooped the water up and had levelled herself. She then seemed to settle very, very quiet, until the last when she rose and seemed to stand twenty seconds, stern in that position (indicating) and then she went down with an awful grating, like a small boat running off a shingley beach. There was no inrush of water, or anything. Mr. Pitman then said to pull back to the scene of the wreck. The ladies started calling out. Two ladies sitting in front where I was pulling said: "Appeal to the officer not to go back. Why should we lose all of our lives in a useless attempt to save others from the ship?" We did not go back. When we left the ship No. 5 had forty-two, including the children and six crew and the officer. Two were transferred with a lady and a child into boat No. 7.

Senator Smith: Of your own knowledge do you

know whether any general call was made for passengers to rouse themselves from their berths; and when it was, or whether there was any other signal given?

Mr. Etches: The second steward (Dodd), sir, was calling all around the ship. He was directing some men to storerooms for provisions for the lifeboats, and others he was telling to arouse all the passengers and to tell them to be sure to take their life preservers with them.

There was no lamp in No. 5. On Monday morning we saw a very large floe of flat ice and three or four bergs between in different places, and on the other bow there were two large bergs in the distance. The field ice was about three-quarters of a mile at least from us between four and five o'clock in the morning. It was well over on the port side of the *Titanic* in the position she was going.

A. Olliver, Q. M. (Am. Inq., p. 526):
There were so many people in the boat when I got into it that I could not get near the plug to put the plug in. I implored the passengers to move so I could do it. When the boat was put in the water I let the tripper go and water came into the boat. I then forced my way to the plug and put it in; otherwise it would have been swamped.

There was no rush when I got into the boat. I heard Mr. Pitman give an order to go back to the ship, but the women passengers implored him not to go. We were then about 300 yards away. Nearly all objected.

A. Shiers, fireman (Br. Inq., p. 48):
He saw no women left. There were about forty men and women in the boat. There was no confusion among the officers and crew. We did not go back when the *Titanic* went down. The women in the boat said: "Don't go back." They said: "If we go back the boat will be swamped." No compass in boat.

Paul Maugé, Ritz kitchen clerk (Br. Inq.):
Witness was berthed in the third-class corridor. Was awakened and went up on deck. Went down again and woke up the chef. Going through the second-class cabin he noticed that the assistants of the restaurant were there and not allowed to go on the Boat Deck. He saw the second or third boat on the starboard side let down into the water, and when it was about ten feet down from the Boat Deck he jumped into it. Before this he asked the chef to jump, but he was too fat and would not do so. (Laughter.) I asked him again when I got in the boat, but he refused.

When his boat was passing one of the lower decks
one of the crew of the *Titanic* tried to pull him
out of the boat. He saw no passengers prevented
from going up on deck. He thinks he was allowed to pass because he was dressed like a passenger.

Mrs. Catherine E. Crosby's affidavit (Am.
Inq., p. 1144):

Deponent is the widow of Captain Edward
Gifford Crosby and took passage with him and
their daughter, Harriette R. Crosby.

At the time of the collision, Captain Crosby
got up, dressed, went out, came back and said to
her: "You will lie there and drown," and went out
again. He said to their daughter: "The boat is
badly damaged, but I think the water-tight compartments will hold her up."

Mrs. Crosby then got up and dressed, as did
her daughter, and followed her husband on deck.
She got into the first or second boat. About thirty-
six persons got in with them.

There was no discrimination between men and
women. Her husband became separated from
her. She was suffering from cold while drifting
around and one of the officers (Pitman) put a
sail around her and over her head to keep her
warm.

George A. Harder, first-class passenger (Am. Inq., p. 1028):

As we were being lowered, they lowered one side quicker than the other, but reached the water safely after a few scares. Someone said the plug was not in, and they could not get the boat detached from the tackle. Finally, a knife was found and the rope cut. We had about forty-two people in the boat—about thirty women, Officer Pitman, a sailor and three men of the crew. We rowed some distance from the ship—it may have been a quarter or an eighth of a mile. We were afraid of the suction. Passengers said: "Let us row a little further." They did so. Then this other boat, No. 7, came along. We tied alongside. They had twenty-nine in their boat, and we counted at the time thirty-six in ours, so we gave them four or five of our people in order to make it even.

After the ship went down we heard a lot of cries and a continuous yelling and moaning. I counted about ten icebergs in the morning. Our boat managed very well. It is true that the officer did want to go back to the ship, but all the passengers held out and said: "Do not do that; it would only be foolish; there would be so many around that it would only swamp the boat." There was no light in our boat.

C. E. H. Stengel, first cabin passenger (Am. Inq., p. 975):

Senator Smith: Did you see any man attempt to enter these lifeboats who was forbidden to do so?

Mr. Stengel: I saw two. A certain physician * in New York, and his brother, jumped into the same boat my wife was in. Then the officer, or the man who was loading the boat said: "I will stop that. I will go down and get my gun." He left the deck momentarily and came right back again. I saw no attempt of anyone else to get into the lifeboats except these two gentlemen that jumped into the boat after it was started to lower.

Senator Bourne: When you were refused admission into the boat in which your wife was, were there a number of ladies and children there at the time?

Mr. Stengel: No, sir, there were not. These two gentlemen had put their wives in and were standing on the edge of the deck and when they started lowering away, they jumped in. I saw only two.

N. C. Chambers, first-class passenger (Am. Inq., 1041):

Witness referring to boat No. 5 as appearing sufficiently loaded says: "However, my wife said

* Dr. H. W. Frauenthal.

she was going in that boat and proceeded to jump in, calling to me to come. As I knew she would get out again had I not come, I finally jumped into the boat, although I did not consider it, from the looks of things, safe to put many more in. As I remember it, there were two more men, both called by their wives, who jumped in after I did. One of them, a German I believe, told me as I recollect it on the *Carpathia* that he had looked around and had seen no one else, and no one to ask whether he could get in, or not, and had jumped in. Witness describes the difficulty in finding whether the plug was in, or not, and recalls someone calling from above: "It's your own blooming business to see that the plug is in anyhow."

Mrs. C. E. H. Stengel, first-class passenger, writes as follows:

"As I stepped into the lifeboat an officer in charge said: 'No more; the boat is full.' My husband stepped back, obeying the order. As the boat was being lowered, four men deliberately jumped into it. One of them was a Hebrew doctor—another was his brother. This was done at the risk of the lives of all of us in the boat. The two companions of this man who did this were the ones who were later transferred to boat No. 7, to which we were tied. He weighed about 250 pounds and wore two life preservers. These men who jumped in struck me and a little child. I was rendered unconscious and two of my ribs were very badly dislocated. With this exception there was absolutely no confusion and no disorder in the loading of our boat."

Mrs. F. M. Warren, first-class passenger's account:

. . . Following this we then went to our rooms, put on all our heavy wraps and went to the foot of the grand staircase on Deck D, again interviewing passengers and crew as to the danger. While standing there Mr. Andrews, one of the designers of the vessel, rushed by, going up the stairs. He was asked if there was any danger but made no reply. But a passenger who was afterwards saved told me that his face had on it a look of terror. Immediately after this the report became general that water was in the squash courts, which were on the deck below where we were standing, and that the baggage had already been submerged.

At the time we reached the Boat Deck, starboard side, there were very few passengers there, apparently, but it was dark and we could not estimate the number. There was a deafening roar of escaping steam, of which we had not been conscious while inside.

The only people we remembered seeing, except a young woman by the name of Miss Ostby, who had become separated from her father and was with us, were Mr. Astor, his wife and servants, who were standing near one of the boats which was being cleared preparatory to being lowered. The Astors did not get into this boat. They all went back inside and I saw nothing of them again until Mrs. Astor was taken onto the *Carpathia*.

We discovered that the boat next to the one the Astors had been near had been lowered to the level of the deck, so went towards it and were told by the officers in charge to get in. At this moment both men and women came crowding toward the spot. I was the second person assisted in. I supposed that Mr. Warren had followed, but saw when I turned that he was standing back and assisting the women. People came in so rapidly in the darkness that it was impossible to distinguish them, and I did not see him again.

The boat was commanded by Officer Pitman and manned by four of the *Titanic's* men. The lowering of the craft was accomplished with great difficulty. First one end and then the other was dropped at apparently dangerous angles, and we feared that we would swamp as soon as we struck the water.

Mr. Pitman's orders were to pull far enough away to avoid suction if the ship sank. The sea was like glass, so smooth that the stars were clearly reflected. We were pulled quite a distance away and then rested, watching the rockets in terrible anxiety and realizing that the vessel was rapidly sinking, bow first. She went lower and lower, until the lower lights were extinguished, and then suddenly rose by the stern and slipped from sight. We had no light on our boat and were left in intense darkness save from an occasional glimmer of light from other lifeboats and one steady green light on one of the ship's boats which the officers of the *Carpathia* afterwards said was of material assistance in aiding them to come direct to the spot.

With daylight the wind increased and the sea became choppy, and we saw icebergs in every direction; some lying low in the water and others tall, like ships, and some of us thought they were ships. I was on the second boat picked up.

From the time of the accident until I left the ship there was nothing which in any way resembled a panic. There seemed to be a sort of aimless confusion and an utter lack of organized effort.

BOAT No. 3.*

No disorder in loading or lowering this boat.

Passengers: Mesdames Cardeza and maid (Anna Hard), Davidson, Dick, Graham, Harper, Hays and maid (Miss Pericault), Spedden and maid (Helen Wilson) and son Douglas and his trained nurse, Miss Burns, and Misses Graham and Shutes.

Men: Messrs. Cardeza and man-servant (Lesneur), Dick, Harper and man-servant (Hamad Hassah) and Spedden.

Men who helped load women and children in this boat and sank with the ship: Messrs. Case, Davidson, Hays and Roebling.

Crew: Seamen: Moore (in charge), Forward Pascoe. Steward: McKay; Firemen: "5 or 6"; or "10 or 12."

Total: 40.†

INCIDENTS

G. Moore, A. B. (Am. Inq., 559):
When we swung boat No. 3 out I was told by the first officer to jump in the boat and pass the

---

* Third boat lowered on starboard side 1.00 (Br. Rpt., p. 38).
† British Report (p. 38) says 15 crew, 10 men passengers, 25 women and children. Total 50.

ladies in, and when there were no more about
we took in men passengers. We had thirty-two
in the boat, all told, and then lowered away. Two
seamen were in the boat. There were a few men
passengers and some five or six firemen. They
got in after all the women and children. I took
charge of the boat at the tiller.

Mrs. Frederick O. Spedden, first-class passenger's account:

. . . Number 3 and Number 5 were both
marked on our boat. Our seaman told me that
it was an old one taken from some other ship,*
and he didn't seem sure at the time which was the
correct number, which apparently was 3.

We tied up to a boat filled with women once,
but the rope broke and we got pretty well separated from all the other lifeboats for some time.
We had in all about forty in our boat, including
ten or twelve stokers in the bow with us who
seemed to exercise complete control over our coxswain, and urged him to order the men to row
away from the sinking *Titanic,* as they were in
mortal terror of the suction. Two oars were lost
soon after we started and they didn't want to
take the time to go back after them, in spite of

---

*" All boats were new and none transferred from an-
other ship," President Ismay's testimony.

some of the passengers telling them that there was absolutely no danger from suction. All this accounts for the fact of our being some distance off when the ship went down. We couldn't persuade the coxswain to turn around till we saw the lights of the *Carpathia* on the horizon. It was then that we burned some paper, as we couldn't find our lantern. When the dawn appeared and my small boy Douglas saw the bergs around us and remarked: "Oh, Muddie, look at the beautiful north pole with no Santa Claus on it," we all couldn't refrain from smiling in spite of the tragedy of the situation.

No more accurately written or interesting account (one which I freely confess moves me to tears whenever re-read) has come to my notice than the following, which I have the consent of the author to insert in its entirety:

WHEN THE "TITANIC" WENT DOWN
By
Miss Elizabeth W. Shutes

Such a biting cold air poured into my stateroom that I could not sleep, and the air had so

strange an odor,* as if it came from a clammy
cave. I had noticed that same odor in the ice
cave on the Eiger glacier. It all came back to
me so vividly that I could not sleep, but lay in
my berth until the cabin grew so very cold that
I got up and turned on my electric stove. It
threw a cheerful red glow around, and the room
was soon comfortable; but I lay waiting. I have
always loved both day and night on shipboard,
and am never fearful of anything, but now I was
nervous about the icy air.

Suddenly a queer quivering ran under me, apparently the whole length of the ship. Startled
by the very strangeness of the shivering motion,
I sprang to the floor. With too perfect a trust
in that mighty vessel I again lay down. Some
one knocked at my door, and the voice of a friend
said: "Come quickly to my cabin; an iceberg has
just passed our window; I know we have just
struck one."

No confusion, no noise of any kind, one could
believe no danger imminent. Our stewardess
came and said she could learn nothing. Looking
out into the companionway I saw heads appearing
asking questions from half-closed doors. All
sepulchrally still, no excitement. I sat down
again. My friend was by this time dressed; still

* Seaman Lee testifies to this odor.

her daughter and I talked on, Margaret pretending to eat a sandwich. Her hand shook so that the bread kept parting company from the chicken. Then I saw she was frightened, and for the first time I was too, but why get dressed, as no one had given the slightest hint of any possible danger? An officer's cap passed the door. I asked: "Is there an accident or danger of any kind?" "None, so far as I know," was his courteous answer, spoken quietly and most kindly. This same officer then entered a cabin a little distance down the companionway and, by this time distrustful of everything, I listened intently, and distinctly heard, "We can keep the water out for a while." Then, and not until then, did I realize the horror of an accident at sea. Now it was too late to dress; no time for a waist, but a coat and skirt were soon on; slippers were quicker than shoes; the stewardess put on our life-preservers, and we were just ready when Mr. Roebling came to tell us he would take us to our friend's mother, who was waiting above.

We passed by the palm room, where two short hours before we had listened to a beautiful concert, just as one might sit in one's own home. With never a realizing sense of being on the ocean, why should not one forget?—no motion, no noise of machinery, nothing suggestive of a

ship. Happy, laughing men and women constantly passing up and down those broad, strong
staircases, and the music went on and the ship
went on—nearer and nearer to its end. So short
a life, so horrible a death for that great, great
ship. What is a more stupendous work than a
ship! The almost human pieces of machinery,
yet a helpless child, powerless in its struggle
with an almighty sea, and the great boat sank,
fragile as a rowboat.

How different are these staircases now! No
laughing throng, but on either side stand quietly,
bravely, the stewards, all equipped with the white,
ghostly life-preservers. Always the thing one
tries not to see even crossing a ferry. Now only
pale faces, each form strapped about with those
white bars. So gruesome a scene. We passed on.
The awful good-byes. The quiet look of hope in
the brave men's eyes as the wives were put into
the lifeboats. Nothing escaped one at this fearful
moment. We left from the Sun Deck, seventy-
five feet above the water. Mr. Case and Mr.
Roebling, brave American men, saw us to the
lifeboat, made no effort to save themselves, but
stepped back on deck. Later they went to an
honored grave.

Our lifeboat, with thirty-six in it, began lowering to the sea. This was done amid the greatest

confusion. Rough seamen all giving different orders. No officer aboard. As only one side of the ropes worked, the lifeboat at one time was in such a position that it seemed we must capsize in mid-air. At last the ropes worked together, and we drew nearer and nearer the black, oily water. The first touch of our lifeboat on that black sea came to me as a last good-bye to life, and so we put off—a tiny boat on a great sea— rowed away from what had been a safe home for five days. The first wish on the part of all was to stay near the *Titanic*. We all felt so much safer near the ship. Surely such a vessel could not sink. I thought the danger must be exaggerated, and we could all be taken aboard again. But surely the outline of that great, good ship was growing less. The bow of the boat was getting black. Light after light was disappearing, and now those rough seamen put to their oars and we were told to hunt under seats, any place, anywhere, for a lantern, a light of any kind. Every place was empty. There was no water—no stimulant of any kind. Not a biscuit—nothing to keep us alive had we drifted long. Had no good *Carpathia,* with its splendid Captain Rostron, its orderly crew, come to our rescue we must have all perished. Our men knew nothing about the position of the stars, hardly how to pull together.

Two oars were soon overboard. The men's hands were too cold to hold on. We stopped while they beat their hands and arms, then started on again. A sea, calm as a pond, kept our boat steady, and now that mammoth ship is fast, fast disappearing. Only one tiny light is left—a powerless little spark, a lantern fastened to the mast. Fascinated, I watched that black outline until the end. Then across the water swept that awful wail, the cry of those drowning people. In my ears I heard: "She's gone, lads; row like hell or we'll get the devil of a swell." And the horror, the helpless horror, the worst of all—need it have been?

To-day the question is being asked, "Would the *Titanic* disaster be so discussed had it not been for the great wealth gathered there?" It surely would be, for at a time like this wealth counts for nothing, but man's philanthropy, man's brains, man's heroism, count forever. So many men that stood for the making of a great nation, morally and politically, were swept away by the sinking of that big ship. That is why, day after day, the world goes on asking the why of it all. Had a kind Providence a guiding hand in this? Did our nation need so mighty a stroke to prove that man had grown too self-reliant, too sure of his own power over God's sea? God's part was the saving of the few souls on that calmest of oceans on that fearful night. Man's part was the pushing of the good ship, pushing against all reason, to save what?—a few hours and lose a thousand souls—to have the largest of ships arrive in port even a few hours sooner than anticipated. Risk all, but push, push on, on. The icebergs could be avoided. Surely man's experience ought to have lent aid, but just so surely it did not.

In years past a tendency to live more simply away from pomp and display led to the founding of our American nation. Now what are we demanding to-day? Those same needless luxuries. If they were not demanded they would not be supplied. Gymnasiums, swimming pools, tea rooms, had better give way to make space for the necessary number of lifeboats; lifeboats for the crew, also, who help pilot the good ship across the sea.

Sitting by me in the lifeboat were a mother and daughter (Mrs. Hays and Mrs. Davidson). The mother had left a husband on the *Titanic,* and the daughter a father and husband, and while we were near the other boats those two stricken women would call out a name and ask, "Are you there?" "No," would come back the awful answer, but these brave women never lost courage, forgot their own sorrow, telling me to sit close to them to keep warm. Now I began to wish for the warm velvet suit I left hanging in my cabin. I had thought of it for a minute, and then had quickly thrown on a lighter weight skirt. I knew the heavier one would make the life-preserver less useful. Had I only known how calm the ocean was that night, I would have felt that death was not so sure, and would have dressed for life rather than for the end. The life-preservers helped to keep us warm, but the night was bitter cold, and it grew colder and colder, and just before dawn, the coldest, darkest hour of all, no help seemed possible. As we put off from the *Titanic* never was a sky more brilliant, never have I seen so many falling stars. All tended to make those distress rockets that were sent up from the sinking ship look so small, so dull and futile. The brilliancy of the sky only intensified the blackness of the water, our utter loneliness on the sea. The other boats had drifted away from us; we must wait now for dawn and what the day was to bring us we dare not even hope. To see if I could not make the night seem shorter, I tried to imagine myself again in Japan. We had made two strange night departures there, and I was unafraid, and this Atlantic now was calmer than the Inland sea had been at that time. This helped a while, but my hands were freezing cold, and I had to give up pretending and think of the dawn that must soon come.

Two rough looking men had jumped into our boat as we were about to lower, and they kept striking matches, lighting cigars, until I feared we would have no matches left and might need them, so I asked them not to use any more, but they kept on. I do not know what they looked like. It was too dark to really distinguish features clearly, and when the dawn brought the light it brought something so wonderful with it no one looked at anything else or anyone else. Some one asked: "What time is it?" Matches were still left; one was struck. Four o'clock! Where had the hours of the night gone? Yes, dawn would soon be here; and it came, so surely, so strong with cheer. The stars slowly disappeared, and in their place came the faint pink glow of another day. Then I heard, "A light, a ship." I could not, would not, look while there was a bit of doubt, but kept my eyes away. All night long I had heard, "A light!" Each time it proved to be one of our other lifeboats, someone lighting a piece of paper, anything they could find to burn, and now I could not believe. Someone found a newspaper; it was lighted and held up. Then I looked and saw a ship. A ship bright with lights; strong and steady she waited, and we were to be saved. A straw hat was offered (Mrs. Davidson's) ; it would burn longer. That same ship that had come to save us might run us down. But no; she is still. The two, the ship and the dawn, came together, a living painting. White was the vessel, but whiter still were those horribly beautiful icebergs, and as we drew nearer and nearer that good ship we drew nearer to those mountains of ice. As far as the eye could reach they rose. Each one more fantastically chiselled than its neighbor. The floe glistened like an ever-ending meadow covered with new-fallen snow. Those same white mountains, marvellous in their purity, had made of the just ended night one of the blackest the sea has ever known. And near them stood the ship which had come in such quick response to the *Titanic's* call for help. The man who works over hours is always the worthwhile kind, and the Marconi operator awaiting a belated message had heard the poor ship's call for help, and we few out of so many were saved.

From the *Carpathia* a rope forming a tiny swing was lowered into our lifeboat, and one by one we were drawn into safety. The lady pulled up just ahead of me was very large, and I felt myself being jerked fearfully, when I heard some one say: "Careful, fellers; she's a lightweight."

I bumped and bumped against the side of the ship until I felt like a bag of meal. My hands were so cold I could hardly hold on to the rope, and I was fearful of letting go. Again I heard: "Steady, fellers; not so fast!" I felt I should let go and bounce out of the ropes; I hardly think that would have been possible, but I felt so at the time. At last I found myself at an opening of some kind and there a kind doctor wrapped me in a warm rug and led me to the dining room, where warm stimulants were given us immediately and everything possible was done for us all. Lifeboats kept coming in, and heart-rending was the sight as widow after widow was brought aboard. Each hoped some lifeboat ahead of hers might have brought her husband safely to this waiting vessel. But always no.

I was still so cold that I had to get a towel and tie it around my waist. Then I went back to the dining-room and found dear little Louis,* the French baby, lying alone; his cold, bare feet had become unwrapped. I put a hot water bottle against this very beautiful boy. He smiled his thanks.

Knowing how much better I felt after taking the hot stimulant, I tried to get others to take

* One of the Navratil children whose pathetic story has been fully related in the newspapers.

something; but often they just shook their heads and said, "Oh, I can't."

Towards night we remembered we had nothing —no comb, brush, nothing of any kind—so we went to the barber-shop. The barber always has everything, but now he had only a few tooth-brushes left. I bought a cloth cap of doubtful style; and felt like a walking orphan asylum, but very glad to have anything to cover my head. There were also a few showy silk handkerchiefs left. On the corner of each was embroidered in scarlet, "From a friend." These we bought and we were now fitted out for our three remaining days at sea.

Patiently through the dismal, foggy days we lived, waiting for land and possible news of the lost. For the brave American man, a heart full of gratitude, too deep for words, sends out a thanksgiving. That such men are born, live and die for others is a cause for deep gratitude. What country could have shown such men as belong to our American manhood? Thank God for them and for their noble death.

EMERGENCY BOAT No.   *

No disorder in loading or lowering this boat.

* This was the fourth boat to leave the starboard side.

Passengers: Lady Duff Gordon and maid (Miss Francetelli).

Men: Lord Duff Gordon and Messrs. Solomon and Stengel.

Total: 5.

Crew: Seamen: Symons (in charge), Horswell. Firemen: Collins, Hendrickson, Pusey, Shee, Taylor.

Total: 7.

Grand Total: 12.

INCIDENTS

G. Symons, A. B. (Br. Inq.):

Witness assisted in putting passengers in Nos. 5 and 3 under Mr. Murdoch's orders, women and children first. He saw 5 and 3 lowered away and went to No. 1. Mr. Murdoch ordered another sailor and five firemen in. Witness saw two ladies running out of the Saloon Deck who asked if they could get in the boat. Murdoch said: "Jump in." The officer looked around for more, but none were in sight and he ordered to lower away, with the witness in charge. Before leaving the Boat Deck witness saw a white light a point and a half on the port bow about five miles away.

Just after boat No. 1 got away, the water was up to C Deck just under where the ship's name is.

Witness got about 200 yards away and ordered the crew to lay on their oars. The ship's stern was well up in the air. The foremost lights had disappeared and the only light left was the mast light. The stern was up out of the water at an angle of forty-five degrees; the propeller could just be seen. The boat was pulled away a little further to escape suction; then he stopped and watched.

After the *Titanic* went down he heard the people shrieking for help, but was afraid to go back for fear of their swarming upon him, though there was plenty of room in the boat for eight or a dozen more. He determined on this course himself as *"master of the situation."* * About a day before landing in New York a present of five pounds came as a surprise to the witness from Sir Cosmo Duff Gordon.

The President: You state that you were surprised that no one in the boat suggested that you should go back to the assistance of the drowning people?

Witness: Yes.

The President: Why were you surprised?

Witness: I fully expected someone to do so.

The President: It seemed reasonable that such a suggestion should be made?

* Italics are mine.—Author.

Witness: Yes; I should say it would have been reasonable.

The President: You said in America to Senator Perkins that you had fourteen to twenty passengers in the boat?

Witness: I thought I had; I was in the dark.

The President: You were not in the dark when you gave that evidence.

Witness said he thought he was asked how many people there were in the boat, all told.

The Attorney General: You meant that the 14 to 20 meant everybody?

Witness: Yes.

The Attorney General: But you know you only had twelve all told?

Witness: Yes.

The President: You must have known perfectly well when you gave this evidence that the number in your boat was twelve. Why did you tell them in America that there were fourteen to twenty in the boat?

Witness: I do not know; it was a mistake I made then and the way they muddled us up.

The Attorney General: It was a very plain question. Did you know the names of any passengers?

Witness: I knew Sir Cosmo Duff Gordon's name when we arrived in America.

The Attorney General: Did you say anything in America about having received the five pounds?

Witness: No, sir; and I was not asked.

The Attorney General: You were asked these very questions in America which we have been putting to you to-day about going back?

Witness: Yes, sir.

The Attorney General: Why did you not say that you heard the cries, but in the exercise of your discretion as "master of the situation" you did not go back?

Witness: They took us in three at a time in America and they hurried us through the questions.

The Attorney General: They asked you: "Did you make any effort to get there," and you said: "Yes; we went back and could not see anything." But you said nothing about your discretion. Why did you not tell them that part of the story? You realized that if you had gone back you might have rescued a good many people?

Witness: Yes.

The Attorney General: The sea was calm, the night was calm and there could not have been a more favorable night for rescuing people?

Witness: Yes.

The testimony at the American Inquiry above

referred to, because of which this witness was called to account, follows:

G. Symons, L. O. (Am. Inq., p. 573):

I was in command of boat No. 1.

Senator Perkins: How many passengers did you have on her?

Mr. Symons: From fourteen to twenty.

Senator Perkins: Were they passengers or crew?

Mr. Symons: There were seven men ordered in; two seamen and five firemen. They were ordered in by Mr. Murdoch.

Senator Perkins: How many did you have all told?

Mr. Symons: I would not say for certain; it was fourteen or twenty. Then we were ordered away.

Senator Perkins: You did not return to the ship again?

Mr. Symons: Yes; we came back after the ship was gone and saw nothing.

Senator Perkins: Did you rescue anyone that was in the water?

Mr. Symons: No, sir; we saw nothing when we came back.

Witness then testified that there was no confusion or excitement among the passengers. It was just the same as if it was an everyday affair.

He never saw any rush whatever to get into either of the two boats. He heard the cries of the people in the water.

Senator Perkins: Did you say your boat could take more? Did you make any effort to get them?

Mr. Symons: Yes. We came back, but when we came back we did not see anybody or hear anybody.

He says that his boat could have accommodated easily ten more. He was in charge of her and was ordered away by Officer Murdoch. Did not pull back to the ship again until she went down.

Senator Perkins: And so you made no attempt to save any other people after you were ordered to pull away from the ship by someone?

Mr. Symons: I pulled off and came back after the ship had gone down.

Senator Perkins: And then there were no people there?

Mr. Symons: No, sir; I never saw any.

C. E. H. Stengel, first-class passenger (Am. Inq., p. 971):

There was a small boat they called an Emergency boat in which were three people, Sir Duff Gordon, his wife and Miss Francatelli. I asked to get into the boat. There was no one else around that I could see except the people working at the boats. The officer said: "Jump in." The railing was rather high. I jumped onto it and rolled into the boat. The officer said: "That's the funniest thing I have seen to-night," and laughed heartily. After getting down part of the way the boat began to tip and somebody "hollered" to stop lowering. A man named A. L. Soloman also asked to get in with us. There were five passengers, three stokers and two seamen in the boat.

Senator Smith: Do you know who gave instructions?

Mr. Stengel: I think between Sir Cosmo Duff Gordon and myself we decided which way to go. We followed a light that was to the bow of the ship. . . .Most of the boats rowed toward that light, and after the green lights began to burn I suggested that it was better to turn around and go towards them. They were from another lifeboat. When I got into the boat it was right up against the side of the ship. If it had not been, I would have gone right out into the water because I rolled. I did not step in it; I just simply rolled. There was one of the icebergs particularly that I noticed—a very large one which looked something like the Rock of Gibraltar.

THE DUFF GORDON EPISODE

Charles Hendricksen, leading fireman (Br. Inq.):

When the ship sank we picked up nobody. The passengers would not listen to our going back. Of the twelve in the boat, seven were of the crew. Symons, who was in charge, said nothing and we all kept our mouths shut. None of the crew objected to going back. It was a woman who objected, Lady Duff Gordon, who said we would be swamped. People screaming for help could be heard by everyone in our boat. I suggested going back. Heard no one else do so. Mr. Duff Gordon upheld his wife.

After we got on the *Carpathia* Gordon sent for them all and said he would make them a present. He was surprised to receive five pounds from him the day after docking in New York.

Hendricksen recalled.

Witness cross examined by Sir Cosmo Duff Gordon's counsel.

What did you say about Sir Cosmo's alleged statement preventing you from going back?

Witness: It was up to us to go back.

Did anyone in the boat say anything to you about going back?

Witness: Lady Duff Gordon said something to the effect that if we went back the boat would be swamped.

Who was it that first said anything about Sir Cosmo making a presentation to the crew?

Witness: Fireman Collins came down and said so when we were on board the *Carpathia.*

Before we left the *Carpathia* all the people rescued were photographed together. We members of the crew wrote our names on Lady Duff Gordon's life-belt. From the time we first left off rowing until the time the vessel sank, Lady Duff Gordon was violently seasick and lying on the oars.

A. E. Horswell, A. B. (Br. Inq.) :

Witness said it would have been quite a safe and proper thing to have gone back and that it was an inhuman thing not to do so, but he had to obey the orders of the coxswain. Two days after boarding the *Carpathia* some gentlemen sent for him and he received a present.

J. Taylor, fireman (Br. Inq.) :

Witness testifies that No. 1 boat stood by about 100 yards to avoid suction and was 200 yards off when the *Titanic* sank. He heard a suggestion made about going back and a lady passenger talked of the boat's being swamped if they did so.

Two gentlemen in the boat said it would be dangerous.

Did your boat ever get within reach of drowning people?

Witness: No.

How many more could the boat have taken in?

Witness: Twenty-five or thirty in addition to those already in it.

Did any of the crew object to going back?

Witness: No.

Did you ever hear of a boat's crew consisting of six sailors and one fireman?

Witness: No.

Lord Mersey: What was it that Sir Cosmo Duff Gordon said to you in the boat?

Witness: He said he would write to our homes and to our wives and let them know that we were safe.

Witness said he received five pounds when he was on board the *Carpathia*.

R. W. Pusey, fireman (Br. Inq.):

After the ship went down we heard cries for a quarter of an hour, or twenty minutes. Did not go back in the direction the *Titanic* had sunk. I heard one of the men say: "We have lost our kit," and then someone said: "Never mind, we will give you enough to get a new kit." I was surprised that no one suggested going back. I was surprised that I did not do so, but we were all half dazed. It does occur to me now that we might have gone back and rescued some of the strugglers. I heard Lady Duff Gordon say to Miss Francatelli: "You have lost your beautiful nightdress," and I said: "Never mind, you have saved your lives; but we have lost our kit"; and then Sir Cosmo offered to provide us with new ones.

Sir Cosmo Duff Gordon (Br. Inq.):
No. 7 was the first boat I went to. It was just being filled. There were only women and the boat was lowered away. No. 3 was partially filled with women, and as there were no more, they filled it up with men. My wife would not go without me. Some men on No. 3 tried to force her away, but she would not go. I heard an officer say: "Man No. 1 boat." I said to him: "May we get in that boat?" He said: "With pleasure; I wish you would." He handed the ladies in and then put two Americans in, and after that he said to two or three firemen that they had better get in. When the boat was lowered I thought the *Titanic* was in a very grave condition. At the time I thought that certainly all the women had gotten off. No notice at all was taken

in our boat of these cries. No thought entered my mind about its being possible to go back and try to save some of these people. I made a promise of a present to the men in the boat.

There was a man sitting next to me and about half an hour after the *Titanic* sank a man said to me: "I suppose you have lost everything?" I said: "Yes." He said: "I suppose you can get more." I said: "Yes." He said: "Well, we have lost all our kit, for we shall not get anything out of the Company, and our pay ceases from to-night." I said: "Very well, I will give you five pounds each towards your kit."

Were the cries from the *Titanic* clear enough to hear the words, "My God, My God"?

No. You have taken that from the story in the American papers.

Mr. Stengel in his evidence in New York said, "Between Mr. Duff Gordon and myself we decided the direction of the boat."

That's not so; I did not speak to the coxswain in any way.

Lady Duff Gordon (Br. Inq.):
After the three boats had been gotten away my husband and I were left standing on the deck. Then my husband went up and said, might we

not get into this boat, and the officer said **very** politely: "If you will do so I should be very pleased." Then somebody hitched me up at the back, lifted me up and pitched me into the boat. My husband and Miss Francatelli were also pitched into the boat; and then two Americans were also pitched in on top of us. Before the *Titanic* sank I heard terrible cries.

Q. Is it true in an article signed by what purports to be your signature that you heard the last cry which was that of a man shouting, "My God, My God"?

A. Absolutely untrue.

Address by Mr. A. Clement Edwards, M. P., Counsel for Dock Workers' Union (Br. Inq.):

Referring to the Duff Gordon incident he said that the evidence showed that in one of the boats there were only seven seamen and five passengers. If we admitted that, this boat had accommodation for twenty-eight more passengers.

The primary responsibility for this must necessarily be placed on the member of the crew who was in charge of the boat—Symons, no conduct of anyone else in the boat, however reprehensible, relieving that man from such responsibility.

Here was a boat only a short distance from the ship, so near that the cries of those struggling in the water could be heard. Symons had been told to stand by the ship, and that imposed upon him a specific duty. It was shown in Hendricksen's evidence that there was to the fullest knowledge of those in the boat a large number of people in the water, and that someone suggested that they should return and try to rescue them. Then it was proved that one of the ladies, who was shown to be Lady Duff Gordon, had said that the boat might be swamped if they went back, and Sir Cosmo Duff Gordon had admitted that this also represented his mental attitude at the time. He (Mr. Edwards) was going to say, and to say quite fearlessly, that a state of mind which could, while within the hearing of the screams of drowning people, think of so material a matter as the giving of money to replace kits was a state of mind which must have contemplated the fact that there was a possibility of rescuing some of these people, and the danger which might arise if this were attempted.

He was not going to say that there was a blunt, crude bargain, or a deal done with these men: "If you will not go back I will give you five pounds"; but he was going to suggest as a right and true inference that the money was mentioned at that time under these circumstances to give such a sense of ascendancy or supremacy to Sir Cosmo Duff Gordon in the boat that the view to which he gave expression that they should not go back would weigh more with the men than if he had given it as a piece of good advice. There were twenty-eight places on that boat and no one on board had a right to save his own life by avoiding any possible risk involved in filling the vacant places. To say the least of it, it was most reprehensible that there should have been any offer of money calculated to influence the minds of the men or to seduce them from their duty.

From the address of the Attorney-General, Sir Rufus Isaacs, K. C., M. P. (Br. Inq.) :

In regard to boat No. 1, I have to make some comment. This was the Emergency boat on the starboard side, which figured somewhat prominently in the inquiry on account of the evidence which was given in the first instance by Hendricksen, and which led to the calling of Sir Cosmo Duff Gordon. Any comment I have to make in regard to that boat is, I wish to say, not directed to Sir Cosmo or his wife. For my part, I would find it impossible to make any harsh or severe comment on the conduct of any woman who, in circumstances such as these, found herself on the water in a small boat on a dark night, and was afraid to go back because she thought there was a danger of being swamped. At any rate, I will make no comment about that, and the only reason I am directing attention to No. 1 boat is that it is quite plain that it was lowered with twelve persons in it instead of forty. I am unable to say why it was that that boat was so lowered with only five passengers and seven of the crew on board, but that circumstance, I contend, shows the importance of boat drill.

As far as he knew from the evidence, no order was given as to the lowering of this boat. He regretted to say that he was quite unable to offer any explanation of it, but he could not see why the boat was lowered under the circumstances. The point of this part of the inquiry was two-fold—(1) the importance of a boat drill; (2) that you should have the men ready.

No doubt if there had been proper organization there would have been a greater possibility of saving more passengers. What struck one was that no one seemed to have known what his duty was or how many persons were to be placed in the boat before it was lowered. In all cases no boat had its complement of what could be carried on this particular night. The vessel was on her first passage, and if all her crew had been engaged on the next voyage no doubt things would have been better, but there was no satisfactory organization with regard to calling passengers and getting them on deck. Had these boats had their full complement it would have been another matter, but the worst of them was this boat No 1, because the man, Symons, in charge did not exercise his duty. No doubt he was told to stand by, but he went quite a distance away. His evidence was unsatisfactory, and gave no proper account why he did not return. He only said that he "exercised his discretion," and that he was "master of the situation." There was, however, no explanation why he went away and why he did not go back except that he would be swamped. That was no explanation. I can see no justification for his not going back. From the evidence, there were no people on the starboard deck at the time. They must have been mistaken in making that statement, because, as they knew, four more boats were subsequently lowered with a number of women and children. The capacity of this boat was forty. No other boat went away with so small a proportion as compared with its capacity, and there was no other boat which went away with a larger number of the crew. I confess it is a thing which I do not understand why that boat was lowered when she was. Speaking generally, the only boats that took their full quantity were four. One had to see what explanation could be given of that. In this particu-

lar case it happened that the officers were afraid
the boats would buckle. Then they said that no
more women were available, and, thirdly, it was
contemplated to go back. It struck one as very
regrettable that the officers should have doubts
in their minds on these points with regard to the
capacity of the boats.

BOAT NO. 9 *

No disorder when this boat was loaded and
lowered.

Passengers: Mesdames Aubert and maid (Mlle
Segesser), Futrelle, Lines; Miss Lines, and second and third-class.

Men: Two or three.

Said good-bye to wife and sank with ship: Mr.
Futrelle.

Crew: Seamen: Haines (in charge), Wynne,
Q. M., McGough, Peters; Stewards Ward, Widgery and others.

Total: 56.

INCIDENTS

A. Haines, boatswain's mate (Am. Inq., 755):
Officer Murdoch and witness filled boat 9 with
ladies. None of the men passengers tried to get
into the boats. Officer Murdoch told them to

* The fifth boat lowered on starboard side, 1.20 (Br. Rpt.,
p. 38).

stand back. There was one woman who refused
to get in because she was afraid. When there
were no more women forthcoming the boat was
full, when two or three men jumped into the bow.
There were two sailors, three or four stewards,
three or four firemen and two or three men passengers. No. 9 was lowered from the Boat Deck
with sixty-three people in the boat and lowered
all right. Officer Murdoch put the witness in
charge and ordered him to row off and keep
clear of the ship. When we saw it going down
by the head he pulled further away for the safety
of the people in the boat: about 100 yards away
at first. Cries were heard after the ship went
down. He consulted with the sailors about going
back and concluded with so many in the boat it
was unsafe to do so. There was no compass in
the boat, but he had a little pocket lamp. On
Monday morning he saw from thirty to fifty icebergs and a big field of ice miles long and large
bergs and "growlers," the largest from eighty to
one hundred feet high.

W. Wynne, Q. M. (Br. Inq.):
Officer Murdoch ordered witness into boat No.
9. He assisted the ladies and took an oar. He
says there were fifty-six all told in the boat, forty-
two of whom were women. He saw the light of

a steamer—a red light first, and then a white one
—about seven or eight miles away. After an
interval both lights disappeared. Ten or fifteen
minutes afterwards he saw a white light again in
the same direction. There was no lamp or compass in the boat.

W. Ward, steward (Am. Inq., 595):
Witness assisted in taking the canvas cover off
of boat No. 9 and lowered it to the level of the
Boat Deck.*

Officer Murdoch, Purser McElroy and Mr. Ismay were near this boat when being loaded. A
sailor came along with a bag and threw it into
the boat. He said he had been sent to take charge
of it by the captain. The boatswain's mate,
Haines, was there and ordered him out. He got
out. Either Purser McElroy or Officer Murdoch
said: "Pass the women and children that are here
into that boat." There were several men standing around and they fell back. There were quite
a quantity of women but he could not say how
many were helped into the boat. There were no
children. One old lady made a great fuss and
absolutely refused to enter the boat. She went

* Brice, A. B. (Am. Inq., p. 648) and Wheate, Ass't. 2nd
Steward (Br. Inq.), say No. 9 was filled from A Deck with
women and children only.

back to the companionway and forced her way in and would not get into the boat. One woman, a French lady, fell and hurt herself a little. Purser McElroy ordered two more men into the boat to assist the women. When No. 9 was being lowered the first listing of the ship was noticeable.

From the rail to the boat was quite a distance to step down to the bottom of it, and in the dark the women could not see where they were stepping. Purser McElroy told witness to get into the boat to assist the women. Women were called for, but none came along and none were seen on deck at the time. Three or four men were then taken into the boat until the officers thought there were sufficient to lower away with safety.

No. 9 was lowered into the water before No. 11. There was some difficulty in unlashing the oars because for some time no one had a knife. There were four men who rowed all night, but there were some of them in the boat who had never been to sea before and did not know the first thing about an oar, or the bow from the stern. Haines gave orders to pull away. When 200 yards off, rowing was stopped for about an hour. Haines was afraid of suction and we pulled away to about a quarter of a mile from the ship. The ship went down very gradually for a while by the head. We could just see the ports as she

dipped. She gave a kind of a sudden lurch forward. He heard a couple of reports like a vol-
ley of musketry; not like an explosion at all. His
boat was too full and it would have been mad-
ness to have gone back. He thinks No. 9 was
the fourth or fifth boat picked up by the *Carpathia*. There was quite a big lot of field ice and
several large icebergs in amongst the field; also
two or three separated from the main body of the
field.

J. Widgery, bath steward (Am. Inq., 602):
Witness says that all passengers were out of
their cabins on deck before he went up.

When he got to the Boat Deck No. 7 was about
to be lowered, but the purser sent him to No. 9.
The canvas had been taken off and he helped
lower the boat. Purser McElroy ordered him
into the boat to help the boatswain's mate pass in
women. Women were called for. An elderly
lady came along. She was frightened. The
boatswain's mate and himself assisted her, but
she pulled away and went back to the door (of
the companionway) and downstairs. Just before
they left the ship the officer gave the order to
Haines to keep about 100 yards off. The boat
was full as it started to lower away. When they
got to the water he was the only one that had a

knife to cut loose the oars. He says that the balance of his testimony would be the same as that of Mr. Ward, the previous witness.

BOAT NO. 11 *

No disorder when this boat was loaded and lowered.

Passengers: Women: Mrs. Schabert and two others of first cabin; all the rest second and third class. Fifty-eight women and children in all.

Men: Mr. Mock, first cabin, and two others.

Crew: Seamen: Humphreys (in charge), Brice; *Stewards:* Wheate, MacKay, McMicken, Thessinger, Wheelton; *Fireman* ————; *Stewardess:* Mrs. Robinson.

Total: 70.

INCIDENTS

W. Brice, A. B. (Am. Inq., 648):
This boat was filled from A Deck. An officer said: "Is there a sailor in the boat?" There was no answer. I jumped out and went down the fall into the bow. Nobody was in the stern. I went aft and shipped the rudder. By that time the boat had been filled with women and children. We had a bit of difficulty in keeping the boat clear of a big body of water coming from the ship's side.

* Sixth boat lowered on starboard side, 1.25 (Br. Rpt., p. 38).

The after block got jammed, but I think that must have been on account of the trip not being pushed right down to disconnect the block from the boat. We managed to keep the boat clear from this body of water. It was the pump discharge. There were only two seamen in the boat, a fireman, about six stewards and fifty-one passengers. There were no women and children who tried to get into the boat and were unable to do so. There was no rush and no panic whatever. Everything was done in perfect order and discipline.

Mr. Humphreys, A. B., was in charge of No. 11. There was no light or lantern in our boat. I cut the lashing from the oil bottle and cut rope and made torches. The ship sank bow down first almost perpendicularly. She became a black mass before she made the final plunge when boat was about a quarter of a mile away. Boat No. 9 was packed. Passengers were about forty-five women and about four or five children in arms.

E. Wheelton, steward (Am. Inq.) :
As I made along B Deck I met Mr. Andrews, the builder, who was opening the rooms and looking in to see if there was anyone in, and closing the doors again. Nos. 7, 5 and 9 had gone. No. 11 boat was hanging in the davits. Mr. Murdoch said: "You go too." He shouted: "Women

and children first." He was then on the top deck standing by the taffrail. The boat was loaded with women and children, and I think there were eight or nine men in the boat altogether, including our crew, and one passenger.

"Have you got any sailors in?" asked Mr. Murdoch. I said: "No, sir." He told two sailors to jump into the boat. We lowered away. Everything went very smooth until we touched the water. When we pushed away from the ship's side we had a slight difficulty in hoisting the after block. We pulled away about 300 yards. We rowed around to get close to the other boats. There were about fifty-eight all told in No. 11. It took all of its passengers from A Deck except the two sailors. I think there were two boats left on the starboard side when No. 11 was lowered. The eight or nine men in the boat included a passenger. A quartermaster (Humphreys) was in charge.

C. D. MacKay, steward (Br. Inq.):
No. 11 was lowered to A Deck. Murdoch ordered me to take charge. We collected all the women (40) on the Boat Deck, and on A Deck we collected a few more. The crew were five stewards, one fireman, two sailors, one forward and one aft. There was Wheelton, McMicken,

Thessenger, Wheate and myself. The others were strangers to the ship. There were two second-class ladies, one second-class gentleman, and the rest were third-class ladies. I found out that they were all third-class passengers. We had some difficulty in getting the after fall away. We went away from the ship about a quarter of a mile. No compass. The women complained that they were crushed up so much and had to stand. Complaints were made against the men because they smoked.

J. T. Wheate, Ass't. 2nd Steward (Br. Inq.):
Witness went upstairs to the Boat Deck where Mr. Murdoch ordered the boats to the A Deck where the witness and seventy of his men helped pass the women and children into boat No. 9, and none but women and children were taken in. He then filled up No. 11 with fifty-nine women and children, three male passengers and a crew of seven stewards, two sailors and one fireman. He could not say how the three male passengers got there. The order was very good. There was nobody on the Boat Deck, so the people were taken off on the A Deck.

Philip E. Mock, first cabin passenger [letter]:
No. 11 carried the largest number of passengers of any boat—about sixty-five. There were

only two first cabin passengers in the boat besides my sister, Mrs. Schabert, and myself. The remainder were second-class or stewards and stewardesses. We were probably a mile away when the *Titanic's* lights went out. I last saw the ship with her stern high in the air going down. After the noise I saw a huge column of black smoke slightly lighter than the sky rising high into the sky and then flattening out at the top like a mushroom.

I at no time saw any panic and not much confusion. I can positively assert this as I was near every boat lowered on the starboard side up to the time No. 11 was lowered. With the exception of some stokers who pushed their way into boat No. 3 or No. 5, I saw no man or woman force entry into a lifeboat. One of these was No. 13 going down, before we touched the water.

From address of the Attorney-General, Sir Rufus Isaacs, K. C., M. P.

"No. 11 took seventy, and carried the largest number of any boat."

BOAT NO. 13 *

No disorder when this boat was loaded and lowered.

* Seventh boat lowered on starboard side, 1.25 (Br. Rpt., p. 38).

Passengers: Women: Second cabin, including Mrs. Caldwell and her child Alden. All the rest second and third-class women.

Men: Dr. Dodge only first cabin passenger. Second cabin, Messrs. Beasley and Caldwell. One Japanese.

Crew: Firemen: Barrett (in charge), Beauchamp, Major and two others. *Stewards:* Ray, Wright and another; also baker ————.

Total: 64.

INCIDENTS

Mr. Lawrence Beesley's book, already cited, gives an excellent description of No. 13's history, but for further details, see his book, *The Loss of the SS. Titanic,* Houghton, Mifflin Co., Boston.

F. Barrett, leading stoker (Br. Inq.):

Witness then made his escape up the escape ladder and walked aft on to Deck A on the starboard side, where only two boats were left, Nos. 13 and 15. No. 13 was partly lowered when he got there. Five-sixths in the boat were women. No. 15 was lowered about thirty seconds later. When No. 13 got down to the water he shouted: "Let go the after fall," but, as no one took any notice, he had to walk over women and cut the fall himself. No. 15 came down nearly on top of them, but they just got clear. He took charge of the boat until he got so cold that he had to give up to someone else. A woman put a cloak over him, as he felt so freezing, and he could not remember anything after that. No men waiting on the deck got into his boat. They all stood in one line in perfect order waiting to be told to get into the boat. There was no disorder whatever. They picked up nobody from the sea.

F. D. Ray, steward (Am. Inq., 798):

Witness assisted in the loading of boat No. 9 and saw it and No. 11 boat lowered, and went to No. 13 on A Deck. He saw it about half filled with women and children. A few men were ordered to get in; about nine to a dozen passengers and crew. Dr. Washington Dodge was there and was told that his wife and child had gone away in one of the boats. Witness said to him: "You had better get in here then," and got behind him and pushed him and followed after him. A rather large woman came along crying and saying: "Do not put me in the boat; I don't want to get in one. I have never been in an open boat in my life." He said: "You have got to go and you may as well keep quiet." After that there was a small child rolled in a blanket thrown into the boat to him. The woman that brought it got into the boat afterwards.

We left about three or four men on the deck at the rail and they went along to No. 15 boat. No. 13 was lowered away. When nearly to the water, two or three of them noticed a very large discharge of water coming from the ship's side which he thought was the pumps working. The hole was about two feet wide and about a foot deep with a solid mass of water coming out. They shouted for the boat to be stopped from being lowered and they responded promptly and stopped lowering the boat. They pushed it off from the side of the ship until they were free from this discharge. He thinks there were no sailors or quartermasters in the boat because they apparently did not know how to get free from the tackle. Knives were called for to cut loose. In the meantime they were drifting a little aft and boat No. 15 was being lowered immediately upon them about two feet from their heads and they all shouted again, and they again replied very promptly and stopped lowering boat No. 15. They elected a fireman (Barrett) to take charge. Steward Wright was in the boat; two or three children and a very young baby seven months old. Besides Nos. 9, 11, and 13, No. 15 was lowered to Deck A and filled from it. He saw no male passengers or men of the crew whatever ordered out or thrown out of these lifeboats on the starboard side. Everybody was very orderly and there was no occasion to throw anybody out. In No. 13 there were about four or five firemen, one baker, three stewards; about nine of the crew. Dr. Washington Dodge was the only first-class passenger and the rest were third-class. There was one Japanese. There was no crowd whatever on A Deck while he was loading these boats. No. 13 was full.

Extracts from Dr. Washington Dodge's address: "The Loss of the *Titanic*," a copy of which he kindly sent me:

I heard one man say that the impact was due to ice. Upon one of his listeners' questioning the authority of this, he replied: "Go up forward and look down on the fo'castle deck, and you can see for yourself." I at once walked forward to the end of the promenade deck, and looking down could see, just within the starboard rail, small fragments of broken ice, amounting possibly to several cartloads. As I stood there an incident occurred which made me take a more serious view of the situation, than I otherwise would.

Two stokers, who had slipped up onto the promenade deck unobserved, said to me: "Do you think there is any danger, sir?" I replied: "If there is any danger it would be due to the

vessel's having sprung a leak, and you ought to
know more about it than I." They replied, in
what appeared to me to be an alarmed tone:
"Well, sir, the water was pouring into the stoke
'old when we came up, sir." At this time I observed quite a number of steerage passengers,
who were amusing themselves by walking over
the ice, and kicking it about the deck. No ice or
iceberg was to be seen in the ocean.

I watched the boats on the starboard side, as
they were successively filled and lowered away.
At no time during this period, was there any
panic, or evidence of fear, or unusual alarm. I
saw no women nor children weep, nor were there
any evidences of hysteria observed by me.

I watched all boats on the starboard side, comprising the odd numbers from one to thirteen, as
they were launched. Not a boat was launched
which would not have held from ten to twenty-
five more persons. Never were there enough
women or children present to fill any boat before
it was launched. In all cases, as soon as
those who responded to the officers' call were
in the boats, the order was given to "Lower
away."

What the conditions were on the port side of
the vessel I had no means of observing. We were
in semi-darkness on the Boat Deck, and owing to

the immense length and breadth of the vessel, and the fact that between the port and the starboard side of the Boat Deck, there were officers' cabins, staterooms for passengers, a gymnasium, and innumerable immense ventilators, it would have been impossible, even in daylight, to have obtained a view of but a limited portion of this boat deck. We only knew what was going on within a radius of possibly forty feet.

Boats Nos. 13 and 15 were swung from the davits at about the same moment. I heard the officer in charge of No. 13 say: "We'll lower this boat to Deck A." Observing a group of possibly fifty or sixty about boat 15, a small proportion of which number were women, I descended by means of a stairway close at hand to the deck below, Deck A. Here, as the boat was lowered even with the deck, the women, about eight in number, were assisted by several of us over the rail of the steamer into the boat. The officer in charge then held the boat, and called repeatedly for more women. None appearing, and there being none visible on the deck, which was then brightly illuminated, the men were told to tumble in. Along with those present I entered the boat. Ray was my table steward and called to me to get in.

The boat in which I embarked was rapidly

lowered, and as it approached the water I observed, as I looked over the edge of the boat, that the bow, near which I was seated, was being lowered directly into an enormous stream of water, three or four feet in diameter, which was being thrown with great force from the side of the vessel. This was the water thrown out by the condenser pumps. Had our boat been lowered into the same it would have been swamped in an instant. The loud cries which were raised by the occupants of the boat caused those who were sixty or seventy feet above us to cease lowering our boat. Securing an oar with considerable difficulty, as the oars had been firmly lashed together by means of heavy tarred twine, and as in addition they were on the seat running parallel with the side of the lifeboat, with no less than eight or ten occupants of the boat sitting on them, none of whom showed any tendency to disturb themselves—we pushed the bow of the lifeboat, by means of the oar, a sufficient distance away from the side of the *Titanic* to clear this great stream of water which was gushing forth. We were then safely lowered to the water. During the few moments occupied by these occurrences I felt for the only time a sense of impending danger.

We were directed to pull our lifeboat from the

steamer, and to follow a light which was carried in one of the other lifeboats, which had been launched prior to ours. Our lifeboat was found to contain no lantern, as the regulations require; nor was there a single sailor, or officer in the boat. Those who undertook to handle the oars were poor oarsmen, almost without exception, and our progress was extremely slow. Together with two or three other lifeboats which were in the vicinity, we endeavored to overtake the lifeboat which carried the light, in order that we might not drift away and possibly become lost. This light appeared to be a quarter of a mile distant, but, in spite of our best endeavors, we were never enabled to approach any nearer to it, although we must have rowed at least a mile.

BOAT NO. 15.*

No disorder in loading or lowering this boat.

Passengers: All third-class women and children (53) and

Men: Mr. Haven (first-class) and three others (third-class) only. Total: 4.

Crew: Firemen: Diamond (in charge), Cavell, Taylor; *Stewards:* Rule, Hart. Total: 13.

Grand Total (Br. Rpt., p. 38): 70.

* Br. Rpt., p. 38, places this next to last lowered on starboard side at 1.35.

INCIDENTS

G. Cavell, trimmer (Br. Inq.) :

The officer ordered five of us in the boat. We took on all the women and children and the boat was then lowered. We lowered to the first-class (i. e. A) deck and took on a few more women and children, about five, and then lowered to the water. From the lower deck we took in about sixty. There were men about but we did not take them in. They were not kept back. They were third-class passengers, I think—sixty women, Irish. Fireman Diamond took charge. No other seaman in this boat. There were none left on the third-class decks after I had taken the women.

S. J. Rule, bathroom steward (Br. Inq.) :

Mr. Murdoch called to the men to get into the boat. About six got in. "That will do," he said, "lower away to Deck A." At this time the vessel had a slight list to port. We sent scouts around both to the starboard and port sides. They came back and said there were no more women and children. We filled up on A Deck—sixty-eight all told—the last boat to leave the starboard side. There were some left behind. There was a bit of a rush after Mr. Murdoch said we could fill the boat up with men standing by. We very nearly came on top of No. 13 when we lowered away. A man, Jack Stewart, a steward, took charge. Nearly everybody rowed. No lamp. One deckhand in the boat, and men, women and children. Just before it was launched, no more could be found, and about half a dozen men got in. There were sixty-eight in the boat altogether. Seven members of the crew.

J. E. Hart, third-class steward (Br. Inq., 75):
Witness defines the duties and what was done by the stewards, particularly those connected with the steerage.

"Pass the women and children up to the Boat Deck," was the order soon after the collision. About three-quarters of an hour after the collision he took women and children from the C Deck to the first-class main companion. There were no barriers at that time. They were all opened. He took about thirty to boat No. 8 as it was being lowered. He left them and went back for more, meeting third-class passengers on the way to the boats. He brought back about twenty-five more steerage women and children, having some little trouble owing to the men passengers wanting to get to the Boat Deck. These were all third-class people whom we took to the only boat left on the starboard side, viz., No. 15. There were a large number already in the boat, which was then lowered to A Deck, and five women, three children and a man with a baby in his arms taken in, making about seventy people in all, including thirteen or fourteen of the crew and fireman Diamond in charge. Mr. Murdoch ordered witness into the boat. Four men passengers and fourteen crew was the complement of men; the rest were women and children.

When boat No. 15 left the boat deck there were other women and children there—some first-class women passengers and their husbands. Absolute quietness existed. There were repeated cries for women and children. If there had been any more women there would have been found places for them in the boat. He heard some of the women on the A Deck say they would not leave their husbands.

There is no truth in the statement that any of the seamen tried to keep back third-class passengers from the Boat Deck. Witness saw masthead light of a ship from the Boat Deck. He did his very best, and so did all the other stewards, to help get the steerage passengers on the Boat Deck as soon as possible.

ENGELHARDT BOAT "C." *

No disorder in loading or lowering this boat.

Passengers: President Ismay, Mr. Carter. Balance women and children.

Crew: Quartermaster Rowe (in charge). Steward Pearce. Barber Weikman. Firemen, three.

Stowaways: Four Chinamen, or Filipinos.

Total: 39.

INCIDENTS

G. T. Rowe, Q. M. (Am. Inq., p. 519, and Br. Inq.):

To avoid repetition, the testimony of this witness before the two Courts of Inquiry is consolidated:

He assisted the officer (Boxhall) to fire distress signals until about five and twenty minutes past one. At this time they were getting out the starboard collapsible boats. Chief Officer Wilde wanted a sailor. Captain Smith told him to get into the boat "C" which was then partly filled. He found three women and children in there with

* Br. Rpt., p. 38, makes this last boat lowered on starboard side at 1.40.

no more about. Two gentlemen got in, Mr. Ismay and Mr. Carter. Nobody told them to get
in. No one else was there. In the boat there
were thirty-nine altogether. These two gentlemen, five of the crew (including himself), three
firemen, a steward, and near daybreak they found
four Chinamen or Filipinos who had come up between the seats. All the rest were women and
children.

Before leaving the ship he saw a bright light
about five miles away about two points on the
port bow. He noticed it after he got into the
boat. When he left the ship there was a list to
port of six degrees. The order was given to
lower the boat, with witness in charge. The rub
strake kept on catching on the rivets down the
ship's side, and it was as much as we could do to
keep off. It took a good five minutes, on account
of this rubbing, to get down. When they reached
the water they steered for a light in sight, roughly
five miles. They seemed to get no nearer to it
and altered their course to a boat that was carrying a green light. When day broke, the *Carpathia* was in sight.

In regard to Mr. Ismay's getting into the boat,
the witness's testimony before the American
Court of Inquiry is cited in full:

Senator Burton: Now, tell us the circumstances

under which Mr. Ismay and that other gentleman got into the boat.

Mr. Rowe: When Chief Officer Wilde asked if there were any more women and children, there was no reply, so Mr. Ismay came into the boat.

Senator Burton: Mr. Wilde asked if there were any more women and children? Can you say that there were none?

Mr. Rowe: I could not see, but there were none forthcoming.

Senator Burton: You could see around there on the deck, could you not?

Mr. Rowe: I could see the fireman and steward that completed the boat's crew, but as regards any families I could not see any.

Senator Burton: Were there any men passengers besides Mr. Ismay and the other man?

Mr. Rowe: I did not see any, sir.

Senator Burton: Was it light enough so that you could see anyone near by?

Mr. Rowe: Yes, sir.

Senator Burton: Did you hear anyone ask Mr. Ismay and Mr. Carter to get in the boat?

Mr. Rowe: No, sir.

Senator Burton: If Chief Officer Wilde had spoken to them would you have known it?

Mr. Rowe: I think so, because they got in the after part of the boat where I was.

Alfred Pearce, pantryman, third-class (Br. Inq.) :

Picked up two babies in his arms and went into a collapsible boat on the starboard side under Officer Murdoch's order, in which were women and children. There were altogether sixty-six passengers and five of the crew, a quartermaster in charge. The ship had a list on the port side, her lights burning to the last. It was twenty minutes to two when they started to row away. He remembers this because one of the passengers gave the time.

J. B. Ismay, President International Mercantile Marine Co. of America, New Jersey, U. S. A. (Am. Inq., pp. 8, 960) :

There were four in the crew—one quartermaster, a pantryman, a butcher and another. The natural order would be women and children first. It was followed as far as practicable. About forty-five in the boat. He saw no struggling or jostling or any attempts by men to get into the boats. They simply picked the women out and put them into the boat as fast as they could—the first ones that were there. He put a great many in—also children. He saw the first lifeboat lowered on the starboard side. As to the circumstances of his departure from the ship, the boat was there. There was a certain number of men in the boat and the officer called and asked if there were any more women, but there was no response. There were no passengers left on the deck, and as the boat was in the act of being lowered away he got into it. The *Titanic* was sinking at the time. He felt the ship going down. He entered because there was room in it. Before he boarded the lifeboat he saw no passengers jump into the sea. The boat rubbed along the ship's side when being lowered, the women helping to shove the boat clear. This was when the ship had quite a list to port. He sat with his back to the ship, rowing all the time, pulling away. He did not wish to see her go down. There were nine or ten men in the boat with him. Mr. Carter, a passenger, was one. All the other people in the boat, so far as he could see, were third-class passengers.

Examined before the British Court of Inquiry by the Attorney-General, Sir Rufus Isaacs, Mr. Ismay testified:

I was awakened by the impact; stayed in bed a little time and then got up. I saw a steward who could not say what had happened. I put a coat on and went on deck. I saw Captain Smith. I asked him what was the matter and he said we had struck ice. He said he thought it was serious. I then went down and saw the chief engineer, who said that the blow was serious. He thought the pumps would keep the water under control. I think I went back to my room and then to the bridge and heard Captain Smith give an order in connection with the boats. I went to the boat deck, spoke to one of the officers, and rendered all the assistance I could in putting the women and children in. Stayed there until I left the ship. There was no confusion; no attempts by men to get into the boats. So far as I knew all the women and children were put on board the boats and I was not aware that any were left. There was a list of the ship to port. I think I remained an hour and a half on the *Titanic* after the impact. I noticed her going down by the head, sinking. Our boat was fairly full. After all the women and children got in and there were no others on that side of the deck, I got in while the boat was being lowered. Before we got into the boat I do not know that any attempt was made to call up any of the passengers on the Boat Deck, nor did I inquire.

And also examined by Mr. A. C. Edwards, M. P., counsel for the Dock Workers' Union. Mr. Ismay's testimony was taken as follows:

Mr. Edwards: You were responsible for determining the number of boats?

Mr. Ismay: Yes, in conjunction with the shipbuilders.

Mr. Edwards: You knew when you got into the boat that the ship was sinking?

Mr. Ismay: Yes.

Mr. Edwards: Had it occurred to you apart perhaps from the captain, that you, as the representative managing director, deciding the number of lifeboats, owed your life to every other person on the ship?

The President: That is not the sort of question which should be put to this witness. You can make comment on it when you come to your speech if you like.

Mr. Edwards: You took an active part in directing women and children into the boats?

Mr. Ismay: I did all I could.

Mr. Edwards: Why did you not go further and send for other people to come on deck and fill the boats?

Mr. Ismay: I put in everyone who was there and I got in as the boat was being lowered away.

Mr. Edwards: Were you not giving directions and getting women and children in?

Mr. Ismay: I was calling to them to come in.

Mr. Edwards: Why then did you not give instructions or go yourself either to the other side of the deck or below decks to get people up?

Mr. Ismay: I understood there were people there sending them up.

Mr. Edwards: But you knew there were hundreds who had not come up?

Lord Mersey: Your point, as I understand it now, is that, having regard for his position as managing director, it was his duty to remain on the ship until she went to the bottom?

Mr. Edwards: Frankly, that is so, and I do not flinch from it; but I want to get it from the witness, inasmuch as he took it upon himself to give certain directions at a certain time, why he did not discharge his responsibility after in regard to other persons or passengers.

Mr. Ismay: There were no more passengers who would have got into the boat. The boat was being actually lowered away.

Examined by Sir Robert Finley for White Star Line:

Mr. Finley: Have you crossed very often to and from America?

Mr. Ismay: Very often.

Mr. Finley: Have you ever, on any occasion, attempted to interfere with the navigation of the vessel on any of these occasions?

Mr. Ismay: No.

Mr. Finley: When you left the deck just before getting into the collapsible boat, did you hear the officer calling out for more women?

Mr. Ismay: I do not think I did; but I heard them calling for women very often.

Mr. Edwards: When the last boat left the *Titanic* you must have known that a number of passengers and crew were still on board?

Mr. Ismay: I did.

Mr. Edwards: And yet you did not see any on the deck?

Mr. Ismay: No, I did not see any, and I could only assume that the other passengers had gone to the other end of the ship.

From an address (Br. Inq.) by Mr. A. Clement Edwards, M. P., Counsel for Dock Workers' Union:

What was Mr. Ismay's duty?

Coming to Mr. Ismay's conduct, Mr. Edwards said it was clear that that gentleman had taken upon himself to assist in getting women and children into the boats. He had also admitted that when he left the *Titanic* he knew she was doomed, that there were hundreds of people in the ship, that he didn't know whether or not there were any women or children left, and that

he did not even go to the other side of the Boat
Deck to see whether there were any women and
children waiting to go. Counsel submitted that
a gentleman occupying the position of managing
director of the company owning the *Titanic*, and
who had taken upon himself the duty of assisting
at the boats, had certain special and further duties
beyond an ordinary passenger's duties, and that he
had no more right to save his life at the expense
of any single person on board that ship than the
captain would have had. He (Mr. Edwards)
said emphatically that Mr. Ismay did not discharge his duty at that particular moment by
taking a careless glance around the starboard side
of the Boat Deck. He was one of the few persons
who at the time had been placed in a position of
positive knowledge that the vessel was doomed,
and it was his clear duty, under the circumstances,
to see that someone made a search for passengers
in other places than in the immediate vicinity of
the Boat Deck.

Lord Mersey: Moral duty do you mean?

Mr. Edwards: I agree; but I say that a
managing director going on board a liner, com-
mercially responsible for it and taking upon himself certain functions, had a special moral obligation and duty more than is possessed by one
passenger to another passenger.

Lord Mersey: But how is a moral duty relative to this inquiry? It might be argued that there was a moral duty for every man on board that every woman should take precedence, and I might have to inquire whether every passenger carried out his moral duty.

Mr. Edwards agreed that so far as the greater questions involved in this case were concerned this matter was one of trivial importance.

From address of Sir Robert Finlay, K. C., M. P., Counsel for White Star Company (Br. Inq.):

It has been said by Mr. Edwards that Mr. Ismay had no right to save his life at the expense of any other life. He did not save his life at the expense of any other life. If Mr. Edwards had taken the trouble to look at the evidence he would have seen how unfounded this charge is. There is not the slightest ground for suggesting that any other life would have been saved if Mr. Ismay had not got into the boat. He did not get into the boat until it was being lowered away.

Mr. Edwards has said that it was Mr. Ismay's plain duty to go about the ship looking for passengers, but the fact is that the boat was being lowered. Was it the duty of Mr. Ismay to have remained, though by doing so no other life could have been saved? If he had been impelled to

commit suicide of that kind, then it would have
been stated that he went to the bottom because
he dared not face this inquiry. There is no observation of an unfavorable nature to be made
from any point of view upon Mr. Ismay's conduct. There was no duty devolving upon him of
going to the bottom with his ship as the captain
did. He did all he could to help the women and
children. It was only when the boat was being
lowered that he got into it. He violated no point
of honor, and if he had thrown his life away in
the manner now suggested it would be said he did
it because he was conscious he could not face this
inquiry and so he had lost his life.

ENGELHARDT BOAT "A."

Floated off the ship.

Passengers: T. Beattie,* P. D. Daly,‡ G.
Rheims, R. N. Williams, Jr., first-class; O.
Abelseth,‡ W. J. Mellers, second-class; and Mrs.
Rosa Abbott,‡ Edward Lindley,† third-class.

Crew: Steward: E. Brown. Firemen: J.
Thompson, one unidentified body,* Seaman:
one unidentified body.⁑

---

*Body found in boat by Oceanic.
†Died in boat.
‡Pulled into boat out of sea.

An extraordinary story pertains to this boat. At the outset of my research it was called a "boat of mystery," occasioned by the statements of the *Titanic's* officers. In his conversations with me, as well as in his testimony, Officer Lightoller stated that he was unable to loosen this boat from the ship in time and that he and his men were compelled to abandon their efforts to get it away. The statement in consequence was that this boat "A" was not utilized but went down with the ship. My recent research has disabused his mind of this supposition. There were only four Engelhardt boats in all as we have already learned, and we have fully accounted for "the upset boat B," and "D," the last to leave the ship in the tackles, and boat "C," containing Mr. Ismay, which reached the *Carpathia's* side and was unloaded there. After all the mystery we have reached the conclusion that boat "A" did not go down with the ship, but was the one whose occupants were rescued by Officer Lowe in the early morning, and then abandoned with three dead bodies in it. This also was the boat picked up nearly one month later by the *Oceanic* nearly 200 miles from the scene of the wreck.

I have made an exhaustive research up to date

for the purpose of discovering how Boat A left
the ship. Information in regard thereto is obtained from the testimony before the British
Court of Inquiry of Steward Edward Brown,
from first-class passenger R. N. Williams, Jr.,
and from an account of William J. Mellers, a
second cabin passenger as related by him to Dr.
Washington Dodge. Steward Brown, it will be
observed, testified that he was washed out of the
boat and yet "did not know whether he went
down in the water." As he could not swim, an
analysis of his testimony forces me to believe
that he held on to the boat and did not have
to swim and that boat "A" was the same one
that he was in when he left the ship. I am
forced to the same conclusion in young Williams'
case after an analysis of his statement that he
took off his big fur overcoat in the water and
cast it adrift while he swam twenty yards
to the boat, and in some unaccountable way
the fur coat swam after him and also got
into the boat. At any rate it was found in
the boat when it was recovered later as shown
in the evidence.

I also have a letter from Mr. George Rheims,
of Paris, indicating his presence on this same boat
with Messrs. Williams and Mellers and Mrs.
Abbott and others.

INCIDENTS

Edward Brown, steward (Br. Inq.):

Witness helped with boats 5, 3, 1 and C, and then helped with another collapsible; tried to get it up to the davits when the ship gave a list to port. The falls were slackened but the boat could not be hauled away any further. There were four or five women waiting to get into the boat. The boat referred to was the collapsible boat "A" which they got off the officers' house. They got it down by the planks, but witness does not know where the planks came from. He thinks they were with the bars which came from the other boats; yet he had no difficulty in getting the boat off the house. The ship was then up to the bridge under water, well down by the head. He jumped into the boat then and called out to cut the falls. He cut them at the aft end, but cannot say what happened to the forward fall. He was washed out of the boat *but does not know whether he went down in the water.** He had his lifebelt on and came to the top. People were all around him. They tore his clothes away struggling in the water. He could not swim, but got into the collapsible boat "A." Only men were in it, but they picked up a woman and some men

* Italics are mine.—Author.

afterwards, consisting of passengers, stewards
and crew.   There were sixteen men.   Fifth
Officer Lowe in boat No. 14 picked them up.

O. Abelseth (Am. Inq.) :
Witness describes the period just before the
ship sank when an effort was made to get out
the collapsible boats on the roof of the officers'
house.   The officer wanted help and called out:
"Are there any sailors here?"   It was only about
five feet to the water when witness jumped off.
It was not much of a jump.   Before that he could
see the people were jumping over.   He went under
and swallowed some water.   A rope was tangled
around him.   He came on top again and tried
to swim.   There were lots of men floating around.
One of them got him on the neck and pressed
him under the water and tried to get on top, but
he got loose from him.   Then another man hung
on to him for a while and let go.   Then he swam
for about fifteen or twenty minutes.   Saw something dark ahead of him; swam towards it and
it was one of the Engelhardt boats ("A").   He
had a life-preserver on when he jumped from
the ship.   There was no suction at all.   "I will
try and see," he thought, "if I can float on the
lifebelt without help from swimming," and he
floated easily on the lifebelt.   When he got on

boat "A" no one assisted him, but they said when he got on: "Don't capsize the boat," so he hung on for a little while before he got on.

Some were trying to get on their feet who were sitting or lying down; others fell into the water again. Some were frozen and there were two dead thrown overboard. On the boat he raised up and continuously moved his arms and swung them around to keep warm. There was one lady aboard this raft and she (Mrs. Abbott) was saved. There were also two Swedes and a first-class passenger. He said he had a wife and child. There was a fireman also named Thompson who had burned one of his hands; also a young boy whose name sounded like "Volunteer." He and Thompson were afterwards at St. Vincent's Hospital. In the morning he saw a boat with a sail up, and in unison they screamed together for help. Boat A was not capsized and the canvas was not raised up, and they could not get it up. *They stood all night in about twelve or fourteen inches of water**—their feet in water all the time. Boat No. 14 sailed down and took them aboard and transferred them to the *Carpathia*, he helping to row. There must have been ten or twelve saved from boat A; one man was from New Jersey, with whom he came in company from London.

* Italics are mine.—Author.

At daybreak he seemed unconscious. He took him by the shoulder and shook him. "Who are you?" he said; "let me be; who are you?" About half an hour or so later he died.

In a recent letter from **Dr. Washington Dodge** he refers to a young man whom he met on the *Carpathia,* very much exhausted, whom he took to his stateroom and gave him medicine and medical attention. This young man was a gentleman's valet and a second cabin passenger. This answers to the description of William J. Mellers, to whom I have written, but as yet have received no response. Dr. Dodge says he believes this young man's story implicitly: He, Mellers, "was standing by this boat when one of the crew was endeavoring to cut the fastenings that bound it to the vessel just as the onrush of waters came up which tore it loose. It was by clinging to this boat that he was saved."

R. N. Williams, Jr., in his letter writes me as follows:
"I was not under water very long, and as soon as I came to the top I threw off the big fur coat I had on. I had put my lifebelt on under the coat. I also threw off my shoes. About twenty yards away I saw something floating. I swam to it and

found it to be a collapsible boat. I hung on to it and after a while got aboard and *stood up in the middle of it. The water was up to my waist.** About thirty of us clung to it. When Officer Lowe's boat picked us up eleven of us were alive; all the rest were dead from cold. My fur coat was found attached to this Engelhardt boat 'A' by the *Oceanic*, and *also a cane marked 'C. Williams.'* This gave rise to the story that my father's body was in this boat, but this, as you see, is not so. How the cane got there I do not know."

Through the courtesy of Mr. Harold Wingate of the White Star Line in letters to me I have the following information pertaining to boat "A":

"One of the bodies found in this boat was that of Mr. Thompson Beattie. We got his watch and labels from his clothes showing his name and that of the dealer, which we sent to the executor. Two others were a fireman and a sailor, both unidentified. The overcoat belonging to Mr. Williams I sent to a furrier to be re-conditioned, but nothing could be done with it except to dry it out, so I sent it to him as it was. *There was no cane in the boat.* The message from the *Oceanic* and the words 'R. N. Williams, *care of*

*Italics are mine.—Author.

Duane Williams,' were twisted by the receiver of
the message to 'Richard N. Williams, *cane of
Duane Williams,*' * which got into the press, and
thus perpetuated the error.

"There was also a ring found in the boat whose
owner we eventually traced in Sweden and restored the property to her. We cannot account
for its being in the boat, but we know that her
husband was a passenger on the *Titanic*—Edward
P. Lindell, a third-class passenger. The widow's
address is, care of Nels Persson, Helsingborg,
Sweden."

Rescue of the occupants of boat "A" at daylight Monday morning is recorded in the testimony of Officer Lowe and members of the crew
of his boat No. 14 and the other boats 12, 10, 4
and "D" which were tied together. No. 14 we
recall was emptied of passengers and a crew
taken from all the boats referred to went back
to the wreck. The substance of the testimony
of all of them agrees and I need only cite that
of Quartermaster Bright, in charge of boat "D,"
as follows:

A. Bright, Q. M. (in charge) (Am. Inq., 834) :
Just at daylight witness saw from his place in

*Italics are mine.—Author.

boat "D" one of the other collapsible boats, "A,"
that was awash just flush with the water. Officer
Lowe came and towed witness's boat to the other
collapsible one that was just awash and took from
it thirteen men and one woman who were in the
water up to their ankles. They had been singing
out in the dark. As soon as daylight came they
could be seen. They were rescued and the boat
turned adrift with two dead bodies in it, covered
with a lifebelt over their faces.

Admiral Mahan on Ismay's duty:
Rear Admiral A. T. Mahan, retired, in a
letter which the *Evening Post* publishes, has this
to say of J. Bruce Ismay's duty:

In the *Evening Post* of April 24 Admiral
Chadwick passes a distinct approval upon the
conduct of Mr. Ismay in the wreck of the *Titanic*
by characterizing the criticisms passed upon it as
the "acme of emotionalism."

Both censure and approval had best wait upon
the results of the investigations being made in
Great Britain. Tongues will wag, but if men like
Admiral Chadwick see fit to publish anticipatory
opinions those opinions must receive anticipatory
comment.

Certain facts are so notorious that they need

no inquiry to ascertain. These are (1) that before the collision the captain of the *Titanic* was solely responsible for the management of the ship; (2) after the collision there were not boats enough to embark more than one-third of those on board, and, (3) for that circumstance the White Star Company is solely responsible, not legally, for the legal requirements were met, but morally. Of this company, Mr. Ismay is a prominent if not the most prominent member.

For all the loss of life the company is responsible, individually and collectively: Mr. Ismay personally, not only as one of the members. He believed the *Titanic* unsinkable; the belief relieves of moral guilt, but not of responsibility. Men bear the consequences of their mistakes as well as of their faults. He—and Admiral Chadwick—justify his leaving over fifteen hundred persons, the death of each one of whom lay on the company, on the ground that it was the last boat half filled; and Mr. Ismay has said, no one else to be seen.

No one to be seen; but was there none to be reached? Mr. Ismay knew there must be many, because he knew the boats could take only a third. The *Titanic* was 882 feet long; 92 broad; say, from Thirty-fourth street to a little north of Thirty-seventh. Within this space were congregated over 1,500 souls, on several decks. True, to find any one person at such a moment in the intricacies of a vessel were a vain hope; but to encounter some stragglers would not seem to be. Read in the *Sun* and *Times* of April 25 Col. Gracie's account of the "mass of humanity, men and women" that suddenly appeared before him after the boats were launched.

In an interview reported in the New York *Times* April 25 Admiral Sir Cyprian Bridge, a very distinguished officer, holds that Mr. Ismay was but a passenger, as other passengers. True, up to a certain point. He is in no sense responsible for the collision; but when the collision had occurred he confronted a wholly new condition for which he was responsible and not the captain, viz., a sinking vessel without adequate provision for saving life. Did no obligation to particularity of conduct rest upon him under such a condition?

I hold that under the conditions, so long as there was a soul that could be saved, the obligation lay upon Mr. Ismay that that one person and not he should have been in the boat. More than 1,500 perished. Circumstances yet to be developed may justify Mr. Ismay's actions completely, but such justification is imperatively required. If this be "the acme of emotionalism" I must be content to bear the imputation.

Admiral Chadwick urges the "preserving a life so valuable to the great organization to which Mr. Ismay belongs." This bestows upon Mr. Ismay's escape a kind of halo of self-sacrifice. No man is indispensable. There are surely brains enough and business capacity enough in the White Star company to run without him. The reports say that of the rescued women thirty-seven were widowed by the accident and the lack of boats. Their husbands were quite as indispensable to them as Mr. Ismay to the company. His duty to the ship's company was clear and primary; that to the White Star company so secondary as to be at the moment inoperative.

We should be careful not to pervert standards. Witness the talk that the result is due to the system. What is a system, except that which individuals have made it and keep it? Whatever thus weakens the sense of individual responsibility is harmful, and so likewise is all condonation of failure of the individual to meet his responsibility.

Boilers arranged in Harland and Wolff's works

Café Parisienne

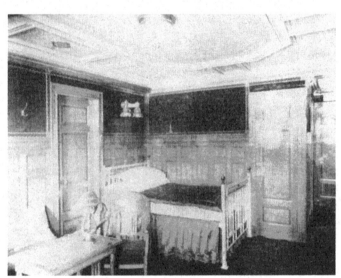

Suite Bedroom (B.57)

The Gymnasium

Overturned lifeboat on which twenty-eight survivors spent the night.

The Sinking
of the
S.S. TITANIC

April 14–15, 1912

John B. Thayer

In memory of
John Borland Thayer
1862–1912

PREFACE

This account of the sinking of the S.S. "TITANIC" has been written primarily as a family record for the information of my children and perhaps their children in memory of my Father, John Borland Thayer, the third of that name, who lost his life in the disaster.

Just as no two happenings in the stream of space time are identical, no two ships either destroyed by an "Act of God" in peace time, or of an "Enemy" in time of war, sink in the same manner or under the same conditions. And due to the great size of modern ships no two individuals no matter how close they may be together on shipboard have the same description of experience to relate, should they be so fortunate as to survive the ordeal. Therefore, every account by an individual survivor of such a disaster probably has some new reader interest to those interested in stories of the sea.

It takes the many separate accounts pieced together to give the true composite history of the whole happening and I hope this attempt at a true description of the "TITANIC" disaster may have some historical value.

The ship was carrying twenty-two hundred and eight persons. Seven hundred and three persons left the ship in the lifeboats, leaving fifteen hundred and fifty-three to go down with the ship. Forty-two of these were saved; twenty-eight were on the bottom of an overturned lifeboat, and of this number I was one; and fourteen were in the half submerged collapsible boat, among whom was my good friend Richard Norris Williams, who also lost his Father. Only about one in every thirty-six who went down with the ship was saved, and I happened to be one of those.

The whole event passes before me now in nineteen hundred and forty, as vividly and with the same clarity, as twenty-eight years ago in nineteen hundred and twelve. Nevertheless, in writing this story I have referred to statistics and a brief article prepared by me shortly after the disaster.

I want to emphasize some of the everyday conditions under which we were then living, to show how much humanity was shocked by the approaching disaster.

These were ordinary days, and into them had crept only gradually the telephone, the talking machine, the automobile. The airplane due to have so soon such a stimulating yet devastating effect on civilization, was only a few years old, and the radio as known today, was still in the scientific laboratory. The Marconi Wireless had just come into commercial use, and the Morse Code for help was "C.Q.D.," as our modern "S.O.S." was just making its appearance. The safety razor had just been invented, and its use was gradually spreading. Upon rising in the morning, we looked forward to a normal day of customary business progress. The conservative morning paper seldom had headlines larger than half an inch in height. Upon reaching the breakfast table, our perusal of the morning paper was slow and deliberate. We did not nervously clutch for it, and rapidly scan the glaring headlines, as we are inclined to do today. Nothing was revealed in the morning, the trend of which was not known the night before. We knew that our morning coffee came from Brazil; that it was grown as a free crop, without destruction of the surplus; that it was purchased from the small corner grocer, a friend, at a price established by competition, without the loading and build-up, due to many hidden taxes; and that it was not "dated." These days were peaceful and ruled by economic theory and practice built up over years of slow and hardly perceptible change. There was peace, and the world had an even tenor to its ways.

A dollar could be exchanged for four shillings, four marks, or five francs. In exchange for a five-dollar gold piece or a five-dollar bill, one could pocket a pound note or a gold sovereign.

As an individual, returning to Haverford School outside of Philadelphia, I confidently knew that after graduation in the Spring, and according to plans for my future laid down by my Father in deference to my nebulous ambitions, I would attend College at Princeton, New Jersey, and from there go to London, Paris, Berlin, and Vienna, where I would serve an apprenticeship in private and commercial banking houses, and would return to practice commercial or private banking in the United States. It could be planned. It was planned. It was a certainty.

In those days one could freely circulate around the world, in both a physical and an economic sense, and definitely plan for the future, unhampered by class, nationality, or government.

True enough, from time to time there were events—catastrophes—like the Johnstown Flood, the San Francisco Earthquake, or floods in China—which stirred the sleeping world, but not enough to keep it from resuming its slumber. It seems to me that the disaster about to occur was the event, which not only made the world rub its eyes and awake, but woke it with a start, keeping it moving at a rapidly accelerating pace ever since, with less and less peace, satisfaction, and happiness.

Today the individual has to be contented with rapidity of motion, nervous emotion, and economic insecurity. To my mind the world of today awoke April 15th, 1912.

THE SINKING OF THE
S.S. "TITANIC"

APRIL 14–15, 1912

The S.S. "TITANIC" of the White Star Line, largest ship the world had ever known, sailed from Southampton on her maiden voyage to New York, on April 10th, 1912. She was built by Messrs. Harland & Wolff, at Belfast. She was a fabricated steel vessel of gigantic dimensions, registered at Liverpool, her gross tonnage was 46,328 tons, her length over all being 852 feet, with a breadth of 92 feet, and a depth of 65 feet. The distance from the keel to the top of the funnel was 175 feet. She had a double bottom extending the full length of the ship, with a space five to six feet between the inner and outer plates, and was divided into sixteen water tight compartments, with access to each compartment through water-tight doors. The rudder alone weighed 100 tons. She was driven by three enormous screws, the center one weighing 22 tons, the other two 38 tons each, and was capable of making 23 knots. The last word in luxury, the world thought her unsinkable.

Captain E. J. Smith, her commander, Commodore of the White Star Line Fleet, was on his last round trip from Southampton, before having to retire on age. In his thirty-eight years of service he had never met with a serious accident. On this trip he had under him a splendid complement of officers and men.

The "TITANIC" had a passenger certificate to carry 3547 passengers and crew. She carried sixteen lifeboats and four Engelhart collapsible boats, all of which had a total carrying capacity of 1167 persons, or approximately 60 to 65 in each boat. She carried 3560 life belts or their equivalent.

The "TITANIC" was a wonderfully safe vessel. The life-saving equipment should surely have been sufficient to take care of any normal eventualities.

On this maiden voyage the ship carried a total of 2208 persons, of whom 1316 were passengers and 892 crew. There were 332 first-class passengers, 277 second-class passengers, and 709 third-class passengers. I have in my safe deposit box an original first-class passenger list. It was carried off the ship in the pocket of the overcoat worn by my Mother.

There were a great many prominent people on the passenger list and because it was her maiden voyage there were on board many of those responsible for the building of the ship and the management of the steamship line. Some of these were: Thomas Andrews, one of the ship's designers; Archie Frost, the builders' Chief Engineer, including his approximately twenty assistants; J. Bruce Ismay, President of the International Mercantile Marine Company and Chairman of the Board and Managing Director of the Oceanic Steam Navigation Company, Limited, owners of the White Star Line; all observing the performance of the ship, and all of whom were often with my Father and myself, during the few days we were aboard the ship.

My Father, John B. Thayer, Second Vice-President of the Pennsylvania Railroad, my Mother, Marian Longstreth

Morris Thayer, my Mother's maid, Margaret Fleming, and I, were all in one party that sailed first-class from Southampton.

We had no more than started down the narrow channel, and were commencing to make headway under our own power, when we passed the American Liner S.S. "ST. PAUL," tied up to the S.S. "OCEANIC" which was lying alongside the dock. The suction created by our port propeller, as we made a turn in the narrow channel, broke the strong cables mooring her to the S.S. "OCEANIC" causing her stern to swing toward us at a rapid rate. It looked as though there would surely be a collision. Her stern could not have been more than a yard or two from our side. It almost hit us. Luckily, the combined efforts of several tugs, which had quickly made fast to her, pulled her stern back. This narrowly averted collision was considered an ill-omen by all those accustomed to the sea.

We called at Cherbourg, and from there proceeded to Queenstown.

We left Queenstown at one-thirty in the afternoon of Thursday, April 11th. The weather was fair and clear, the ship palatial, the food delicious. Almost everyone was counting the days till we would see the Statue of Liberty.

I occupied a stateroom adjoining that of my Father and Mother on the port side of "C" deck; and, needless to say, being seventeen years old, I was all over the ship.

Sunday, April 14th, dawned bright and clear. It looked as if we were in for another very pleasant day. I spent most of that day walking around the decks with my Mother and Father. We had short chats with many of the other promenaders, among whom I particularly remember J. Bruce Ismay,

Thomas Andrews, and Charles M. Hays, who was President of the Grand Trunk Railway of Canada; with all of whom we spent quite a lot of time.

It became noticeably colder as the afternoon wore on. I remember Mr. Ismay showing us a wire regarding the presence of ice and remarking that we would not reach that position until around nine P.M. We went to our staterooms about six-thirty to dress for dinner. My Father and Mother were invited out to dinner that night, so I dined alone at our regular table. After dinner I was enjoying a cup of coffee, when a man about twenty-eight or thirty years of age drew up, and introduced himself as Milton C. Long, son of Judge Charles M. Long, of Springfield, Massachusetts. He was travelling alone. We talked together for an hour or so. Afterwards I put on an overcoat and took a few turns around the deck.

It had become very much colder. It was a brilliant, starry night. There was no moon and I have never seen the stars shine brighter; they appeared to stand right out of the sky, sparkling like cut diamonds. A very light haze, hardly noticeable, hung low over the water. I have spent much time on the ocean, yet I have never seen the sea smoother than it was that night; it was like a mill-pond, and just as innocent looking, as the great ship quietly rippled through it. I went onto the boat deck—it was deserted and lonely. The wind whistled through the stays, and blackish smoke poured out of the three forward funnels; the fourth funnel was a dummy for ventilation purposes. It was the kind of a night that made one feel glad to be alive.

About eleven o'clock I went below to my stateroom. After a short conversation with my Father and Mother, and saying good night to them, I stepped into my room to put on pajamas expecting to have another delightful night's rest like the four preceding.

The ship was so large and extensive that all I can tell about the tragedy is only a small part of all that actually occurred. I will try to recount all that I actually saw or heard, or heard from others and afterwards verified.

We were steaming along at 22 or 23 knots, not reducing speed at all, in spite of the many warnings of the presence of ice, which had come in from other ships during the afternoon and evening. We were out for a record run.

I had called "Good Night" to my Father and Mother in the next room. In order to get plenty of air I had half opened the port, and the breeze was coming through with a quiet humming whistle. There was the steady rhythmic pulsation of the engines and screws, the feel and hearing of which becomes second nature to one, after a few hours at sea. It was a fine night for sleeping, and with the day's air and exercise, I was sleepy.

I wound my watch—it was 11:45 P.M.—and was just about to step into bed, when I seemed to sway slightly. I immediately realized that the ship had veered to port as though she had been gently pushed. If I had had a brimful glass of water in my hand not a drop would have been spilled, the shock was so slight.

Almost instantaneously the engines stopped. The sudden quiet was startling and disturbing. Like the subdued quiet in a sleeping car, at a stop, after a continuous run. Not a sound except the breeze whistling through the half open port. Then there was the distant noise of running feet and muffled voices, as several people hurried through the passageway. Very shortly the engines started up again—slowly—not with the bright vibration to which we were accustomed, but as though they were tired. After very few revolutions they again stopped.

I hurried into my heavy overcoat and drew on my slippers. All excited, but not thinking anything serious had occurred, I called in to my Father and Mother that "I was going up on deck to see the fun." Father said he would put on his clothes and come right up and join me. It was bitterly cold. I walked around the deck looking over the side from time to time. As far as I could see, there was nothing to be seen, except something scattered on the well deck forward, which I afterwards learned was ice. There was no sign of any large iceberg. Only two or three people were on deck when I arrived, but many rapidly gathered. My Father joined me very soon. He and I moved around the deck trying to discover what happened and finally found one of the crew who told us we had hit an iceberg, which he tried to point out to us, but which we could not see in spite of the brilliant night, as possibly our eyes were not accustomed to the dark after coming out of the lighted ship.

The ship took on a very slight list to starboard. We did not know it at the moment, but we learned afterward that the iceberg had ripped open probably four of her larger forward compartments on the starboard side; and also that if we had only hit the ice head on, instead of making too late an attempt to avoid it, the ship would in all probability have survived the collision.

About fifteen minutes after the collision she developed a list to port and was distinctly down by the head.

Here we were eight hundred miles out from New York, off the Grand Banks, our position Latitude 41 degrees 46 minutes North, Longitude 50 degrees 14 minutes West. No one yet thought of any serious trouble. The ship was unsinkable.

It was now shortly after midnight. My Father and I came in from the cold deck to the hallway or lounge. There were quite a few people standing around questioning each other in a dazed kind of way. No one seemed to know what next to do. We saw, as they passed, Mr. Ismay, Mr. Andrews, and some of the ship's officers. Mr. Andrews told us he did not give the ship much over an hour to live. We could hardly believe it, and yet if he said so, it must be true. No one was better qualified to know.

I was still just dressed in pajamas and overcoat. At about 12:15 A.M. the stewards passed the word around for every one to get fully clothed and put on life preservers, which were in each stateroom. We went below right away and found my Mother and her maid fully dressed. I hurried into my clothes—a warm greenish tweed suit and vest with another mohair vest underneath my coat. We all tied on life preservers, which were really large thick cork vests. On top of these we put our overcoats.

We than hurried up to the lounge on "A" deck, which was now crowded with people, some standing, some hurrying, some pushing out onto the deck. My friend Milton Long came by at that time and asked if he could stay with us. There was a great deal of noise. The band was playing lively tunes without apparently receiving much attention from the worried moving audience.

It has been more or less definitively established by the investigations into the disaster, held both in the United States and in England, that the S.S. "CALIFORNIAN" passed the

S.S. "TITANIC" at about 12:30 A.M., and did see the distress rockets which were continually sent up. She must have seen our blinker light C.Q.D., which was continuously operating. It was determined that her wireless operator signed off after talking to the "TITANIC" at about 11:30 P.M. but possibly even heard our wireless C.Q.D. The Captain apparently paid no attention to any reports from his juniors. While I did not see the masthead lights of the S.S. "CALIFORNIAN" many claim they did see them. My Mother watched them for some time while on the port side, waiting to get into a life boat, and Second Officer Lightoller told me he positively saw them. The ship was at the most not more than ten or twelve miles away. By merely obeying the age old law of the sea, the Captain of the ship had the greatest opportunity ever presented to save over fifteen hundred human lives with the minimum of effort or danger to his own ship.

We all went out onto "A" deck, trying to find where we were supposed to go. They were then uncovering the boats and making preparations to swing them out. Everything was fairly orderly and the crew at least seemed to know what they were doing.

It was now about 12:45 A.M. The noise was terrific. The deep vibrating roar of the exhaust steam blowing off through the safety valves was deafening, in addition to which they had commenced to send up rockets. There was more and more action. After standing there for some minutes talking above the din, trying to determine what we should do next, we finally decided to go back into the crowded hallway where it was warm. Shortly we heard the stewards pass-

ing the word around: "all women to the port side." We then
said good-bye to my Mother at the head of the stairs on "A"
deck and she and the maid went out onto the port side of that
deck, supposedly to get into a lifeboat. Father and I went
out on the starboard side, watching what was going on about
us. It seemed we were always waiting for orders and no orders ever came. No one knew his boat position, as no lifeboat drill had been held. The men had not yet commenced
to lower any of the forward starboard lifeboats, of which
there were four. The noise kept up. The deck seemed to be
well lighted. People like ourselves were just standing around,
out of the way. The stokers, dining-room stewards, and some
others of the crew were lined up, waiting for orders. The
second- and third-class passengers were pouring up onto the
deck from the stern, augmenting the already large crowd.

Finally we thought we had better inquire whether or not
Mother had been able to get a boat. We went into the hall
and happened to meet the Chief Dining-Room Steward. He
told us that he had just seen my Mother, and that she had not
yet been put into a boat. We found her, and were told that
they were loading the forward boats on the port side from
the deck below. The ship had a substantial list to port, which
made quite a space between the side of the ship and the life
boats, swinging out over the water, so the crew stretched
folded steamer chairs across the space, over which the people
were helped into the boats.

We proceeded to the deck below. Father, Mother, and
the maid, went ahead of Long and myself. The lounge on
"B" deck was filled with a milling crowd, and as we went
through the doorway out onto the deck, people pushed be-

tween my Father and Mother, and Long and me. Long and I could not catch up, and were entirely separated from them. I never saw my Father again.

We looked for them, following along to where the port boats were being loaded, but could see nothing of either Father or Mother. Fully believing that they had both been successful in getting into a boat, Long and I went back through the lounge to the starboard side, thinking of what we should do, and not looking further for my Father at all.

It must now have been about 1:25 A.M. The ship was way down by the head with water entirely covering her bow. She gradually came out of her list to port, and if anything, had a slight list to starboard. The crew had commenced to load and lower the forward starboard boats. These could hold over sixty people, but the officers were afraid to load them to capacity, while suspended by falls, bow and stern, sixty feet over the water. They might have buckled, or broken from the falls.

The stern lifeboats, four on the port and four on the starboard side, had already left the ship. One of the first boats to leave carried only twelve people, Sir Cosmo and Lady Duff Gordon, and ten others. Most of the boats were loaded with about forty to forty-five, with the exception of the last few to go, which were loaded to full capacity.

One could see the boats that had already left the ship, standing off about five or six hundred yards. Apparently there was only one light, about which most of them congregated. They were plainly visible and looked very safe on that calm sea.

On deck, the exhaust steam was still roaring. The lights were still strong. The band, with life preservers on, was still playing. The crowd was fairly orderly. Our own situation was too pressing, the scene too kaleidoscopic for me to retain any detailed picture of individual behavior. I did see one man come through the door out onto the deck with a full bottle of Gordon Gin. He put it to his mouth and practically drained it. If ever I get out of this alive, I thought, there is one man I will never see again. He apparently fought his way into one of the last two boats, for he was one of the first men I recognized upon reaching the deck of the S.S. "CARPATHIA." Someone told me afterwards that he was a *State Senator or Congressman* from Virginia or West Virginia.

There was some disturbance in loading the last two forward starboard boats. A large crowd of men was pressing to get into them. No women were around as far as I could see. I saw Ismay, who had been assisting in the loading of the last boat, push his way into it. It was really every man for himself. Many of the crew and men from the stokehole were lined up, with apparently not a thought of attempting to get into a boat without orders. Purser H. W. McElroy, as brave and as fine a man as ever lived, was standing up in the next to last boat, loading it. Two men, I think they were dining-room stewards, dropped into the boat from the deck above. As they jumped he fired twice into the air. I do not believe they were hit, but they were quickly thrown out. McElroy did not take a boat and was not saved. I should say that all this took place on "A" deck, just under the boat deck.

Long and I debated whether or not we should fight our way into one of the last two boats. We could almost see the ship slowly going down by the head. There was so much confusion, we did not think they would reach the water right side up, and decided not to attempt it. I do not know what I thought could happen, but we had not given up hope.

We leaned over the side to watch the next to last boat being lowered. It was terrible. Apparently, for some seconds, there was no one above directing the lowering of the bow and stern falls so that she might be held level. The bow was lowered so fast that the people were almost dumped out into the water. I think, if Long and I, and others, had not yelled up—"Hold the bow," they all would have been spilled out. Finally, in a few minutes, she reached the water safely.

It must now have been about 1:50 A.M., and, as far as we knew, the last boat had gone. We were not aware of the fact that Second Officer Charles Herbert Lightoller and some of the crew were working desperately on top of one of the deck houses to free and launch one of the four Engelhart Collapsible Lifeboats. These boats had strong wooden bottoms with sides which could be raised, and all around the hull ran a canvas covered cork fender with a curved surface.

I argued with Long about our chances. I wanted to jump out and catch the empty lifeboat falls, which were swinging free all the way to the water's edge, with the idea of sliding down and swimming out to the partially filled boats lying off in the distance, for I could swim well. In this way we would be away from the crowd, and away from the suction of the ship when she finally went down. We were still fifty or sixty feet above the water. We could not just jump, for we might hit wreckage or a steamer chair, and be knocked unconscious. He argued against it and dissuaded me from doing so. Thank heaven he did. The temperature of the water was 28 degrees Fahrenheit. Four degrees below freezing.

We then went up a sheltered stairway onto the starboard side of the boat deck. There were crowds of people up there. They all seemed to keep as far as possible from the ship's rail. We stood there talking from about 2:00 A.M. on. We sent messages through each other to our families. At times we were just thoughtful and quiet, but the noise around us did not stop.

So many thoughts passed so quickly through my mind! I thought of all the good times I had had, and of all the future pleasures I would never enjoy; of my Father and Mother; of my Sisters and Brother. I looked at myself as though from some far-off place. I sincerely pitied myself. It seemed so unnecessary, but we still had a chance, if only we could keep away from the crowd and the suction of the sinking ship.

I only wish I had kept on looking for my Father. I should have realized that he would not have taken a boat, leaving me behind. I afterwards heard from my friend, Richard Norris Williams, the tennis player, that his Father and mine were standing in a group consisting of Mr. George D. Widener and his son Harry, together with some others. They were close in under the second funnel, which was very near to where Long and I were.

It was now about 2:15 A.M. We could see the water creeping up the deck, as the ship was going down by the head at a pretty fast rate. The water was right up to the bridge. There must have been over sixty feet of it on top of the bow. As the water gained headway along the deck, the crowd gradually moved with it, always pushing, toward the floating stern and keeping in from the rail of the ship as far as they could. We were a mass of hopeless, dazed humanity, attempting, as the Almighty and Nature made us, to keep our final breath until the last possible moment. The roaring of the exhaust steam suddenly stopped, making a great quietness, in spite of many mixed noises of hurrying human effort and anguish. As I recall it, the lights were still on, even then. There seemed to be quite a ruddy glare, but it was a murky light, with distant people and objects vaguely outlined. The stars were brilliant and the water oily.

Occasionally there had been a muffled thud or deadened explosion within the ship. Now, without warning she seemed to start forward, moving forward and into the water at an angle of about fifteen degrees. This movement, with the water rushing up toward us was accompanied by a rumbling roar, mixed with more muffled explosions. It was like standing under a steel railway bridge while an express train passes overhead, mingled with the noise of a pressed steel factory and wholesale breakage of china.

Long and I had been standing by the starboard rail, about abreast of the second funnel. Our main thought was to keep away from the crowd and the suction. At the rail we were entirely free of the crowd. We had previously decided to jump into the water before she actually went down, so that we might swim some distance away, and avoid what we thought would be terrific suction. Still we did not wish to jump before the place where we were standing would be only a few yards over the water, for we might be injured and not be able to swim.

We had no time to think now, only to act. We shook hands, wished each other luck. I said "Go ahead, I'll be right with you." I threw my overcoat off as he climbed over the rail, sliding down facing the ship. Ten seconds later I sat on the rail. I faced out, and with a push of my arms and hands, jumped into the water as far out from the ship as I could. When we jumped we were only twelve or fifteen feet above the water. I never saw Long again. His body was later recovered. I am afraid that the few seconds elapsing between our going, meant the difference between being sucked into the deck below, as I believe he was, or pushed out by the back wash. I was pushed out and then sucked down.

The cold was terrific. The shock of the water took the breath out of my lungs. Down and down I went, spinning in all directions.

Swimming as hard as I could in the direction which I thought to be away from the ship, I finally came up with my lungs bursting, but not having taken any water. The ship was in front of me, forty yards away. How long I had been swimming under water, I don't know. Perhaps a minute or less. Incidentally, my watch stopped at 2:22 A.M.

The story would not be complete without comment on the discipline and behavior of the crew. They were perfect and did their full and complete duty. To see all the men covered with the dirt and grime of the boiler room, after having drawn the fires from the flooded stokehole, lined up on deck, awaiting orders, was a grand, inspiring sight. It was a tribute to the British Mercantile Marine.

Not a single Engineering Officer or Engineer of the ship was saved. Every one was at his post in the engine room. They kept the lights going till the ship went under. They made the power for the "C.Q.D.," which called for help through the night. Think what panic we might have had if the lights had failed; or worse yet, if the S.S. "CARPATHIA" had been unable to hear our call and learn our position.

Besides the full complement of Engineers on the ship, headed by Chief Engineer William Bell, there were Archie Frost, Harland and Wolff's Chief Engineer, and about twenty assistants, together with Mr. Thomas Andrews, one of the designers of the ship. Every single one died attending to his duty without a chance of being saved.

The ship seemed to be surrounded with a glare, and stood out of the night as though she were on fire. I watched her. I don't know why I didn't keep swimming away. Fascinated, I seemed tied to the spot. Already I was tired out with the cold and struggling, although the life preserver held me head and shoulders above the water.

She continued to make the same forward progress as when I left her. The water was over the base of the first funnel. The mass of people on board were surging back, always back toward the floating stern. The rumble and roar continued, with even louder distinct wrenchings and tearings of boilers and engines from their beds. Suddenly the whole superstructure of the ship appeared to split, well forward to midship, and blow or buckle upwards. The second funnel, large enough for two automobiles to pass through abreast, seemed to be lifted off, emitting a cloud of sparks. It looked as if it would fall on top of me. It missed me by only twenty or thirty feet. The suction of it drew me down and down, struggling and swimming, practically spent.

As I finally came to the surface I put my hand over my head, in order to push away any obstruction. My hand came against something smooth and firm with rounded shape. I looked up, and realized that it was the cork fender of one of the collapsible lifeboats, which was floating in the water bottom side up. About four or five men were clinging to her bottom. I pulled myself up as far as I could, almost exhausted, but could not get my legs up. I asked them to give me a hand up, which they readily did. Sitting on my haunches and holding on for dear life, I was again facing the "TITANIC."

It seemed as though hours had passed since I left the ship; yet it was probably not more than four minutes, if that long. There was the gigantic mass, about fifty or sixty yards away. The forward motion had stopped. She was pivoting on a point just abaft of midship. Her stern was gradually rising into the air, seemingly in no hurry, just slowly and deliberately. The last funnel was about on the surface of the water. It was the dummy funnel, and I do not believe it fell.

Some months after the disaster, however, I had been invited to tell my story of the behavior of the ship to the Engineers and Ship Designers of The William Cramp and Sons' Ship and Engine Building Company, Richmond and Norris Streets, Philadelphia. I described the action in this way: The iceberg cut open about four of the "TITANIC'S" forward compartments, leaving, possibly, at least one buoyant compartment in the bow intact. With the buoyant stern tending to rise, and the bow tending slightly to do the same, the weight of the engines and boilers, which, torn from their beds, crashed in midship, possibly broke the keel downwards, and this in turn forced the superstructure to buckle or push up at the forward expansion joint; causing the funnel to fall.

I did not say she broke into separate parts, but that some bending and breaking did take place. My hearers told me that it was a reasonable supposition and a possible explanation of the final behavior of the ship.

Her deck was turned slightly toward us. We could see groups of the almost fifteen hundred people still aboard, clinging in clusters or bunches, like swarming bees; only to fall in masses, pairs or singly, as the great after part of the ship, two hundred and fifty feet of it, rose into the sky, till it reached a sixty-five or seventy degree angle. Here it seemed to pause, and just hung, for what felt like minutes. Gradually she turned her deck away from us, as though to hide from our sight the awful spectacle.

We had an oar on our overturned boat. In spite of several men working it, amid our cries and prayers, we were being gradually sucked in toward the great pivoting mass. I looked upwards—we were right underneath the three enormous propellers. For an instant, I thought they were sure to come right down on top of us. Then, with the deadened noise of the bursting of her last few gallant bulkheads, she slid quietly away from us into the sea.

There was no final apparent suction, and practically no wreckage that we could see.

I don't remember all the wild talk and calls that were going on on our boat, but there was one concerted sigh or sob as she went from view.

Probably a minute passed with almost dead silence and quiet. Then an individual call for help, from here, from there; gradually swelling into a composite volume of one long continuous wailing chant, from the fifteen hundred in the water all around us. It sounded like locusts on a mid-summer night, in the woods in Pennsylvania.

This terrible continuing cry lasted for twenty or thirty minutes, gradually dying away, as one after another could no longer withstand the cold and exposure. Practically no one was drowned, as no water was found in the lungs of those later recovered. Everyone had on a life preserver.

The partially filled lifeboats standing by, only a few hundred yards away never came back. Why on earth they did not come back is a mystery. How could any human being fail to heed those cries? They were afraid the boats would be swamped by people in the water.

The most heartrending part of the whole tragedy was the failure, right after the "TITANIC" sank, of those boats which were only partially loaded, to pick up the poor souls in the water. There they were, only four or five hundred yards away, listening to the cries, and still they did not come back. If they had turned back several hundred more would have been saved. No one can explain it. It was not satisfactorily explained in any investigation. It was just one of the many "Acts of God" running through the whole disaster.

During this time more and more were trying to get aboard the bottom of our overturned boat. We helped them on until we were packed like sardines. Then out of self-preservation, we had to turn some away. There were finally twenty-eight of us altogether on board. We were very low in the water. The water had roughened up slightly, and was occasionally washing over us. The stars still shone brilliantly.

Photostatic reproduction of pages from the original complete First Class Passenger List.

We were standing, sitting, kneeling, lying, in all conceivable positions, in order to get a small hold on the half inch overlap of the boat's planking, which was the only means of keeping ourselves from sliding off the slippery surface into that icy water. I was kneeling. A man was kneeling on my legs with his hands on my shoulders, and in turn somebody was on him. Once we obtained our original position we could not move. The assistant wireless man, Harold Bride, was lying across, in front of me, with his legs in the water, and his feet jammed against the cork fender, which was about two feet under water.

We prayed and sang hymns. A great many of the men seemed to know each other intimately. Questions and answers were called around—who was on board, and who was lost, or what they had been seen doing? One call that came around was, "Is the Chief aboard?" Whether they meant Mr. Wilde, the Chief Officer, or the Chief Engineer, or Captain Smith, I do not know. I do know that one of the circular life rings from the bridge was there when we got off in the morning. It may be that Captain Smith was on board with us for a while. Nobody knew where the "Chief" was.

About twenty of our whole group were stokers. How they ever withstood the icy temperature after the heat they were accustomed to, is extraordinary, but there was no case of illness resulting. They surely were a grimy, wiry, dishevelled, hard looking lot. Under the surface they were brave human beings, with generous and charitable hearts.

Second Officer Lightoller, I discovered in the morning, was on board. He and some of the crew were trying to launch this boat before the "TITANIC" sank. They were unsuccessful, but she floated off the deck covered with people, all of whom were shortly after washed off. Lightoller himself was washed off and sucked up against one of the ventilator grills. He had a terrific struggle, but finally again was able to reach the boat.

In August 1914, just as war was declared, I sailed on the S.S. "OCEANIC," from New York, to play cricket in and around London, on a Merion Cricket Club team. Lightoller was either Chief Officer or First Officer of the "OCEANIC," I am not certain which. We again went over our experiences and checked our ideas of just what had happened. We agreed on almost everything, with the exception of the splitting or bending of the ship. He did not think it broke at all.

Only four of us were passengers: Colonel Archibald Gracie, Washington, D.C.; A. H. Barkworth, East Riding, Yorkshire, England; W. J. Mellers, Chelsea, London, England; and myself.

Harold Bride helped greatly to keep our hopes up. He told us repeatedly which ships had answered his "C.Q.D." (at that time the Morse Code for help), and just how soon we might expect to sight them. He said time and time again, in answer to despairing doubters, "The 'CARPATHIA' is coming up as fast as she can. I gave her our position. There is no mistake. We should see her lights at about four or a little after."

During all this time nobody dared to move, for we did not know at what moment our perilous support might overturn, throwing us all into the sea. The buoyant air was gradually leaking from under the boat, lowering us further and further into the water.

Sure enough, shortly before four o'clock we saw the masthead light of the "CARPATHIA" come over the horizon and creep toward us. We gave a thankful cheer. She came up slowly, oh, so slowly. Indeed she seemed to wait without getting any nearer. We thought hours and hours dragged by as she stood off in the distance. We had been trying all night to hail our other lifeboats. They did not hear us or would not answer. We knew they had plenty of room to take us aboard, if we could only make them realize our predicament. The "CARPATHIA," waiting for a little more light, was slowly coming up on the boats and was picking them up. With the dawn breaking, we could see them being hoisted from the water. For us, afraid we might over-turn any minute, the suspense was terrible.

The long-hoped-for dawn actually broke, and with it a breeze came up, making our raft rock more and more. The air under us escaped at a more rapid rate, lowering us still further into the water. We had visions of sinking before the help so near at hand could reach us.

With daylight we could see what we were doing and took courage to move, stretch, and untangle ourselves.

One by one those on top of the freezing group stood up, until all of us who could stand were on our feet, with the exception of poor Bride, who could not bear his weight on his, but could only pull his feet and legs slightly out of the water. The waves washed over the upturned bottom more and more, as we sank lower and the water became rougher. To keep our buoyancy, we tried to offset the roll by leaning all together first to one side and then to the other.

About six-thirty, after continued and desperate calling, we attracted the attention of the other life boats. Two of them finally realized the position we were in and drew toward us. Lightoller had found his whistle, and more because of it than our hoarse shouts, their attention was attracted.

It took them ages to cover the three or four hundred yards between us. As they approached, we could see that so few men were in them that some of the oars were being pulled by women. In neither of them was much room for extra passengers, for they were two of the very few boats to be loaded to near capacity. The first took off half of us. My Mother was in this boat, having rowed most of the night. She says she thought she recognized me. I did not see her. The other boat took aboard the rest of us. We had to lift Harold Bride. He was in a bad way and, I think, would have slipped off the bottom of our over-turned boat, if several of us had not held onto him for the last half hour.

It was just about this time that the edge of the sun came above the horizon. Then, to feel its glowing warmth, which we had never expected to see again, was something, never to be forgotten. Even through my numbness I began to realize that I was saved—that I would live.

The "CARPATHIA" was about eight hundred yards away, picking up the people from one boat after another as fast as she could. Gradually we drew along side of her. There was a rope ladder with wooden steps hanging down her side. Most of us climbed up it, although many had to be hauled up in slings or chairs. It was now almost 7:30 A.M. We were the last boat to be gathered in. The only signs of ice were four small, very scattered bergs, 'way off in the distance.

As I reached the top of the ladder, I suddenly saw my Mother. When she saw me, she thought, of course, that my

Father must be with me. She was overjoyed to see me, but it was a terrible shock to hear that I had not seen Father since he had said good-bye to her.

As we talked, somebody gave me a coffee cup full of brandy. It was the first drink of an alcoholic beverage I had ever had. It warmed me as though I had put hot coals in my stomach, and did more too. A man kindly loaned me his pajamas and his bunk, then my wet clothes were taken to be dried, and with the help of the brandy I went to sleep till almost noon. I got up feeling fit and well, just as though nothing bad had happened. After putting on my own clothes, which were entirely dry, I hurried out to look for Mother. We were then passing to the south of a solid ice field, which I was told was over twenty miles long and four miles wide.

I found that Captain Arthur H. Rostron, Commander of the "CARPATHIA," of the Cunard Line, had given up his cabin to my Mother, Mrs. George D. Widener, and Mrs. John Jacob Astor. I slept on the floor of the cabin every night until we reached New York on Thursday evening, April 18th.

The passengers and crew of the "CARPATHIA" were wonderfully good to us, looking to our every need and comfort. Enough cannot be said to describe the bravery of Captain Rostron, in his taking the tremendous responsibility of running through that dense ice field, full speed ahead, to our rescue.

The trip back to New York was one big heartache and misery. There were 705 survivors on board, 1503 having been lost. It seemed as if there were none but widows left, each one mourning the loss of her husband. It was a most pitiful sight. All were hoping beyond hope, even for weeks afterwards, that some ship, somehow, had picked up their loved one, and that he would be eventually among the saved.

Because I had known Ismay so well on board the "TITANIC," the Doctor of the "CARPATHIA," the afternoon that we approached New York, asked me if I would not visit Mr. Ismay in his cabin and talk to him, to see if I could not help relieve the terribly nervous condition he was in.

I immediately went down and as there was no answer to my knock, I went right in. He was seated, in his pajamas, on his bunk, staring straight ahead, shaking all over like a leaf.

My entrance apparently did not dawn on his consciousness. Even when I spoke to him and tried to engage him in conversation, telling him that he had a perfect right to take the last boat, he paid absolutely no attention and continued to look ahead with his fixed stare.

I am almost certain that on the "TITANIC" his hair had been black with slight tinges of gray, but now his hair was virtually snow white.

I have never seen a man so completely wrecked. Nothing I could do or say brought any response.

As I closed the door, he was still looking fixedly ahead.

The final docking in New York at Pier No. 54 North River, when all our friends and relations learned the truth about the extent of the loss, was the last nerve-shattering blow for many people. For those who were ashore, it marked the end of all hope. With the exception of law suits and investigations, it was the closing chapter of the greatest and most distressing disaster of the sea the world has yet seen.